KINSHIP AND GEOGRAPHICAL MOBILITY

INTERNATIONAL STUDIES IN SOCIOLOGY AND SOCIAL ANTHROPOLOGY

CHIEF EDITOR

K. ISHWARAN

VOLUME III

KINSHIP AND GEOGRAPHICAL MOBILITY

LEIDEN
E. J. BRILL
1965

KINSHIP
AND
GEOGRAPHICAL MOBILITY

EDITED BY

RALPH PIDDINGTON

LEIDEN
E. J. BRILL
1965

Reprinted from:
International Journal of Comparative Sociology
Vol. VI, No. 1, 1965

First published in 1965

PRINTED IN THE NETHERLANDS

CONTENTS

Foreword

K. ISHWARAN

York University, Toronto, Canada

EVERY social system incorporates a network of human relations based on kinship. The kinship principle, of mutual rights and obligations based ultimately on blood, is in one form or another universal. In some societies, such as among the Australian aborigines, the rights and duties based on kinship are coextensive with the entire complex of roles. In other societies, such as the industrialized countries of western Europe and North America, the kinship network exists side by side with other forms of social organization. But nowhere is it absent. The blood ties may be fictitious in whole or in part, such as the classificatory kin of stepmother or clansman. But the blood principle, be it reckoned through the mother's side, the father's side, or both, is nowhere entirely absent.

Kinship may fruitfully be studied in its structural aspects. Thus one may describe the various kinds of kinship networks: the clan, the moiety, the extended family, the polygynous family, the monogamous family, etc. This has traditionally been a task assigned to anthropology. One may also explain the particular forms kinship takes by reference to the functions the domestic institution plays for the social system, in the context of other institutions, such as the economic institution, the political institution, or the religious institution. Anthropology and sociology have both theorized here, and workers in both fields have gone on to predict the future course of development, and to make suggestions concerning social planning of the evolution of kinship structures.

Kinship may also, however, be studied in its effects upon individual development. Social psychology is that discipline among the social sciences most adequately fitted to investigate the inter-relationships between the kinship groupings and the individuals who compose them. The divisions between the academic disciplines are largely matters of traditions grown out of historical accident, and there is nothing strange about investigating problems peculiar to all of them in the examination of the undifferentiated phenomena of the real world.

Kinship features differ widely over the world, and there are discernible differences even between different parts of almost every culture. There do seem to be certain broad similarities, however, between the features of kinship systems in the technologically simpler societeis, on the one hand, and the technologically complex societies, on the other. Although our direct experience, and hence our remarks, are based on two societies, the Indian and the Dutch, an examination of other literature will readily convince the reader that the Indian remarks can be generalized to most of the "developing nations", and the Dutch remarks to most of the "developed nations".

The most outstanding difference is in the size of the kinship group. Whereas the average sized household in Holland is of about 4 members, the average size in India is nearly 6, half again as many. And whereas the average Dutchman knows perhaps 50 kinsmen, the average Indian may know 100 or more.

The difference in continuity, though not so immediately apparent as the difference in size, is no less salient. The Indian family group may exist as a residential and social kinship unit for four generations, with a theoretical possibility of even more. The urban Dutch family rarely consists of more than two. The life-span of the Indian family before break-up is hence at least twice as long as that of the Dutch family. In the Dutch family, children may even leave home before marriage, further shortening the temporal duration of the family group. The kinship group in India may exist as a viable mutual aid society through second or even third cousins; the Dutch kinship network, for all practical effects and purposes seems to have no meaning beyond first cousins.

The Dutch family is neolocal, the Indian patrilocal. Authority in the neolocal system almost of necessity is highly circumscribed between adult generations, whereas under the patrilocal system, parental authority generally persists until the death of the parents.

In both societies, monogamy is now enforced by law. (In India, Muslims constitute an exception, being allowed four wives). In India, however, as elsewhere in Africa and Asia, polygamy has been practiced in the past, and one can still find a few polygamous households in almost every town and village.

The relation of the Indian kin group to production is direct. The Dutch kin group, usually, has little or nothing to do with the economic occupations of its members. Partly as a result of this, kinship in India plays a much greater role in the ascription of status than in Holland.

In simpler socities, where the extended family is common, the predominance of kin is both a cause and an effect of an almost total absence of geographical mobility. The nuclear family type, by the same token, is both encouraged by and makes easier the moving of people from place to place.

The emphasis on the nuclear family system is correlated with a process of increasing individualization, the blurring of age and sex roles, geographical dispersion of the kin group, an open class society, an open family system, and rapid technological change. It remains for further research to demonstrate whether an emphasis on extended kin and technological backwardness, or the nuclear family and technological advancement, are in any way casally related, or whether the correlation can be explained on other grounds.

This volume has been edited by Dr. Ralph Piddington, Professor of Anthropology at the University of Auckland, New Zealand, and is the third in a series on international studies in anthropology and sociology. The authors come from many cultures, and we sincerely hope that this publication will be helpful for the student of comparative sociology. We wish to convey our thanks to the editor and to the contributors who have made this publication possible.

This publication is now being issued with the generous support of York University, Toronto, Canada. We take this opportunity to express our gratitude to Dr. Murray G. Ross, President of York University and an eminent sociologist in his own right, for the moral and material assistance he has given the publication. We have every expectation that this publication, already well established, will continue its steady growth with the support of York University and its President.

Finally, to Dean John Saywell, and to Professor Frederick Elkin, chairman of the Department of Sociology at York, whose co-operation has been very helpful in the publication of this issue, our gratitude is feelingly expressed.

Editor's Introduction[1]

RALPH PIDDINGTON

The University of Auckland, Auckland, New Zealand

IT was originally intended to entitle this volume "Kinship and Migration". But the term "migration" usually implies permanent or semi-permanent settlement at the destination of the migrant, or a regular "nomadic" pattern of migration, usually seasonal. I wished to include visits and other occasional contacts between geographically separated kinsfolk.

These contacts may be important in the maintenance of kinship bonds not only between the individuals directly involved, but also indirectly (for example, through the exchange of news or gifts) between clusters of kinsfolk in the two areas concerned. Hence I chose the wider term "geographical mobility" to cover these phenomena.

It has been widely assumed that such modern phenomena as migration, urbanisation, industrialisation and acculturation must necessarily weaken or destroy the system of closely knit kinship bonds outside the nuclear family which characterises most of the "primitive" or "folk" societies with which social anthropologists were in the past largely concerned. This assumption has been questioned, notably by Firth and Garigue, and it seemed to me that it would be of value to discover how far it is valid for a variety of societies living under more or less "modern" conditions. This is the purpose of the present volume.

In the nature of the case, no comprehensive and definitive formulations could be expected to emerge from these essays. But certain tentative conclusions may be suggested.

Firstly, as to geographical mobility, the variety of factors determining it are apparent. There is no single motivation comparable with what Ragnar Numelin called "the wandering spirit" but rather widely differing concatenations of circumstances which induce individuals or groups to move from one area to another. As will emerge, the variety of these circumstances produces different effects on kinship relationships.

The variety of kinship systems, in both "primitive" and "modern" societies, is likewise well known. But there does exist a broad distinction between the former and the latter. In Firth's terminology, regularities of kinship behaviour in the former are normative and in the latter statistical. I propose to call these types of system *obligatory* and *statistically based* respectively, though the difference

1 For references cited in this introduction, please see bibliography at the end of my essay.

between them is relative the two categories are not mutually exclusive. In obligatory systems, for example, you *must* give presents to your mother's brother, or you *must not* marry your father's sister's daughter. In statiscally based systems you may or may not visit uncles, aunts and cousins who have moved from your locality, or you may or may not marry your brother's wife's sister. Yet a large proportion of French Canadians do both of these things – there is thus a discernible regularity of behaviour but without obligation.

One important feature of statistically based systems seems to be that, as has been stressed by Garigue (1958) for Montreal, they are more flexible and can therefore more easily adapt themselves to new conditions. It is important to note that though in most cases kinship bonds do not atrophy, they change their functions under new conditions. This is apparent when we compare Beckett's material with indigenous Australian inter-tribal kinship relations as described, for example, by Stanner (1934). Nzimiro's essay again shows how indigenous kinship systems become modified to meet new circumstances.

One important matter which must be considered in relation to kinship in statistically based systems is social class. Most commonly in societies having social classes based on economic prosperity or political power or both, kinship tends to be of less importance in the upper social strata – see the observations and citations at the beginning of Osterreich's essay. Hubert and Ishwaran illustrate the same tendency in widely differing societies. But while the general tendency seems clear, there are exceptions. In Yankee City, for example, membership of the Upper Upper class is dependent on kinship – i.e. on membership of one of the "old families". The same principle operates, of course, in heredity aristocracies. Perhaps the distinction which I have drawn between the vertical and lateral dimensions of kinship (Part II, Section 4, of my article) is relevant here.

Another factor which may influence kinship is minority status in plural societies (Beckett, Nzimiro, Gould). I myself believe that the importance of kinship among French Canadians is in part a reaction to the situation which Garigue (1963) has described as *dépendance*.

The general conclusion from these essays is that, in spite of the reservations mentioned above, under modern conditions of change kinship bonds outside the nuclear family tend to persist, or more correctly to assume certain new functions. Where this does not occur a variety of specific negative factors operating in particular situations may lead to a weakening of the ties of kinship.[1] This suggestion may prove to have an important bearing on problems of economic development in under-developed areas. Research stemming from the work of Freud and Malinowski has shown the vital strength of motivations developed within the individual family. It now appears that similar, though less strong, motivations may readily emerge from kinship relationships outside the family. This has a bearing on the implications of what one New Zealand

1 The data on Ganda and non-Ganda at the conclusion of Gutkind's essay are of interest in this connection.

economist (referring specifically to the Pacific) has called the "disincentives" in "communal" systems of economy based largely on kinship. If our conclusion is correct, we should think again about the desirability of "individualising" economic motivations and consider whether and in what ways the latent strength of kinship bonds may be employed for constructive socio-economic development. Compare the Appendix by S. C. Christopher.

Two methodological points deserve mention. One is the study of the genesis of kinship attitudes and behaviour in modern societies, to which Ayoub's essay is a valuable contribution. But it cannot be inferred that the childhood conditions which she records will necessarily continue as her informants reach adulthood and old age. Ayoub does not suggest this, but the inference which might carelessly be drawn from her material should be viewed with caution. It might be suggested as an alternative hypothesis that in some modern societies there are four phases (perhaps more) in the development of kinship attitudes during the life cycle of the average individual:

1. To young children kinsfolk are important as a source of affectionate attention and candy.
2. With adolescence new interests deflect attention from kinsfolk; moreover kinship obligations may be partially rejected as part of the protest against authority, specifically that of parents e.g. "You *must* write to your Aunt Emma".
3. In adult life kinship assumes a new and different significance arising from the "advantages" listed by Osterreich, Table V.
4. As old age approaches, kinship once more assumes a new significance. Interest in it arises partly from the necessary waning of other interests, such as occupational pursuits and strenuous physical activities; and partly from the comfort derived from contemplation of younger kinsfolk as an embodiment of the onward flow of human existence, an experience which does not usually characterise younger people for whom life is active and appears to stretch indefinitely into the future.

Secondly, it is necessary to stress the danger of taking at their face value statements by informants as to their attitudes towards kin (cf. in my essay Part II, D. 7, D. 8) whether in verbal answers or responses to questionnaires, as in the case of some of Osterreich's material, which fortunately embodies data on what people *do* as against how they *feel*. My senior students in Auckland carry out annually an assignment in which they are called upon to compile a genealogy and comment on it in an essay. In two cases the informants when first approached by my students said: "The less I know about my kinsfolk the better", and "My brother and I decided we would have nothing to do with the mob." The further commentaries on both genealogies revealed fairly frequent contacts with kinsfolk and an enjoyment of them when they occurred.

I regret the tardy appearance of this volume, though I feel no obligation to make a personal apology. The reason for delay has been the failure of certain persons who had promised contributions to send their MSS after over a year of procrastination. This necessitated the soliciting of other articles at the last moment in order to produce an adequate volume. I am most grateful to the Chief Editor for his initiative and co-operation in this matter, and throughout the period of preparation of this work.

The Child's Control of his Kindred in View of Geographical Mobility and its Effects

MILLICENT R. AYOUB

Fels Research Institute, Antioch College, Yellow Springs, Ohio, U.S.A.

IN the United States, to move is more usual than not to move, especially when a family is young. The idea of voluntarily changing one's place of residence and moving on to another is surely one of the more characteristic features of American life. From the beginning of the nation in the Seventeenth and Eighteenth Centuries, its people have been bred to believe a solution to any difficulty is leaving one place and going elsewhere. This belief is one constant element which crisscrosses the diverse ethnic, religious, and socio-economic differences which otherwise divide the country. Because, the mere fact of being there attests to one's having traveled, or his ancestors' having traveled, having made the long journey from another continent. This fact has meant that no value distinction may be made between the person leaving and the one he has left. Each has had a turn at being both, neither may reproach for desertion without being open to the reminder that the plaintiff is only being paid in kind for his own mobility.

To move is more normal. To remain in one place is the unnatural case. And this can be so because Americans have one great alternative: the frontier available to those who want it and are strong enough to survive its election. The concept that everything human may change its location in space is at the same time both reason and excuse for the move. The physical frontier, the line of lonely settlements has filled up and moved in a generally westerly direction but the illusion it fostered leads the American to assert that the grass *is* greener in the other fellow's yard and being so he has the right to go to that yard (or one like it) and see for himself. The words of the folksong. "The bear went over the mountain, the bear went over the mountain, the bear went over the mountain and what do you think he saw? He saw another mountain, and what do you think he did? He climbed that other mountain..." tells the whole story. Following this line of reason, Americans rear children to the idea that leaving one home for a new one is *familiar*, even though the home may not be. A child sees and knows his relatives, neighbors and friends leaving the homes he connected them with and although he may not envy their departure, its occurrence is not strange to him. Nor will his own be when the time comes for him to make his own change.

For the purpose of learning about the child's appreciation of such constant geographic mobility, we conducted a small study of the effect this movement may have upon the young child's knowledge of the composition of his family cell. We sought to find out whether it has any unity in time and space and whether he shifts his conceptions with the realignment of the segments with which the larger whole is composed. If he knew of an uncle and this uncle moves, is he still Uncle to him and can he be identified as such?

Procedure

We asked ninety-eight boys and girls between the ages of five and thirteen years to name their *parents' siblings and the spouses of these persons*, and further asked them to specify by *name* and *kintype*. We separately ascertained data on these people, including their current place of residence.

The children were drawn from the larger population of the Fels Research Institute, a longitudinal research project in Yellow Springs, Ohio.

In the analysis of the results of this questioning, we relied upon the base line which was what the child's parent told as his version of the truth, that is to say, the number of uncles and aunts the child had and their current location. In many cases the parent duplicated what the child said although he had no way of knowing what it had been. In several instances the stories differed – the parent nominated more people than his child had mentioned; in a few, the child's exceeded the parent's. Where the latter occurred, we double-checked and when the parent replicated his original answer we interpreted the child's answer to be that of a classificatory or fictive connection. (A parent was never informed of his child's "mistakes". The boundary between fact and fantasy is too shadowy to be measured precisely.)

The selection of parents' siblings as the object of inquiry followed from the expectation that nuclear families in the United States normally segment as a household unit with the attainment of adulthood by the offspring and that it was to be the children of these offspring whose cognizance of this fission we would be seeking to evaluate.

The sample tested is divisible by age and sex into four groups:

Boys between five and nine years
Girls between five and nine years
Boys between ten and thirteen years
Girls between ten and thirteen years.

Each child was interviewed separately without forewarning or other preparation. The children were accustomed to testing when at the Fels Research Institute but this was a totally new experience and one they seemed to enjoy. The investigator was in a subordinate position, the child thought. Surely he knew more about his own relatives than any stranger! It was repeatedly emphasized that this was not an intelligence test to which there were "right" and "wrong" answers.

The principal question was worded in two ways to insure the child's understanding the problem. In a pre-test of our interview method, we soon learned that to some children, particularly the younger ones, the terms "brother" and "sister" meant not what they do to an adult, offspring of the same parent, but rather they meant something such as "a small child." Repeatedly, we confounded our subjects by suggesting that an uncle was by definition a brother. "How could that be?" they said in amazement, "He's a big man...", or when asked if a father has any brothers, a boy might say, "Yes, he has me and my brother Johnny." The first wording was: "Do you have any (uncles) (aunts)? What are their names? Are they related to you through your father or your mother"? And thereafter an artificial topic was introduced, the weather, school, baseball. Then the second wording: "Does your (father) (mother) have any (brothers) (sisters)? What are their names?"

The proximity of the child to his kinsmen was previously ascertained from the mother and the distance expressed on a six point scale, rangein from one for same or adjacent residence, to a score of six meaning out of the country.

The results of the study are presented in Table I, a and b, for the boys and Table II, a and b, for the girls. Kinsmen scored "correct" (based on the parent's word) are represented in Column 1, and their proximity to ego in Column 2. Answers or their lack are scored "incorrect" if the parent cannot verify the child's word or if the kinsman is omitted entirely. Column 1 headed N records the total number of dyads of each type which the children of that group could have mentioned, i.e., if there were four boys between the ages of five and nine who had among them a total of six father's brothers, and mentioned all six, the table would read as it stands now. If seventeen father's brothers existed but only six were correctly cited, only six would be in Column 1 and the eleven remaining would be in Column 4 as it is now.

Reading of the tables

From Tables I and II, we may draw several different but related, not contradictory, conclusions about the child's conception of his relatives.

First, it is very clear that younger children do less well than older ones on the problem with which they are faced, and similarly, boys know less than girls do at each age level. The younger group of boys could mention only sixteen out of the total one hundred twenty-three parents' siblings they were "responsible for," a difference of 22.9% lower than the younger girls. The gap narrows with the older children, of whom the boys know only 5.8% less than the older girls. The difference *age* brings is shown better with the boys. Younger girls know only 32.3% less than the older girls do, whereas younger boys drop 49.6% below the older boys.

The four age/sex groups differ somewhat on which kintypes they remember

Table I
Boys

Geographic Proximity of Boys' Parents' Siblings and Spouses And Their Identification by Age of Boy and Kintype of Relatives

Kintype	*N*	*Average Proximity of Correctly Identified*	*N*	*Average Proximity of Mistakenly Identified*
		Age 5–9 years a.		
Father's brother	6	4.0	11	3.6
Father's brother's wife	2	6.0	11	4.1
Father's sister	1	6.0	18	4.0
Father's sister's husband	0	—	14	4.5
Mother's brother	4	5.0	16	4.5
Mother's brother's wife	1	5.0	12	4.2
Mother's sister	1	4.0	14	4.6
Mother's sister's husband	1	4.0	11	4.8
		Age 10–13 years b.		
Father's brother	36	3.6	16	4.1
Father's brother's wife	23	3.3	21	4.6
Father's sister	24	4.0	24	4.5
Father's sister's husband	14	3.7	26	4.8
Mother's brother	43	4.1	6	4.7
Mother's brother's wife	27	4.1	9	4.9
Mother's sister	30	4.2	15	3.9
Mother's sister's husband	21	4.2	14	3.8

Table II
Girls

Geographic Proximity of Girls' Parents' Siblings and Spouses And Their Identification by Age of Girl and Kintype of Relatives

Kintype	*N*	*Average Proximity of Correctly Identified*	*N*	*Average Proximity of Mistakenly Identified*
		Age 5–9 years a.		
Father's brother	15	5.1	14	4.15
Father's brother's wife	5	5.4	16	4.6
Father's sister	8	3.9	28	4.3
Father's sister's husband	3	4.7	27	4.5
Mother's brother	18	3.4	21	4.9
Mother's brother's wife	6	4.7	14	4.6
Mother's sister	17	4.3	12	5.2
Mother's sister's husband	10	4.5	14	5.2
		Age 10–13 years b.		
Father's brother	14	3.5	8	4.2
Father's brother's wife	8	4.1	15	5.1
Father's sister	30	4.3	15	5.3
Father's sister's husband	21	4.0	15	5.2
Mother's brother	19	4.8	3	3.3
Mother's brother's wife	14	4.6	5	4.0
Mother's sister	30	4.9	6	4.8
Mother's sister's husband	21	5.0	6	4.7

most readily. All four knew their consanguine uncles better than they did any other male kintype, and all also knew their father's sisters less well than the rest, greater or lesser residential proximity notwithstanding. The profile of the pattern of knowledge shows younger boys knowing little more than these uncles, and younger girls knowing the same uncles, with mother's sisters a strong second. All groups evince a greater knowledge of consanguines than of affines. Both older and younger girls exhibit a partiality for mother's sister, the older ones only knowing mother's brother a little more often. The younger girls appear to have forgotten aunts by marriage as a group, although remembering their mother's sister's husband almost as well as they know their mother's brother. Older girls describe an almost adult profile, underscoring on one category only, their father's brother's wife.

When we compare the maternal and paternal sides, we find that only the younger boys favor their father's side, and here the difference is slight because of their general weakness. All the rest are able to mention the distaff side more than the other.

We look now to see what difference, if any, geographic proximity makes for a child's knowing or not knowing his aunts and uncles. With the usual caveats on small size of sample, we make the following tentative statements:

1. With older boys and girls, nearness seems to have a positive effect. Older boys identify kin correctly with an average proximity which is 3.85 as compared with 4.35 for those whom they miss. Older girls identify correctly kin who have a proximity rating of 4.4, and err on those who live further away, 4.7.
2. With the younger children, proximity has an inverse effect. Boys know better the ones who live further away, having a Proximity Score of 4.65, compared with those on whom they miss score of 4.3. With the younger girls the direction is the same but not so marked. Girls identify correctly kin who live an average of 4.45, and miss on those who live 4.8 away.

Discussion

Leaving aside the differences which age and sex have produced in amount of knowledge, it is fair to say that older children know better those kinsmen who live in their near vicinity while younger boys and girls know better the ones further away. We may well ask why and how this could be so. I would suggest that these far off uncles and aunts are better known by the small children because from their being more often close to their mothers and they are aware of the special notice the mother may give to the arrival of say a letter from a brother or sister way off in another part of the country. The child will feel personally gratified if he can boast to a schoolmate in Ohio of having an uncle in Arizona with all the intimations of cowboy life which such residence implies. The same applies for an uncle by marriage who is overseas in the army or navy. For the older children, girls particularly, another factor may be operating. The girls are ignorant, or feign ignorance of their father's brother's wife, though they are able to identify a large proportion of every other type of kinsman. We may conjecture that girls of this age are just beginning to shake off maternal control and so are somewhat negative or wary of possible mother surrogates, as their father's brother's wives might be thought to be. Little girls similarly "forget" the father's brother's wife, but that loss of memory is in line with their forgetting other affines. In general, affines are less often remembered than consanguines.

The overall pattern of remembering and forgetting can perhaps be best seen if we combine totals. We find that younger boys know only 23% fewer of their aunts and uncles than younger girls, and know 49.5% less compared with older boys. Younger girls know only 32.3% less than older ones, who in turn know 05.8 more than older boys. Furthermore, as suggested above, the average proximity of those kin correctly identified by the younger children drops sharply when they are able to identify the kin correctly.

Summary

In the effort to discover what, if any, effect the dispersion of children's near relatives had on their conception of the composition of their family, we set ninety-eight boys and girls between the ages of five and thirteen the task of naming and identifying their parents' siblings and their spouses and then looked at the accuracy of these answers in terms of present location of these persons. Speaking generally, it is apparently clear that geographic distance improves only the likelihood of the older child's remembering his aunts and uncles, and may have an inverse effect on the younger boys especially. These boys are the most "childish," in their answers; that is to say, the most often wrong. The younger girls present a pattern of responses more like the older boys than like the older girls, whose answers are nearly perfectly adult.

Kinship, Mobility and Community among Part-Aborigines in Rural Australia

JEREMY R. BECKETT

Monash University

Introduction

THE setting of this study is the "Far West" of New South Wales, a region of semi-arid plains, mainly given over to sheep grazing and supporting only a sparse population. The region's only large town is Broken Hill, a mining centre of about 30,000 inhabitants; the rest are small commercial and servicing centres for the pastoral hinterland: only Bourke, Cobar and Condobolin exceed 2,000, while the three townships of the "Corner" (the extreme north-west of the State), together boast no more than 250. East of the Bogan and South of the Lachlan, sheep grazing gradually gives way to wheat farming, while at Mildura and Griffith there is fruit growing. The population of these areas is less sparse and the towns are larger; however, they figure only marginally in the present account.

In or around most Far Western townships one finds a number of people who are known, locally and officially, as Aborigines. In fact, few of them are "full bloods", the remainder having European ancestry; however, in most situations the important distinction lies between those who have some Aboriginal ancestry and those who have none. The latter are "White People"; the former are "Dark People" (the polite euphemism), "Abos." or "Darkies". The stress on colour is not altogether misplaced. Most Aborigines are physically distinct from White People, ranging from the near-black of the "full blood", to the swarthiness of the "quarter-caste" which might in other places indicate Mediterranean origin; however, there are some who are physically indistinguishable but retain Aboriginal identity because of their known kinship with darker people or their adherence to Aboriginal ways.

Although one may speak of an Aboriginal way of life, this implies little that is tribal. The old tribal groups are dispersed, while local populations are of mixed origin; no boys or girls have been initiated for 50 years or more; the old rules of kinship behaviour, including prescribed marriage, are not merely disregarded but forgotten; tribal languages are scarcely spoken, even at home, and are not being learned by the rising generation. The eating of wild foods, such as kangaroo, is perhaps the only conscious carry-over from tribal times. Loss of their indigenous culture has not, however, made them any more ready to adopt the White 'Australian way of life', as some advocates of "assimilation" seem to think it should. Instead of emulating the industry, thrift and regard for property and comfort, of middle class Europeans – with whom they had little contact – they took as their model the nineteenth century pastoral workers, whose way of life presented many parallels to their own. This white "Nomad Tribe"[1] took little account of property or thrift, preferring to squander their earnings in prodigality and drunkenness; they changed their jobs frequently, affecting a sturdy independence, and took what was almost a pride in enduring rough food and conditions; generosity to friends was perhaps their cardinal virtue. Few Europeans live this way today, and those who do are not highly regarded by the more settled section of the population; however, it has been carried on by Aborigines for several generations, with the difference that they are more or less settled in one place and have large families. The White citizens of outback townships expect from their neighbours a minimum standard of material possession and comfort, cleanliness and sobriety. Not all Europeans conform to this standard, but almost all Aborigines fall short of it. Dirtiness, fecklessness, drunkenness and sexual immorality form a central part of the "no-hoper Abo" stereotype commonly held by White country people. The camps of scrap iron "humpies" and ill-kempt government cottages, which fringe so many country towns, are said to "give the place a bad name" and endanger public health; no White person would go there except on business or for some nefarious purpose.[2] The entry of an Aboriginal family into the body of the town is regarded with misgiving, unless its respectability is firmly established.

Racial antagonism is perhaps strongest in a place like Wilcannia, where the Aboriginal-European ratio is of the order of 300:600 and where the Aboriginal population is a largely post-war phenomenon. Antagonism is less in the Lake Cargelligo district where the ratio is 300:1,500 and where the Aborigines live segregated on a government settlement (Murrin Bridge) 10 miles from town, but this may be only because contacts are so limited as to provide insufficient base for any positive attitude. In either case, there is a marked separation between White and Coloured. Far West Aborigines are integrated into the regional economy as wage-labourers and consumers, and into the governmental system as persons subject to ordinary laws as well as special "protective" laws, and the attentions of a special agency devoted to their "welfare"; however, there are many areas of Australian institutional life where few if any Aborigines penetrate. Bridge situations, which might lead to closer rapport between white and coloured, are few and in fact friendships are rare and intermarriage even more so.[3] The

---

1 "Nomad tribe" was the name given to Australian pastoral workers by the author Anthony Trollope, when he visited Australia during 1870 (Trollope 1876:69); see also Ward (1958:9).

2 A more detailed account of race relations in the Far West can be found in Beckett (1964).

3 In 1957, four Aboriginal women were married to or living with white men around Wilcannia; there were no Murrin Bridge Aborigines married to or living with white people, though in neighbouring Euabalong five women and three men were involved in mixed marriages.

separation is reinforced by the lack of common interests, which makes communication difficult, while initial antipathy and suspicion disincline either side to seek each other out.

Aborigines throughout the Far West – indeed, throughout the Southern half of Australia – share a common culture, but they are not organized in any over-all way. Even local communities rarely engage in any joint enterprise; the nuclear family is the largest group functioning regularly. This low level of organization is possible because Aboriginal society is very much dependent upon European society, particularly as regards the economy and the maintenance of law and order. The norms of Aboriginal society govern inter-personal rather than inter-group relations, and are mostly concerned with casual, short-term types of inter-action. In the absence of any wider co-ordinating principle, face-to-face relations are of primary importance among Aborigines, and local communities are only saved from isolation by the direct contacts their members make in the course of moving about the countryside. Mobility is consequently of considerable social importance.

Since coming under White domination, Far West Aborigines have moved about a good deal, though mostly within the region. Some of these moves have been involuntary, dictated by the authorities or economic circumstances; others have been voluntary. These last follow a pattern which is largely the product of factors within Aboriginal society. Mere proximity need not be a major factor: an Aboriginal may go 200 miles to a place where he is known, rather than 10 miles to a place where he is not. Usually, being *known* means having kinsfolk who will receive him and act as his sponsors in the local community. The area within which he moves – his *beat*, as I shall call it – is defined by the distribution of kin. I shall show that the typical beat is gradually expanding.

In the pages that follow I shall identify the tribes from which most of the present Far West Aborigines are descended and follow their movements up to the present time. I shall then describe the pattern of mobility and indicate some of the factors which go towards determining it.

The Tribes of the Far West

The so-called "tribes" of the Far West were often distinguished only by their use of a particular named language or dialect, however, the approximate territories of these linguistic groups are known[1] and "tribal" identification gives some indication of local origin during the early period.

The Darling River forms the major division in the area: to the south-east lived the Wiradjeri-speaking tribes, the Ngiemba around Cobar, the Wongaibon (also sometimes called Ngiemba) between Cobar and Ivanhoe, and the Wiradjeri proper along the Lachlan River and to the south and east. At the lower ends

1 Australian tribal boundaries have been drawn by Tindale (1940), utilizing a number of sources. See Beckett (1958) for a re-drawing of some of the boundaries in the Corner area.

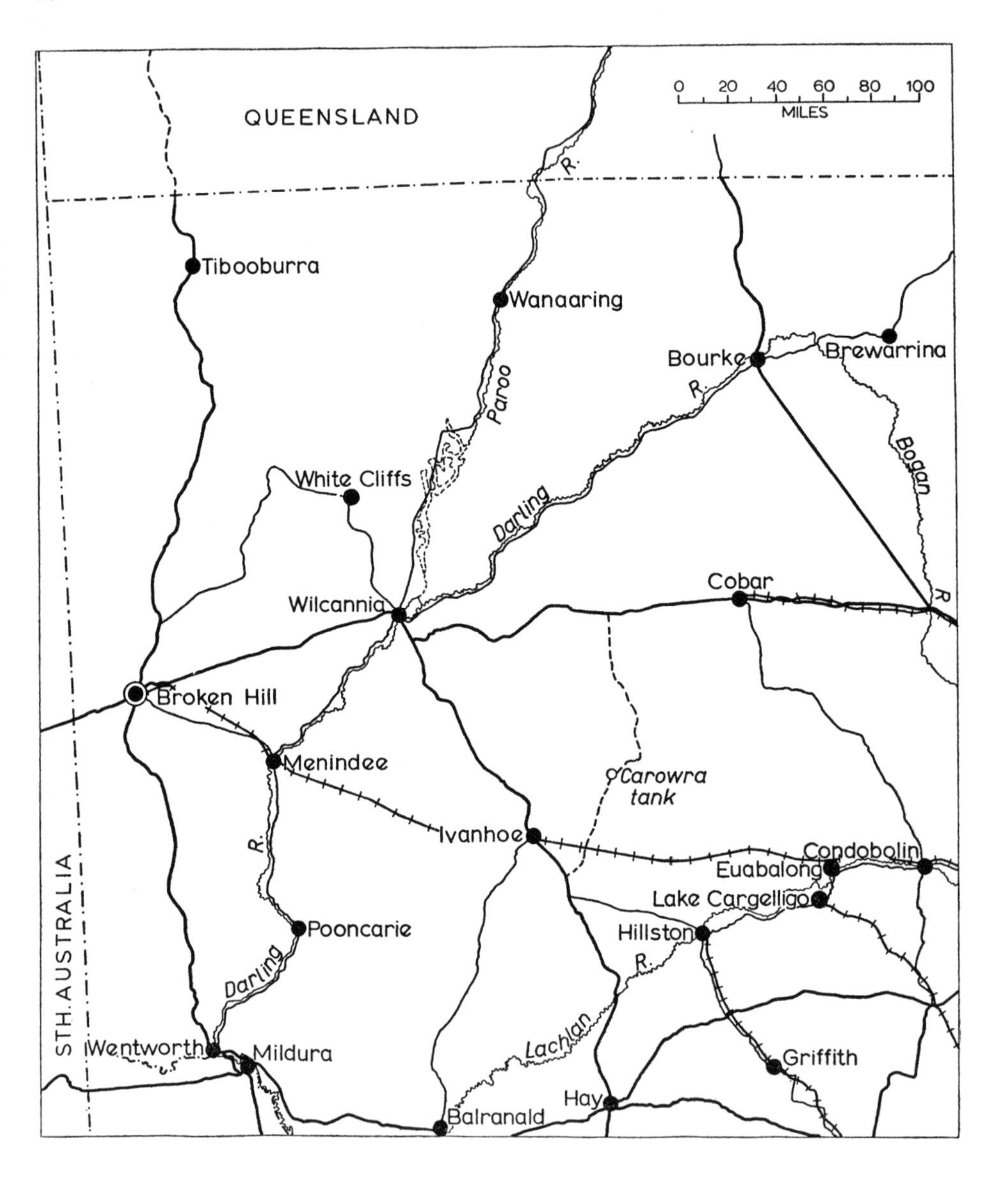

of the Lachlan and Murrumbidgee lived a number of small groups such as the Ita-Ita and Waimbu-Waimbu, about whom very little is known.

Along the Darling, from about Wentworth to Bourke, lived the Bagundji speaking peoples, and back from the river to the north, along the Paroo, and to the northwest as far as the South Australian border, lived a number of tribes who spoke dialects of the same language, most of whom have now died out.

In the Corner region, around Tibooburra, were two more tribes, the Maliangapa and Wonggumara, who were again distinct though related to others across the Queensland border.

The major linguistic divisions seem to have been correlated with cultural differences in kinship organization, ceremonial and mythology,[1] though how far these inhibited contact is hard to tell. According to native tradition, Wongaibon fought with the Lachlan River people, and both they and the Ngiemba fought the Darling River people, but again we do not know whether these hostilities were sufficiently continuous to inhibit contact. Certainly, trade linked widely separated tribes.

The Early Phases of Contact

Europeans settled the Far West early in the second half of the nineteenth century, though the settlement was very sparse for some years. Since the settlement was mainly pastoral, and since native spearing of stock provoked violent clahes in other pastoral areas, we may guess that the same occurred here. Bean speaks of shootings along the Upper Darling (1911:259), and there is a native tradition of a massacre near Menindee, but information concerning this early period is very sparse. In 1883 the N.S.W. Government produced the first of a series of reports on the conditions of Aborigines in the Far West (Protector of Aborigines: 1883). By this time black and white had reached a *modus vivendi*, corresponding to the phase of intelligent parasitism described by Elkin (1951:31). Aborigines camped around the small townships and large station homesteads, living partly from government handouts, partly from what they earned from doing casual stockwork and odd jobs; however, when they wished it was still possible for them to take to the bush, living on wild foods in the traditional manner and organizing the old ceremonies (Beckett, 1958). Depopulation, resulting possibly from shootings, and certainly from epidemics, had reduced the Aborigines to manageable numbers – indeed, it had exterminated some tribes altogether – and they continued to decline for some years to come.

The distribution of Aboriginal population in 1915, the last year in which the N.S.W. Government published detailed figures (Aborigines Protection Board: 1916) is set out in Table I. The figures for 1883, the date of the first survey, are added to indicate the rate of decline over the period. Up to about 1920 the tribal remnants were mostly living on or near their old territories. The possibilities for travelling had increased, however; those still interested travelled into Queensland and South Australia in search of ceremonies; others, more interested in modern things, travelled long distances as drovers or moved about from station to station in search of stock work. One or two men never returned from their travels and a few strangers married local women and stayed,

1 There is a voluminous though often superficial literature on the culture and social organization of the tribes of the Far West, mostly dating from the late nineteenth and early twentieth centuries, see Greenway (1963).

Table 1

Location of Aboriginal Population in the Far West, 1883 and 1915

Location	*1883*	*1915*
Tibooburra	153	17
Milparinka (nr. Tibooburra)	80	33
Wanaaring	109	32
Wilcannia	189	5
Menindee	—	21
Pooncairie	37	26
Cobar	17	28
Ivanhoe	—	43
Mosgiel (nr. Ivanhoe)	99	109
Hillston	80	32
Lake Cargelligo	31	—
Euabalong	66	76
Condobolin	145	53
	1,006	375

but the over-all scene was fairly stable. However, the inter-war period was to bring a more serious upheaval.

The Uprooting

The pattern of life described in the preceding section was disrupted by two main factors: pastoral sub-division and the Great Depression. The sub-division of large pastoral property began during the 1900s and was resumed after the war as a means of settling ex-servicemen. In the Far West, the vast sheep runs with their village-like homesteads, employing large numbers of workers and supporting a small Aboriginal camp (Bean 1945:73–6), were replaced by small family blocks which employed only a few men and could not afford to maintain Aborigines. The evicted Aborigines drifted away to live on the fringes of townships.[1]

The plight of the Wongaibon, who were the largest and also the most backward group in the Far West, was sufficiently serious for the Government Aborigines Protection Board to establish a controlled settlement for them at Carowra Tank, providing a minimum of shelter, food for the indigent, medical care and education (Aborigines Protection Board: 1927). Similar settlements had existed for some time in the more closely settled areas, including one at Brewarrina and another at Darlington Point (near Griffith), but they had not hitherto been considered necessary in the Far West; nor were the other groups in the region sufficiently large to justify the establishment of further settlements.

1 A similar upheaval seems to have occurred on the North Coast of New South Wales (Hausfeld 1963).

During the early 1930s there was serious unemployment throughout the area and for various reasons the Aborigines were particularly affected. Being ineligible for unemployment benefit (Bell 1959:350), they were reduced to seeking government rations and families who had previously lived independently were obliged to settle at Carowra Tank – among them a number from Hillston and the Darling River.

In 1934 the Carowra Tank water supply failed and the people were abruptly shifted to a new settlement outside Menindee. The Protection Board also seized this opportunity to bring Aborigines living at Menindee and Pooncairie under its control. As employment opportunities improved, after the outbreak of war, a number of these families resumed their independent existence and drifted up to Wilcannia. In 1948 the Aborigines Welfare Board transferred the Menindee settlement 200 miles east to Murrin Bridge, near Lake Cargelligo, but while most of the Carowra Tank people were content to "go with the mission" most of the Darling River people were not, preferring to live independently at Menindee or joining their countrymen in Wilcannia. At least ten marriages between the two groups had occurred during the period of co-residence, and when the ways parted most, though not all, husbands followed their wives' people.

The Government also forced a number of Tibooburra Aborigines to move some 300 miles across to its settlement at Brewarrina, during the depression; however, as soon as employment conditions improved the majority moved back west to Bourke, Wilcannia and the Corner region. The population of the Corner has been declining for many years, and the Aboriginal section of it has also been emigrating, mainly to Wilcannia and Bourke. The Wilcannia population, which has now swelled to about 300, consists mainly of Aborigines from the lower Darling, Tibooburra and the Paroo.

By about 1950, then, the Aboriginal population of the Far West had almost all been uprooted from their tribal territories. Few have gone outside the Far West region, but there has been a general movement from the smallest townships and back country, to the more populous centres.

Aggregation and Dispersal of Aboriginal Population in the Recent Period

Since 1950, the main centres of Aboriginal population in the Far West have been Wilcannia, Bourke, Brewarrina, Murrin Bridge (near Lake Cargelligo) and Condobolin, each with more than 200 Aborigines. Euabalong has had about 50, and Hillston, Ivanhoe and Meninda, slightly fewer. Most originate within the region, though not necessarily at the place where they are now resident, and few from within the region have gone far afield.

In Table II the 1957 married populations of Murrin Bridge and Wilcannia are broken down according to origin. Only persons who are or have been

Table 2

Origin of "Married" Aboriginal Residents of Murrin Bridge and Wilcannia in 1957

	Residence	
Origin	*Murrin Bridge*	*Wilcannia*
Condobolin	5	—
Euabalong	3	—
Hillston & Darlington Pt.	12	—
Balranald & Denilaquin	5	—
Carowra Tank & Murrin Bridge	58	11
Darling River	9	30
Wilcannia	1	20
Paroo River & Tibooburra	—	15
Elsewhere	1	5
TOTAL:	94	81

married[1], and thus have families of their own, are included; children up to the age of sixteen or seventeen almost invariably live with their parents; over that age, until marriage, young people wander about so much that some cannot be said to be permanently domiciled anywhere. Married people do move, but infrequently, and they can generally be regarded as being domiciled in a particular locality. Determining "origin" can be difficult when a person has lived in a number of places; however, Aborigines generally associate one another with particular localities which are generally where their early years were spent.

A little over 63% of those living at Murrin Bridge originated in or around Carowra Tank (i.e. persons of Wongaibon descent), or – the younger generation – at Menindee and Murrin Bridge settlements (most of whom are also of at least part-Wongaibon descent). Of the 34 outsiders, eighteen were married into this "core group". This composition had changed very little by 1964, despite some turnover of population, except that there had been a slight reduction in the number of outsiders not married into the core group.

The Wilcannia population is a coming together of several stocks, of which the largest part, 37% in 1957, came from the Darling River (Bagundji). A little over 18% came from the back country, some from around Tibooburra (Maliagnapa) and a few from the Paroo (Barundji). A further 25%, offspring of the others, considered Wilcannia their home. All those originating elsewhere were married into one of these stocks. Here again, this composition had changed very little by 1964, except that a few more outsiders (mainly from Murrin Bridge) had married Wilcannia people and settled there.

It can be seen from Table II that both populations consist largely of persons originating from one or two centres. Table III shows to what extent the people

1 Aborigines distinguish between those couples who are legally married and those who are simply "living"; however, the distinction is of no practical significance and I shall include both types of relation under the heading "married".

Table 3

Distribution of "Married" Far West Aborigines in 1957

	Origin:			
Residence	*Carowra Tank-Murrin Bridge*	*Darlin R.*	*Wilcannia*	*"Corner"*
Condobolin	2	—	—	—
Euabalong	5	—	—	—
Hillston	1	—	—	—
Griffith	1	1	—	—
Murrin Bridge	58	9	1	—
Ivanhoe	3	1	1	—
Menindee	2	5	—	—
Mildura-Wentworth	3	3	—	—
Wilcannia	11	30	20	15
Broken Hill	—	—	—	1
Tibooburra, White Cliffs & Wanaaring	—	—	—	6
Bourke & Brewarrina	—	—	—	8(?)
Far West Sheep Stations	9	2	—	5
Sydney	—	—	—	1
Queensland	3	—	—	1(?)
	98	51	22	37(?)

from these centres were dispersed in 1957. About 55% of the Carowra-Murrin Bridge stock resided at Murrin Bridge; the remainder were scattered about in twos and threes, most of them within the area confined by Lake Cargelligo – Menindee – Wilcannia – Euabalong. Ten lived outside it, but only three of them outside Western N.S.W. This distribution had not changed significantly by 1964, except that rather more young people had gone to live in Wilcannia, as already noted.

Almost 60% of the Darling River people lived at Wilcannia in 1957, while the rest were distributed within an area confined by Wilcannia – Murrin Bridge – Wentworth. Only one lived further afield. This distribution had not changed substantially by 1964, except that a few more had moved down to Wentworth district, and a few up to Bourke. The stocks originating in the Corner were and are more widely dispersed; exact numbers of those living in Bourke and Brewarrina are unfortunately not available, but the majority seem to be living in these two towns and in Wilcannia.

Substantially, the distribution of population living in, or originating from the Far West is the function of factors within Aboriginal society, although European society does impose some limitations. Transport itself is not a serious problem. A regular train service links the townships along the Broken Hill-Condobolin line. Back from the railway, travel is slow, uncomfortable and expensive, except for those few with cars, but it is generally possible to get wherever one wants in the long run, and Aborigines are not averse to spending substantial sums on taxis. Moving the contents of a European house might be difficult and expensive, but Aboriginal possessions are generally so few as to constitute little impediment. Representatives of the Aborigines Welfare Board (the successor to the Aborigines Protection Board) are empowered to expel undesirables from a controlled settlement (i.e. Murrin Bridge), but I know of only one instance in which it was done. Movement into Murrin Bridge is also limited by the lack of vacant houses and the refusal of the Board to permit the erection of temporary dwellings such as tents and scrap-iron "humpies". Elsewhere there is little restriction on the erection of such dwellings and, since most Aborigines are content to live in them, accommodation presents little problem.

Economic factors may perhaps discourage Aborigines from visiting certain places. Their pastoral skills are scarcely exportable to the city, but wherever sheep are raised or unskilled, casual labour is employed there should be opportunities for them. There are firm, though seasonally variable limits on the amount of such labour that any locality can utilize, and when supply exceeds demand employers tend to favour workers who are already tried. However, pastoral workers do not always expect to live close to their place of work. Their families must live near town so that the children can attend school (as they are required by law to do) and since many stations are isolated, they must resign themselves to being absent from home for weeks at a time; under these circumstances, it may not matter greatly whether they work 100 rather than 50 miles away.

External factors do not, then, closely determine the distribution of Aboriginal population, and we must look for clues within Aboriginal society. Overall, we can discern two clear trends; first, the tendency for people of the same origin to be concentrated in one or two main localities; and second, the tendency for people to live near some, though not necessarily all, of their kinsfolk.

In 1957, the following patterns of cohesion among close kin were apparent. Attachment to parents was fairly strong. Of 37 men who had one or both parents living, 14 resided elsewhere; of 48 women, similarly placed, only 11 (24%) resided elsewhere, and of these one had been forcibly removed (from Murrin Bridge) while three lived only ten miles away. In the case of marriage between persons from different settlements, one or other spouse has to live away from his or her parents: thus five of the eleven women and three of the fourteen men living away from a parent were living near parents-in-law. Of 39 sets of married siblings (each numbering two or more persons), 26 (66%) were dispersed; however, only 12 out of 76 married men who had siblings alive (and a much smaller proportion of women) resided where none was present. Three Aborigines who had kinsfolk somewhere resided away from them but near affines, while five lived near neither kin nor affines, having moved outside the Far West region.

Kinship Behaviour and Mobility

The clear tendency for Aborigines to reside near at least some of their close kin can be explained by a closer examination of kinship relations. In terms of stability and sentiment the relationship between mother and children is by far the strongest. Women scarcely ever desert their children, and most never leave home at all: their lives are very largely taken up with domestic duties and it is they who obtain and prepare the food – an important consideration in a society where the supply of meals is often uncertain. In short, the mother is the pivot of the home. The bond is continued in later life, and old women, whose children have grown up, spend their lives visiting one after another, including those who have gone to reside elsewhere. Once widowed, they move in with a son or daughter and often exercise considerable authority over the next generation. The position of fathers is more variable. Divorce is fairly frequent[1] and in these cases the father generally leaves home, though he may maintain some connection with the children. Men who do pastoral work, the majority, are necessarily absent from home for long periods, and their homecomings may be marked by drunkenness and discord (Beckett 1964). Nevertheless, children generally retain some regard for their fathers, and provide a home for those who are widowed. The status of elderly parents is perhaps bolstered by the pension which they receive and which constitutes a small but regular addition to an otherwise uncertain household budget.

Genealogical knowledge goes back one or, at the most, two generations, but since many families are numerous a large number of kinsfolk may still be recognized within this narrow span. Moreover, children often use kin terms for persons to whom they know themselves to be related, though ignorant of the precise link. Vernacular kin terms have now fallen into disuse and are not known to the younger generation; in their place, the standard English terms are used, though probably used more frequently than in most white communities.

The traditional norms of kinship relations have also been abandoned, and there is now very little difference between the norms of behaviour appropriate to the various categories of kin. Briefly, these norms govern the choice of spouses, the sharing of property, particularly food, and the provision of hospitality. Sexual intercourse with first degree kin is universally considered shameful, though it seems to occur very rarely; but it is also said that mating with any consanguineal kin is improper. Where genealogies are no deeper than three generations the prohibition cannot extend beyond second cousins, but in practice marriages between more distant kin are extremely rare. This can be safely concluded, even without genealogies, since, as I show later, so many have taken their spouses from other local groups with whom there was previously no contact. A recent marriage between second cousins once removed[2] evoked no comment,

1 In 1957 approximately 20% of Wilcannia and Murrin Bridge Aborigines who had ever been married (formally or informally), had also been divorced.

2 The boy married his mother's-mother's-sister's (and also mother's-father's-brother's) – daughter's-daughter's-daughter. His father claimed to have been unaware of the connection until I pointed it out.

but this is the only "test case" available to me. In principle, the prohibition is so generally accepted that little attempt is made to justify it; Aborigines sometimes suggest that "close" marriages produce unhealthy children, but this may well be a *post hoc* justification. The old rules forbade marriage with close kin, even when these were in the correct kinship category, but whether this has carried over into the contemporary situation or whether there is an unexpressed disinclination for marrying those with whom one already has defined rights and obligations, is hard to say.

Discussing traditional Aboriginal attitudes to property, Elkin has written:

> "...the goods are to use or to give away or to exchange (mostly ceremonially); food is obtained to eat and to share according to rules..." (1951:165)

Today, ceremonial is defunct and the rules are forgotten, but the general principle still holds. The obligation to share food, clothes and – more doubtfully – money, with kinsfolk who are in need is loosely defined and frequently evaded, but it is nevertheless recognized in principle and is of great social importance.

The sharing of food was important in nomadic times because the fortunes of the chase were uncertain and a regular supply of meat for each family could only be ensured in this way. Today, wild food is a minor item of diet but food supplies are uncertain for other reasons. Aboriginal workers can earn quite substantial wages, but the supply of housekeeping money is irregular: many return after several weeks' work with their wages in a lump sum, which, in the flush of momentary opulence, is quickly dissipated in purchases of liquor, small luxuries, handouts to kin and foodstuffs. The foodstuffs will also be shared with other households in need at the time. Men may spend several idle weeks at home before returning to work, by which time money and food are exhausted and the house-wife obliged to go borrowing. In theory at least, some of those whom she has helped are now well supplied and ready to reciprocate, although there is no strict accounting.

In practice there are some who borrow more than they lend and a few who are little more than parasites, but even these generally get what they want. Women may call the adults *bludgers*[1] but confess that they "don't like to see the little children going short". Families may opt out of this system if they wish; indeed, it is necessary to do so if one intends to adopt a European way of life, which involves accumulating property, but they will be called *flash*[2] and will be placed in a humiliating position if they ever find themselves in need. In a context of irregular work and improvidence, then, sharing food is an economic necessity as well as a civic virtue, and there is a crucial dependence between households.

There is little diffidence in asking for help and great reluctance to refuse; however, requests are generally addressed to kinsfolk and relatedness is implicitly or explicitly regarded as a charter. Those who have known one another for many

---

1 *Bludger* is popular Australian slang for a parasite.

2 *Flash* is nineteenth century Australian and Cockney slang applied to anyone affecting showy or superior ways.

years but are not related may also recognize similar rights and obligations, but with less certainty, while strangers are virtually excluded. An Aboriginal family, then, unless it is prepared to be entirely self-reliant, must live near some kinsfolk with whom it can engage in sharing relations. Persons of Carowra Tank origin living at Murrin Bridge have a very wide range of kin; but those living in Wilcannia are not completely isolated, even if they have no links with the Darling River people. The need is to live near some, but not necessarily all of one's kin.

The right to ask, and the obligation to provide hospitality, only arise in the case of people coming from other places, either as transient visitors or as intending immigrants. In either case, hospitality is provided for long periods without overt complaint and with very little attempt to make the guests "pay their way". Again, these rights are recognized mainly among kinsfolk although strangers are occasionally sponsored by a friend who has met them elsewhere.

Aborigines are generally unwilling to go where they are not known, for a number of reasons. Prior to 1962 the law forbidding the supply of liquor to Aborigines prevented them from seeking accommodation in hotels, and even now many landlords would refuse to accept them as guests; thus the hospitality of other Aborigines is the only alternative. Finding work in a strange locality may also be harder, particularly for the Aboriginal who is shy in the presence of white people, and there is always the risk of being charged with vagrancy if one is unemployed. Aborigines in other regions succeed in overcoming these problems and become quite self-reliant after one or two experiences as servicemen or long-distance drovers, but few in the Far West have served in the armed forces and little long-distance droving is now carried on. A number have been sent to a state capital for medical attention, but they seem to have seen little and made no social contacts there. My suggestion that a spontaneous visit should be made to a city evoked the almost standard response: "I'd get lost".

Far West Aborigines often strike the stranger as shy and they are undoubtedly hesitant about going where they would feel out of place. However, they like to travel where they are known, that is to say, where they have kin or close affines who, even though not personally acquainted, can be asked for hospitality. Considerable value is attached to seeing "a bit of the world", even though that "bit" is only a tiny township which scarcely differs from the one left, and there is a steady traffic between the main centres of Aboriginal population, particularly of old women visiting their married children and young people "taking a trip". Single boys and girls travel a good deal: their lack of domestic responsibilities renders them particularly mobile, but some may also be in search of a spouse from another place.

The rule against marrying kinsfolk drastically reduces the number of eligible partners in some places, notably at Murrin Bridge. The population there is very much inter-related and a large proportion of the Carowra Tank – Murrin Bridge stock are the descendants of three sisters. Boys and girls of the third generation find themselves with a choice of only two or three eligible partners for whom, of course, the competition is intense. Had they been cut off from outside contacts the old rule would certainly have broken down, but contacts – first with Hillston, later with the Darling River (due to the merging at the Menindee settlement) and recently through inter-visiting with Wilcannia and other places – have reduced the strain upon it. Of 119 current marriages involving at least one Aboriginal who originated in the Far West, 89 (almost 75%) were contracted with a spouse who originated from a different locality or – in a few instances – who was a European.

When I returned in 1964, after an interval of seven years, the pattern was essentially the same. Of 26 marriages occurring in the interim, 16 were between persons who normally resided in different localities, having resulted from one partner visiting the locality of the other. Three more were between persons who, though currently living in the same locality, had originated in different ones; while a further four were between persons whose respective parents originated in different localities, though they themselves belonged to the same locality. In short, the process of migration and visiting within the region has resulted in inter-marriage between localized groups which were originally almost endogamous.

Each Aboriginal has a *beat*, an area which is defined by the situation of kinsfolk who will give him hospitality, within which he can travel as much or as little as he pleases, and where he is most likely to find his wife. Proximity is only a minor factor. When first working in Murrin Bridge, I was impressed by the fact that most of the people knew far more about Wilcannia – 200 miles away – and visited it more frequently, than they did Euabalong – only ten miles away – or Condobolin – only thirty. One explanation is that the Murrin Bridge people have lived near these last two places only since 1948, whereas their contacts with the Darling River people go back to 1934 and before; however, one might expect links to have developed after a decade. In fact, over the last seven years only one marriage has been contracted with Condobolin and only one with Euabalong, as against six with Wilcannia.

A child acquires kinship connections through both his parents; if his parents originated from different localities his own constellation of kin[1] is likely to be more widely dispersed than either one of theirs. If he again marries someone from another locality, his children's kin constellation will be still more widely dispersed. Consider the following case:

> Gloria is a Murrin Bridge resident whose mother comes from Carowra Tank and whose father from Hillston. Most of her maternal kin live in the same settlement, but she has a mother's-brother in Mildura and a mother's-sister's son in Wilcannia. Her father's kin live in Hillston, Griffith and Condobolin.
> Gloria has married Mervyn, a Wilcannia resident, whose mother comes from Tibooburra and whose father from the Darling River. His maternal kin live in Wilcannia and Bourke, while his paternal kin live at various points along the lower Darling and at Murrin Bridge.

The marriage is hypothetical – no one yet has kin so widely dispersed as the

1 Piddington has chosen the word "constellation" from several suggested by Firth (1956: 16) "to apply to the aggregate of effective kinsfolk centred round a given individual". (1961: 16)

offspring would have – nevertheless it is most likely to become a reality before long.

Assuming that genealogical knowledge becomes cumulative, and that Aborigines continue to provide visiting kin with a *pied à terre*, *beats* will tend to become more extensive with each new generation. If we further assume that the prohibition on marriage with kin persists, there will be an increasing tendency to seek further afield for marriage partners. For example, a child of Gloria and Mervyn might find a spouse in Bourke, whose kin lay further to the north and east, or in Mildura, whose kin extended south into Victoria. In short, if our assumptions hold, the social insulation of Aborigines in the Far West is breaking down, and will continue to do so with increasing rapidity.

Of course, these assumptions may not hold, for the Aboriginal kinship system is subject to both internal strains and external pressures. Fundamental to the system is the use of genealogy as a means of classifying people. It is particularly appropriate in homogeneous societies whose members are otherwise distinguishable only by sex, age and personal idiosyncracies. Contemporary Aboriginal society is precisely of this character and it generates strong pressures against incipient economic, political or religious differentiation. Gradations of skin colour are also without significance in the Far West. Increasing concern with colour, as in Brewarrina (Fink 1957); living standards, as in Moree (Reay and Sitlington, 1948); or religion, as on the North Coast (Calley 1964), would reduce or modify the use of kinship as a means of classification and a framework for social relations. Such developments would, moreover, conflict with the types of rights and obligations which now make up the substance of kinship relations. Those claiming superiority on grounds of lighter skin colour would scarcely welcome visits from darker relatives; those trying to accumulate property would not welcome the importunings of feckless kin. Similarly, those who have joined some puritanical religion will wish to stand apart from those who remain addicted to drinking and gambling.

Even if these major changes do not occur, it is still not yet certain whether genealogical knowledge will become cumulative or whether more remote ties will be forgotten with each new generation. Till now, genealogies have usually been shallow. However, those kin who are the most remote geographically are not necessarily the most remote genealogically, so that the extension of kin ties over an ever-widening area need not be prevented by the loss of some connections. It is also uncertain whether marriage will be prohibited even with genealogically remote kin, or whether, in emulation of white people, even cousin marriage will come to be considered permissible. Such changes could reduce one of the pressures towards seeking spouses from other localities, but if young people continued to travel for other reasons the probability of their marrying non-kin would be higher than if they stayed at home. Since travel in itself widens the choice of marriage partners, it is this rather than any marriage rule which is the primary determinant of inter-locality marriages.

Yet another assumption made in these prognoses is that more distant groups of Aborigines will be content to marry the Far Westeners, and that their social systems are essentially the same. From the handful of studies already done in surrounding areas, there does seem to be a broad uniformity: most Aborigines live more or less apart from Europeans, while among themselves social relations are organized on kinship lines. Some are even more mobile than their Far West cousins, but the majority seem to confine their journeyings to a set *beat.* However, there are differences in marriage preferences. For example, the main groups of Victorian Aborigines, whose unity derives from common local origin, prefer to marry among themselves, although they recognize a prohibition on first – and sometimes also, second cousin marriages (Barwick 1963: 256–264). This preference seems to be based on an unwillingness to go to live among strangers and the expectation that the other spouse would be unhappy away from his people. Other groups, such as those at Moree, base a like preference on their adherence to higher living standards (Reay and Sitlingon 1948): to these too, Far West Aborigines would scarcely be acceptable. However, the areas immediately on the periphery of the Far West do not seem to be so exclusive, and it is with them that inter-marriage is most likely to occur over the next generation.

Kinship, Mobility and Community

Far West Aborigines distinguish two main classes of humanity: European and Aboriginal, concerning each of which they have fairly well developed stereotypes. Aborigines are deemed to have a common culture in which open-handedness, particularly towards kin, is valued, and any form of exclusiveness or superiority disapproved as an attempt to ape white people. However, while it is expected that all Aborigines will conform to these norms, personal responsibility is accepted only for those who are "known". One is "known" wherever one has lived and wherever one has kin; where one has kin one can also visit and meet the other local people face-to-face. There are no other means whereby one can become "known", even by repute. If we are to speak of an Aboriginal belonging to a community wider than his local residential group, it is his *beat* – the localities where he has kin – who will provide him with a *pied-à-terre.* In this sense, each individual has his own personal community, but inasmuch as people are closely inter-related and tend to marry into the same local groups, communities tend to coincide. Few Far West Aborigines are "known" outside the region, and few living elsewhere are "known" within it.

No Far West Aboriginal has achieved any reputation among Aborigines living outside the region, and only those few outsiders who have received some notice in the mass media – for example, the painter Namatjira and the popular recording artist, Jimmy Little – have achieved any reputation within it. The marked lack of interest in outsiders is an important factor in the Aborigines' lack of political unity. The Welfare Board has for some years encouraged New South Wales Aborigines to elect a representative, but the elections have been conducted on a state-wide basis and it has never been possible to find a candidate known to everyone. For many years the Aboriginal "representative" has come from other parts of the State, leaving the Far West people without any sense of being represented at all. The only one whose name is remembered and occasionally mentioned, was related by marriage through his brother to the Carowra Tank people. For much the same reasons, probably, the religious revivals among Aborigines of other regions have never spread to the Far West. The ideologies of "Hot Gospel" sects and the various groups now working for "Aboriginal Rights" in the more closely settled areas, implicitly at least transcend locality and kinship[1], but it seems as though they must be transmitted initially along the roads provided by kinship.

BIBLIOGRAPHY

Bean, C. E. W., 1911, *Dreadnought of the Darling*. Sydney.
—, 1945, *On the Wool Track*. Sydney.
Beckett, J. R., 1958, "Marginal Men: A Study of Two Half Caste Aborigines". *Oceania*, Vol. XXIX. Sydney.
—, 1964, "Aborigines, Alcohol and Assimilation", in *Aborigines Now*, ed. Reay. Sydney.
Bell, J. H., 1959, "Official Policies towards the Aborigines of New South Wales". *Mankind*, Vol. V, No. 8. Sydney.
Barwick, D. E., 1963, *A Little More than Kin: Regional Affiliation and Group Identity Among Aboriginal Migrants in Melbourne*. Unpublished Thesis. Australian National University.
Calley, M. J., 1964, "Pentecostalism among the Bardjdang", in *Aborigines Now*, ed. Reay. Sydney.
Elkin, A. P., 1951, "Reaction and Interaction: A Food-gathering People and European Settlement in Australia". *American Anthropologist*, Vol. LIII.
Fink, R. A., 1957, "The Caste Barrier – An Obstacle to the Assimilation of Part-Aborigines in North-West New South Wales". *Oceania*, XXVIII.
Firth, R., 1956, *Two Studies of Kinship in London*. London.
Greenway, J., 1963, *Bibliography of Australian Aborigines*. Sydney.
Hausfeld, R. H., 1963, "Dissembled Culture: An Essay on Method". *Mankind*, Vol. VI. No. 2. Sydney.
Lipski, S., 1965, "The Freedom Riders", *The Bulletin*, Vol. 87, No. 4434. Syndey.
Piddington, R., 1961, "A Study of French Canadian Kinship". *International Journal of Comparative Sociology*. Vol. II, No. 1. Dharwar.
Reay, M. & Sitlington, G., 1948, "Class Status in a Mixed-Blood Community, Moree, New South Wales". *Oceania*, Vol. XVIII.
Tindale, N. B., 1940, "Distribution of Australian Aboriginal Tribes". *Transactions of the Royal Society of South Australia*. 64.
Trollope, A., 1876, *Australia and New Zealand*. Melbourne.
Ward, R., 1958, *The Australian Legend*.

1 In this connection, the words of Sydney Aboriginal spokesman and "Freedom Rider", Charles Perkins, are very relevant: "Aborigines used to be very quick to say to someone – 'You're a Barrowville boy, or you're from Queensland or you're a Kempsey boy'. If the kinship ties weren't there they wouldn't have much to do with you. But now there's a growing feeling that we're all part of one people". (Lipski 1965).

Lucknow Rickshawallas: The Social Organization of an Occupational Category[1]

HAROLD A. GOULD

University of Pittsburgh, Pittsburgh, U.S.A.

THIS paper is frankly experimental in that it constitutes an effort to deal not with a community or culture as a whole in the usual social anthropological sense of the word but with an occupational category in an urban center of North India using the combined techniques of the sociologist and the anthropologist. The study deals with social organization, but with social organization in the broader meaning of the term which embraces not only kinship but social stratification, role patterning, demographic structure and certain aspects of economic relationships as well. Ultimately, therefore, we discuss the kinship system and domestic organization of a chance sample[2] of bicycle ricksha drivers in Lucknow, India, but only after a fairly lengthy examination of the place this occupational category occupies in the social structure of a "transitional society". Since our approach is so unorthodox in many ways, this prior preoccupation with the whole setting of our subjects seemed a necessary precondition for talking meaningfully about the characteristics of domestic organization that were found among them. Many difficulties lie in the path of using anthropological methods in urban settings for the study of occupations and these are well appreciated by the author. Subsequent publications on this subject will endeavor to profit from the difficulties and deficiencies evident in this initial, rather imperfect attempt. But it is felt that one must begin somewhere and the present essay represents this first, tenuous step. Building upon the body of concepts elucidated in this paper, for example, a subsequent paper will explore in much detail the domestic organization of scores of families at the top and bottom of the urban occupational

1 My work in India has been made possible by three generous sources. In 1954–55, as a Fulbright Student, I first went to India. In 1959–60, I returned as a Postdoctoral Fellow of the National Science Foundation. From 1960 to 1962, I remained to do further research under two concurrent postdoctoral fellowships provided by the National Institute of Mental Health.

2 A "chance" as opposed to a "random" sample was all that could be obtained under the circumstances. There were no statistics available concerning the social composition of this occupation on the basis of which a systematic sample could be constructed.

hierarchy and compared with the rural kinship system found in the city's hinterland.

General and Theoretical Considerations

The term "rickshawalla" is Hindustani and denotes one who operates a three-wheeled conveyance that is propelled and steered in the same fashion as a conventional bicycle. Two passengers are normally accommodated on the seat behind the driver although, by overloading, more are sometimes carried. Throughout India the bicycle ricksha meets a need for cheap, individualized transportation much in the same fashion as the taxicab does in the United States. The rickshawalla's is a low-status occupation because the work is exhausting, the pay is low, and little training or education is needed. In middle-sized Indian cities in particular, such as Lucknow, there are hundreds of these vehicles on the streets and it is clear on the basis of even superficial observation that a large percentage of their drivers are recent arrivals from rural areas who are qualified to do little other than menial tasks such as this.

Lucknow had a population of around 625,000 in 1959[1]. It is the capital of Uttar Pradesh, India's most populous province (70 million people), and is predominantly a center of politics, administration, trade and education. Heavy industry in the province is located in Kanpur, forty miles to the south. Although the number varies from year to year, it is estimated that between two and four thousand rickshas ply their trade in the city and its environs[2]. Normally, ownership of bicycle rickshas is separate from their operation. Owners are sometimes middle class individuals, such as teachers, clerks and shopkeepers, who purchase and maintain from one to four rickshas as a side-investment to bring in a modest added income. This category probably accounts for the majority of bicycle rickshas in operation. However, there are also some large-scale entrepreneurs who may own dozens or scores of bicycle rickshas and whose primary income is derived from this source. In all cases, owners rent their vehicles to prospective rickshawallas for from twelve annas to two-and-a-half ruppees (15c to 50c) a day[3]. Rarely does one encounter a driver who owns his own ricksha mainly because the cost of ownership (Rs 450 or $ 100 for a new one) is prohibitive for those who typically find their way into the occupation.

This investigation of the social life of rickshawallas was part of an overall examination of the phenomenon of social mobility in India, with particular reference to the question of what takes place when people steeped in the values of a caste system confront the economic, social, and cultural order that is

1 According to the 1951 Census of India, the population of Lucknow was 496, 961; by 1961, the Census indicated a population of 655, 673. This is a growth-rate of approximately 1.6% per year which means that by 1959 around 128,000 had been added to the population.

2 Mukerjee and Singh (1961:35) say that there were 412 bicycle rickshas in Lucknow in 1943–44 which number had increased to more than 2,500 in 1954–55.

3 The rate of exchange is Rs 4. 75 to the dollar.

engendered by the spreading industrialization, bureaucratization and urbanization of Indian society. Underlying our study, therefore, are a number of theoretical assumptions which must be rendered explicit.

Viewed in social structural terms, industrialization implies much more than the adoption of machinery and the erection of factories. As is well known, it involves the altering of fundamental relationships among men in many spheres of social life so that, if carried to its ultimate conclusions, industrialization means the achievement of a new form of human society. Certainly the primary change which industrialization brings about at the level of social structure is the widespread bureaucratization of work of all kinds. Both the direct and indirect consequences of industrialization conduce to this. Use of machines in the context of factories necessitates the proliferation of work-relationships based upon considerations of efficiency, skill, training, etc., to the comparative exclusion of personal considerations. The concomitant growth in transportation, communications, administration, education, urbanization and the sheer demographic scale of society, help carry bureaucratized social relationships into all remaining major work situations in society. Personal relationships remain, of course, and perform important functions, even within bureaucratic structures themselves, as I have noted elsewhere (Gould 1963), but it is accurate to say that the fulfilled industrial society is to a high degree characterized by the dominance of bureaucratic relationships[1].

By contrast, complex preindustrial societies reveal much specialization of work but little bureaucratization of work roles. Technology supports only modest urbanization because it cannot free the majority from the necessity of residing in agricultural communities where they must directly create their subsistence. It supports only modest populations because it cannot provide answers to disease, famine, and premature mortality. Nor is technology sufficiently advanced to enable productive activities to be removed from the context of kin groups. Specialization of tasks tends to be by household and clusters of households and therefore tends to be hereditary, since under these conditions, occupations are inherited along with other family property and are inculcated as an integral aspect of childhood socialization.

In terms of social stratification, the social structure of work in the two types of society, the industrial and complex preindustrial, imply fundamentally different approaches to the recruitment of personnel into occupational roles. We may characterize the social stratification found in the industrial and complex preindustrial societies as achievement-oriented and ascription-oriented respectively. That is, the fundamentally bureaucratic nature of work in the former must be associated with a value system which implicitly assumes that any given occupational role and its role-occupant are distinct and seperable so that in response to the needs of efficiency, etc., individuals are free to move from one occupational role to another. "Promotion" and "firing" are policies that

1 The original statement of this position is contained in, "Castes, Outcastes and the Sociology of Stratification". (Gould, 1960).

are possible mainly because a value system makes possible distinguishing between the work role as an abstract position in the social structure and the individual who concretely occupies that role. For the fundamentally ascription-oriented stratification of the complex nonindustrial society is associated with a value system which implicitly assumes that to a high degree, where not totally, the work a man does and the man himself are indistinguishable.

Traditional India, of course, is a noteworthy instance of the latter. Her caste system fuses occupational role and role-occupant with respect to thousands of specialized tasks. The system arose, in large part, due to the capacity of a particular segment of the society, the Brahman caste, to successfully propagate its values until they had become the values of the whole society. A key feature of this value system, from the standpoint of its effect on social organization, was the conception that religious sanctity is possible only through abstention from certain occupations and tasks. Ritual purity or Twice Born status depended upon the ability of certain castes to compel others to absorb the impurities thought to inhere in certain kinds of work, especially work involving contact with "blood, death and dirt" (cf. Passin, 1955). Thus, the disposal of dead animals, the manufacture of leather goods, washing clothes, barbering, sweeping, plowing and many other occupations became permanently assigned to groups who were then socially interdicted in varying degrees because of their association with these occupations. This added further rigidity to a social order which even before the emergence of Hinduism had been a typical nonindustrial complex society with ascription-oriented social stratification. We may infer the latter from the archaeological descriptions that are available on the early, pre-Aryan Indus Valley Civilization (Wheeler, 1953; Piggott, 1950).

With the coming of European rule to India and, within this framework, the coming of modern economic, social and political institutions, the foundation was laid for the competing, achievement-oriented stratification system. However, the new technological order and its social structural concomitants has even now failed to replace completely the earlier traditional social order and its technological base, as is well known: This is the sociological basis for calling India a "transitional society". What is meant is that social structures and cultural values associated with both industrial society and complex preindustrial society impinge upon the population in varying ways and degrees to produce highly complex permutations of behavior at all levels of Indian life. In the occupational order, important loci of the two competing stratification systems are the city and the village. Although no absolute dichotomy can be defended in this regard, it is nevertheless true that the caste system in its fullest contemporary development is to be found operating in villages where numbers are small, relations intimate, and technology still supports a peasant economy. Thus, the values and personality systems which caste societies both create and utilize are paramount there. By contrast, cities are the focus of economic structures, bureaucratic institutions and cultural values which machine-age technology requires and sustains.

Although it can certainly be argued that nearly everyone in India is in some sense "marginal" as between caste and class values, it is as certainly true that many of those in urban menial occupations like ricksha driving, where the turnover of personnel is rapid and no education or specialized skills are required, are especially so. For a significant number will have only recently migrated from villages where some or all of their kinsmen still reside and where caste discipline remains viable. They will have found themselves in an urban occupational environment where modifications in thinking and behaving are immediately required by the inherent demands of the situation. Even those whose ties are not immediately traceable to a rural background must nevertheless reveal evidence of the behavioral transformation that had to be made in the process of becoming urbanized. Let us now turn to our sample of rickshawallas to illustrate these and other facts about an urban, menial occupation in India today.

Social Composition

In considering the social composition of our sample, one is immediately struck by how completely the occupational feature of caste disintegrates in the modern economic order. It has to be recognized as one of the truly significant changes which occur in the transition from the caste to the class system. Neither caste, ethnic community nor nationality retain any exclusive importance as a determinant of who shall drive a ricksha. As Table 1 shows, twelve castes are

Table 1

Caste, Ethnic and National Composition of a Sample of Fifty Rickshawallas in Lucknow, India, 1959

Community, Nationality, Caste	*Traditional Occupation*	*Current Caste Occupation*	*Number*	
Plains Hindu				
Brahman	Priest	Priest/Cultivator	4	(27)
Thakur	Warrior/Ruler	Cultivator	4	
Ahir	Cowherd	Cowherd/Cultivator	1	
Gujar	Grazier	Cultivator	1	
Kurmi	Cultivator	Cultivator	1	
Murau	Veg. Cultivator	Cultivator	2	
Kumhar	Potter	Cultivator	1	
Kahar	Water Carrier	Variable occupations	4	
Kori	Weaver	Menial occupations	2	
Jaiswara	Scavanger/Tanner	Menial occupations	5	
Chamar	Scavanger/Tanner	Scavanger/Menial occup's	1	
Luniya	Grave digger	Menial occupations	1	
Nepali Hindu				
Chetri	Warrior	Variable occupations	4	(4)
Muslim	Non-Hindu	Variable occupations	19	(19)
Total:			50	(50)

represented among the twentyseven subjects who are defined as Plains Hindu, by which is meant Hindus who are citizens of India. They range from the highest and purest Brahman caste to the lowest and most defiled Chamar and Luniya castes. Four subjects are Nepali Hindus who migrated to Lucknow from their native land in search of employment. Finally, nineteen are Muslims and therefore technically not a part of the traditional caste order at all.

It was found, in addition, that rickshawallas showed no marked tendencies to segregate themselves by caste or ethnic community in the primary groups they formed during working hours. Much as there are taxi stands in American cities, there are ricksha stands scattered throughout a city like Lucknow. At many of these places cliques of ricksha drivers had formed. There was even a degree of hierarchy involved in this which stemmed from the fact that some stands were situated in better places than others in terms of potentiality for making money. Skill, strength and personality mattered as much as anything in determining who won acceptance into cliques which monopolized the most lucrative stands in the city. One at the gate of Lucknow's best hotel is a case in point. It naturally ranked high because of the quality of the hotel's clientele, which included a large number of transient foreigners whose ignorance of correct fares and tendency to pity the plight of rickshawallas makes them susceptible to being overcharged[1]. The core group at this stand consisted of two Muslims, a Nepali, a Chamar, a Jaiswara and a Kahar. These men sat together, gambled together and ate together on the job. Their economic cooperation was not confined to sharing the business of carrying passengers either; it extended to other activities as well, prime among which were transmitting bets on horses to bookmakers and providing prostitutes to hotel patrons. These "elite" rickshawallas all possessed an above-average knowledge of city life. The Chamar, Jaiswara and two Muslims were urban born and had spent many years as rickshawallas because they saw the occupation as a means of combining mobility with a reasonably good income for menial work. The Nepali had migrated to Lucknow in childhood and had spent many years working around army posts. He was very strong, unmarried, unencumbered by lineal kin ties, and outspoken in his preference for rickshadriving as a source of excitement and money. The only one with any meaningful village ties left was the Kahar, but poverty had not been a strong motive for his leaving the rural area. His kin group owned considerable land and livestock in the village and he had departed in company with his father in the aftermath of severe conflicts among the agnates.

---

1 These rickshawallas consciously exploited the known tendency of Americans, in particular, to express pity in pecuniary terms. After delivering an American to his destination, the rickshawalla would dramatically protest that whatever fare his passenger had given was pathetically inadequate for the service that had been rendered. Often this performanci would result in the rickshawalla receiving five to ten times the amount normally paid for the distance actually traveled. Among themselves, rickshawallas joked and boasted about their successes in extracting large overpayments from foreigners in this fashion. The larger the overpayment they succeeded in obtaining, the higher their status rose in the eyes of the peer group.

Whatever tendencies there were for cliques to reflect homogeneous characteristics these were found to prevail in residential areas of the city and even here it was the ethnic community rather than the caste that was the significant variable. That is, Muslim neighborhoods revealed a number of rickshawalla factions that were entirely Muslim whereas Hindu neighborhoods revealed a number that were entirely Hindu. At any rate, under no circumstances were there indications that a "rickshawalla caste" was forming or would ever form in the occupational milieu of the city.

Despite the disappearance of caste as an *occupational* factor in the urban division of labor, it cannot be simply asserted that caste had entirely disappeared from the life of either the migrant or urban-born rickshadriver. On the contrary, in other respects, caste remained an extremely crucial element in the social life of both. What we must realize in order to understand this point is that the achievement-oriented stratification system rooted in modern technology and occupations succeeds in detaching work from its caste contexts without necessarily altering the extent to which other features of caste continue to operate. It will be recalled that a caste is endogamous, and within the religious sphere of experience is regarded as a kind of moral status which precisely expresses the cumulative consequences of a past existence. It has become for the ordinary Hindu the basis of his self-hood and social identity and in this sense a very real part of his personality system. Like the traditional caste occupation itself, these features of caste are rooted in and sustained by the kin group and the local community and they continue to be after involvement in the modern economic order causes the former to be abandoned. Villagers who have come to the city to work, and urban-born workers as well, whose connections with their rural past are broken, equally experience the persistence of caste and other traditional values in their family life. This is most clearly demonstrated by the finding that among our sample of fifty rickshawallas, despite their common urban occupation and widespread fraternization on the job, not a single case of intercaste marriage was recorded. This means that not only had the Plains Hindus maintained their caste endogamy without exception but that the Nepalis and Muslims had done so with equal fidelity.

In other respects too, rickshawallas showed little inclination to engage in social fraternization outside the occupational context. All said they normally dine only with members of their own caste or ethnic group under domestic conditions despite the fact that during working hours they constantly violated the rule enjoining commensal exclusiveness. Respondents saw no inconsistency in this; they held that their work is part of one domain with its specific necessities respecting social interaction while their domestic or non-work life is part of quite another. Such compartmentalization of behavior appears to be a major mechanism whereby the urban Hindu and Muslim both successfully balance the social requirements arising from the opposing ascription and achievement-oriented values which sustain the caste and class systems respectively. It is a mechanism not confined to the menial worker either, as I propose to show in subsequent publications, but generally prevalent in varying degrees at all levels

Table 2

Village and Extravillage Occupations of Sherupur Residents, by Caste

Caste	*Traditional Occupation*	*Village Occupation*	*Extravillage Occupation*
Brahman	Priest	Agriculture	Land manager Store proprietor
Thakur	Warrior/Ruler	Agriculture	Railroad switchman Ekka driver Factory laborer Army private Store clerk Government Farm laborer
Kayastha	Accountant	Agriculture	Railroad ticket clerk Mason
Ahir	Cowherd	Cowherd/Agriculture	Government dairy Railway coolie Store clerk Coal miner Urban dairy proprietor Ekka driver
Kurmi	Agriculture	Agriculture	Government Farm laborer Holy man Cowherd Machine operator Weaver
Murau	Veg. Cult.	Veg. Cult./Agric.	Store clerk Railroad signalman Apprentice mechanic Government Farm laborer
Sonar	Goldsmith	Any metal work	Sugar mill worker
Lohar	Blacksmith	Blacksmith/Agric.	Government Farm laborer
Kahar	Water Carrier	Roasting grams Shopkeeper Menial labor	Coal miner
Kori	Weaver	Menial labor Midwife Scavanger	Farm laborer Rickshadriver Manual laborer Ekka driver University student
Chamar	Scavanger Leatherworker	Scavanger Midwife Agriculture Leatherworker	Farm laborer

of Indian society. Its operation is perhaps best illustrated among those who are still truly marginal between the city and the village, however. These individuals take their appropriate places in the caste system while in their villages despite the fact that when they are in the city they engaged in an occupation which, in terms of conditions of employment, remuneration, etc., equates all individuals so engaged regardless of caste status. In Sherupur, for example, pseudonym for a village in eastern Uttar Pradesh which I have studied over the years, we find that many men now residing in the community either presently hold or in the past have held jobs in the modern occupational order which cut across traditional caste lines in every conceivable way. As Table 2 illustrates, persons who are from Lohar, Murau, Kurmi, Ahir and Thakur castes have held jobs on government-run farms which are operated strictly on an achievement-oriented basis like any modern business. Jobs on the railways, another government-owned enterprise, are part of the occupational history of a Murau, Ahir, Kayastha and Thakur. But such common occupational backgrounds are never made the basis for serious claims of caste equality within the village social system in the sense of intermarriage and interdining or of refusing to honor the traditional division of labor. Obviously this is the case because the new social order has as yet failed to effect any transformation of rural technology sufficient to necessitate replacement of the traditional division of labor with its roots in the corporate kin group and the religious system. In the city too the situation is similar. Persons remain profoundly dependent on the corporate kin group for maintenance because the standard of living is extremely low, unemployment is high, and technology remains so primitive in the domestic domain that the provision of food and other amenities can best be handled on a collective basis. Equally, people remain dependent on caste ties because outside the kin group the caste is the most important real and potential source of support and preferential treatment wherever they go. Although hiring and firing in the modern occupational order are ostensibly, and to an important extent in reality, based upon achievement criteria, it is nevertheless true that the uncompromising application of these criteria can be and is modified by ties of friendship, kinship and caste. Caste is the lateral extension of the personal obligational system inherent in kinship ties to embrace as wide an arc of individuals as possible. When the occupational feature of caste drops out in the face of bureaucratized economic activities this personal-obligation feature remains viable, and its functional importance is no doubt attested to by the tenacity with which caste endogamy is being maintained even in the face of the most persistent urban pressures. To put it another way, preferential access to scarce economic and affective resources are assured by caste ties.

Some Demographic Aspects

Age is the first demographic feature of our sample that will be considered. Note that in Table 3 four age-categories are distinguished for purposes of classifying respondents. These reflect certain relationships between maturation and socialization that I have elsewhere (Gould 1959) held to be general for India. Thus, the period from twelve through twenty is called "Youth" when puberty occurs and individuals serve their social apprenticeship which prepares them to assume a full measure of adult responsibilities. These responsibilities commence, at the latest, by the age of twenty-one and the first phase of their exercise, called "Young Adulthood", pertains to the time when persons are in their physical prime and are making their maximal productive contributions to their kin group and society. The second phase, which is called "Later Adulthood", begins at about thirty-six and is the time when persons attain emotional and intellectual maturity and thus make their maximum leadership contributions to their kin group and society. By the time people are entering their fifties, this "mature" phase is giving way to "Old Age", where both mental and physical faculties are beginning to slow down; it is at this time that the status of "elder" begins to emerge in which the direct exercise of power is progressively supplanted by the receipt of veneration.

Table 3

Age, Marital Status and Residence of Fifty Bicycle Rickshawallas in Lucknow, India, 1959

	Rural		*Urban*		*Married*		*Unmarried*		*Total*	
Age Category	*No.*	*Per Cent*	*No.*	*Per Cent*	*No.*	*Per Cent*	*No.*	*Per Cent*	*No.*	*Per Cent*
Youth (12–20)	5	16%	6	33%	2	18%	9	82%	11	22%
Young Adulthood (21–35)	20	63%	12	67%	17	53%	15	47%	32	64%
Later Adulthood (36–50)	5	16%	—	—	3	60%	2	40%	5	10%
Old Age (above 50)	2	5%	—	—	1	50%	1	50%	2	4%
Total:	32	100%	18	100%	23	46%	27	54%	50	100%

The age structure of the sample reveals, then, what one would expect for as physically taxing a job as rickshawalla. That is, most are in the categories we have above called Youth and Young Adulthood. Specifically, all were fifteen or above and most were thirty-five or less. As Table 3 shows, however, some older men were working as rickshawallas also and all of these were migrants from rural areas. This was an unanticipated finding for which I have at hand no certain explanation. It is possible that urban-born men who reach "senior status" have had many more years to reconnoitre the job market and obtain somewhat more attractive occupations in relation to their physical and emotional capacities. It is also likely that these men have their younger kin nearer at hand to accord them the support and veneration which is normally the prerogative of aging individuals in India.

Four of these older, rural-born rickshawallas were married and three were not. Two of the latter had been married but their wives had died long ago and they had never remarried. The four married men said they had come to Lucknow in search of any employment they could obtain because their economic situation in the village was desperate. All of these claimed they actually prefer village life and would resume it as soon as pecuniary circumstances permitted. The unwed, older rickshawallas will be discussed later in a different context because they have characteristics in common with some other members of the sample.

Clearly, the proportion of rickshawallas who are unmarried is higher than for the ordinary village population at comparable age levels. In Sherupur, seventy to eighty percent of the men in the Youth to Old Age range are married. This suggests that the occupation appeals strongly to individuals who, for whatever the reasons, have comparatively weak domestic ties. It was obvious that most of the single men interviewed saw rickshadriving as a means of maximizing their spatial mobility in the city, as well as earning a living. For within the framework of this occupation a great deal of time was available for interaction with peer groups all over Lucknow. At the various ricksha stands gambling, gossiping, smoking, drinking and other forms of idle-time activity were constantly occurring which strongly appealed to restless young men. Rickshadriving, despite the physical exertion involved, has a certain quality of excitement and irresponsibility connected with it that must be regarded as one of its major latent sources of appeal and gratification.

The fore going is further attested by the fact that the majority of the married men were what might be called "functional bachelors" as far as their life in Lucknow was concerned. Of eighteen who were from villages, ten (56%) had left their conjugal unit behind in their natal village whereas eight of fourteen (58%) of the single men born in villages had come to Lucknow unaccompanied by any other close kinsman.

Of the rickshawallas who were migrants to Lucknow, most came from the three most backward regions of the province – viz., the eastern, central and Himalayan border districts of Uttar Pradesh. Conditions in Western U.P. are vastly superior to those in its other parts. Poverty in the other districts is extensive because there is little modern economic activity and even agricultural technology lags far behind the more progressive parts of India. With jobs difficult to obtain in the face of low productivity and rising populations, menial workers have long flowed out of these regions toward centers of greater economic vitality. Table 4 gives the region of origin of those in the sample who had migrated to Lucknow in their own lifetime. The area involved has a maximum radius of three hundred miles. However, the region containing Lucknow (viz., the central districts) supplied less migrants than did the more remote eastern districts, a fact which by itself tells much about the difficult economic conditions there.

Table 4

Region of Origin of Rickshawallas Born Outside Lucknow

Region of Origin	*Rural Born*	*Urban Born*	*Total*
Eastern Districts	17	–	17
Central Districts	9	1	10
Himalayan Districts	5	–	5
Western Districts	1	–	1
Total:	32	1	33

Another important feature of migration patterns concerns the differences among various status levels respecting the time when migration took place. Our "N" of fifty is too small to undertake fine distinctions of status and time, of course; but if we combine elite and middle caste Hindus in the sample and contrast them with low caste Hindus, Nepalis, and Muslims in terms of whether those falling in each category have been in Lucknow ten years or less, on the one hand, or above ten years or Lucknow-born, on the other, then an important finding emerges. A preponderance of the higher status rickshawallas (64%) are relatively recent arrivals in Lucknow by contrast with those of lower status. In

Table 5

General Status Level of Lucknow Rickshawallas and Amount of Time Since Coming to the City

General Status Level		*Less than Ten Years in Lucknow*	*More than Ten Years in Lucknow or Lucknow-Born*	*Total*
Elite and Middle Caste Hindus	(N)	9	5	14
	(%)	64%	36%	100%
Low Caste Hindus, Nepalis and Muslims	(N)	13	22	35
	(%)	36%	64%	100%
Total:		22	27	49*

* One subject's record is unclear.

the latter case, it is being assumed that having been born in Lucknow implies migration at least one generation ago by a kinsman, an assumption fully supported by the interview data. The overall picture suggests that a shift in the status of migrants has taken place in fairly recent times. Whereas heretofore lower status people were leaving rural areas to seek menial jobs in the city, today the motivation to do so has been stronger among higher status people. Niehoff (1959, 34) in his study of industrial workers in Kanpur, found a similar differential pattern of mobility. Says he:

> "Until 1930 there were very few caste Hindus working in the factories. From 1931 to 1945 they consistently increased in proportion to the low castes and Moslems. Then industry slackened off and their migration decreased, but considerably less than in the case of the low castes. This change is probably more a matter of choice than necessity by the high caste men, since those who bear the brunt of economic privation during hard years in the villages are the low caste people... This change in part represents a new attitude toward the work by the high caste people".

Niehoff cites the new land reapportionment laws and like reforms as contributing to the greater readiness of higher caste Hindus to leave the villages; by "new attitude" he means development of a willingness to labor in factories at occupations which traditional caste values once interdicted for the Twice

Born. What really underlies these observations, of course, is the fact that since the movement to gain independence for India really got underway, and culminated in the winning of freedom in 1947, a series of progressively more comprehensive reforms in the economic, political and social life of the country, coupled with rapid technological changes, have effectively altered the power position of the traditional elites everywhere. In the villages, this has meant not only reduction in the amount of land and other economic resources controlled by Brahamans, Thakurs, and other high castes but a weakening of their capacity to preserve the old pattern of intercaste etiquette through which their traditional paramountcy was socially expressed. Using Srinivas' parlance (1952), "Sanskritization" has become easier and easier for the lower castes and as a consequence the traditional status hierarchy has become diluted. This process is obviously connected with the opportunities for previously servile castes to achieve ownership of land and other resources by virtue of the very reforms which subtracted these things in some measure from the assets of the elite castes. Thus, both symbolically and materially, it can be said that lower caste people have more of a stake in rural life today than they did before. By contrast, high caste migrants to the city are no doubt a reaction to their loss of status and means in the rural areas. They seek to improve both by entering the heretofore tabooed, or at least deprecated, occupations as a means of gaining entrée into the domain from whence the greatest rewards and gratifications to be had in today's India increasingly flow. I have discussed this matter in more detail elsewhere (Gould 1961, 1962).

The pattern of land holdings reveals that the possession of property in villages was indeed generally common among those who were migrants to Lucknow in their own lifetime, regardless of status, which is what the foregoing would rather lead us to expect. A total of thirty subjects had close kin (i.e., siblings, parents, grandparents and close collaterals in varying combinations) still residing in villages; twenty-seven of thirty-two who were rural born did and three of eighteen who were urban-born did. Of the thirty, twenty-six reported that their family owned land while only four reported complete landlessness. Regarding amounts of land, a Brahman rickshawalla said his kin group owned 350 *kachha bighas*[1] and a Kurmi declared that his kin group had 150. These two stood out, to be sure, and it was possible to confirm from other sources the validity of their statements. There was, in fact, no noticeable tendency to deliberately misrepresent land holdings. Other than the above two exceptional cases, respondents indicated possession of lands varying from tiny plots of no more than a *kachha bigha* to as much as fifty. Half of all respondents (15) said they had twenty or more *kachha bighas*; of them, seven were high and middle caste Hindus whereas eight were low caste Hindus, Nepalis and Muslims. Thus land impoverishment *per se* cannot be the determinant factor in decisions to migrate; rather, there is a subtle interweaving of economic with other less tangible factors like relative

1 A *kachha bigha* is $2\frac{1}{2}$ times smaller than a *pukka bigha*; the latter is equal to two-thirds of an acre; therefore, a *kacha bigha* is approximately four-tenths of an acre.

status deprivation, the modes of acting out deviancy, etc. At the same time, the fact that only three of eighteen urban-born rickshawallas report any ownership of land at all vividly shows that the pursuit of urban occupations beyond one generation has been associated with a virtually complete cessation of rural property ties.

Family and Kinship

Studies of urbanization and industrialization have widely assumed that the adoption of city living causes the automatic dissolution of extended families and their replacement by nuclear, neolocal units. Economic, demographic and ideological conditions allegedly make this transition inevitable. Thus Mukerjee and Singh (1961:37), in their social survey of Lucknow, assert:

> "The urban family at present is in transition towards the natural family (*sic*) comprising the couple and their unmarried children. But the transition is in no way complete, and many families still exhibit the features of a joint family – with several generations and a large number of relations living together".

Unfortunately such a viewpoint has been derived from an uncritical application of generalizations appropriate to the West's experience with industrialization. This is a dangerous procedure on a number of grounds, but particularly so in a country like India where unilineal kinship systems and caste, both rare or nonexistent in even the preindustrial West, occupy such important places. Bloch (1961) has pointed out that medieval feudalism arose in Europe in part as a response to the weakness of kinship institutions at a time when wider principles of interdependence and mutual obligation were required.

But the important point to keep in mind is that in all societies all of the changes which may occur in the composition of kin groups through time are not *structural* changes. Thus, since the transition from a non-industrial, ascription-oriented society to an industrial, achievement-oriented society represents a major series of changes in the structure of technology and significant social groups, it becomes essential that genuine structural change be differentiated from other structural activities, whether in regard to kinship or any other feature of society, if a truly accurate assessment of change is to be made. Furthermore, it will always be important to learn how much structural alteration in a given dimension of society is actually *necessary* to fulfill basic functional requirements of mechanized, bureaucratized productive activities. This latter may, in fact, become a most crucial variable in determining the eventual form which non-western societies will take after they have achieved their maximum absorption of industrialization.

The need for distinguishing between true structural changes in kinship systems and merely normal rearrangements of personnel through time has been cogently stated by Fortes (1958:2). He declares:

> "...what are the institutional mechanisms and customary activities of social reproduction in a particular society and how do they operate?... In all human societies, the workshop,

so to speak, of social reproduction, is the domestic group... The domestic group goes through a cycle of development analogous to the growth cycle of a living organism. The group as a unit retains the same form, but its members, and the activities which unite them, go through a regular sequence of changes during the cycle which culminates in the dissolution of the original unit and its replacement by one or more units of the same kind".

Such an approach is definitely necessary if we are to understand the precise character of the kinship structure which was found to prevail among our sample of Lucknow rickshawallas. To do this it is first necessary to examine some features of the North Indian kinship system which affect all inhabitants of the region equally. An entire tradition of Hindu law, ultimately traced back to Manu, lies behind and legitimizes the principles of relationship, descent and inheritance; this is known as Mitakshara Succession (cf, Mulla 1952).[1] In brief, the following principles are included: (a) the "normal conditon" (Mulla 1952) of the Hindu family is jointness, that is, it is a "coparcenary unit" which owes maintenance to all its members "in severalty"; (b) property is inherited through male agnates; (c) females may not inherit the chief wealth of the joint family; (d) females become members of their husbands' joint families upon marriage and cease being members of their natal families; (e) residence is patrilocal/virilocal; and (f) any adult male agnate may call for partition of the coparcenary any time he deems it in his interests to do so.

The rule permitting any male agnate to call for partition appears to have been a means of assuring that younger brothers could not be deprived of a share in the property of the joint family after the father's death. For without such a rule, the leadership of the family, devolving upon the eldest brother as next in the line of succession, might be used as a weapon against younger generational equivalents. However, despite this "safetyvalve mechanism", traditional legal treatises make it clear that, ideally, the solidarity of brothers is a desired end of society, a fact which constitutes an implicit admission that under Mitakshara Law the relationship between brothers is faught with ambivalence.

Whether there was greater or less solidarity among brothers in classical times

1 The basic premises of Hindu Law supposedly emanate from the period of the *smrtis* (lit.: "What is remembered"), around 600 to 300 B.C. Prior to this time the Sanskrit texts seem unconcerned with detailed legal commentaries but with brief, axiomatic allusions to legal points in the hymns and incantations which make up the bulk of the earlier literature. By the first centuries of the Christian Era, considerable proliferation of legal viewpoints had occurred in response to the emergence of a tradition of critical commentary. The Mitakshara School had its origins at this time in the legal codes compiled by Yajnavalkya (circa. 100–300 A.D.). These were elaborated over the succeeding centuries and brought to a high degree of organization in the Indian Middle Ages by Vijnaneswara (1075–1125?); his treatises are still considered to be authoritative sources of Mitakshara legal doctrine. There are other systems of Hindu Law but these need not concern us here since they do not apply to the region in question. The Succession Act of 1956 radically alters the premises of Mitakshara Succession by making wives and daughters entitled to equal shares with male agnates in the partitioned property of the joint family. As the provisions of this act are resorted to in practice, major changes in the Indian Kinship system must inevitably take place. However, up to the present, customary practice adheres to Mitakshara principles of inheritance and descent despite their formal supercession by the 1956 Succession Act.

than we find today is a question which cannot be fruitfully explored here. All that can be said is that with the coming of European rule, modern technology, bureaucracy, modern jurisprudence, the pecuniary economy, rapidly growing populations and rising property values, a definite pattern or cycle or fission became established in domestic groups and persists up to the present. Basically it is this: Domestic groups divide in every generation because after the father dies the sons eventually invoke their right to partition the coparcenary. There are a number of interrelated reasons for this. As the father ages, the sons are maturing, marrying and having children of their own. This works counter to the unilineal interests of the kin group because it means that each son progressively develops conjugal loyalties to his own wife and children which often lead to conflicts with his lineal loyalties. With the removal of the father's strong patriarchal authority, these conflicting sets of loyalties become overwhelming because no basis exists for the reassertion of this authority with equal force at the intragenerational level. The right to partition effectively nullifies the possibility of an all-powerful eldest brother.

Viewed in the overall, we can say that contemporary social conditions, male agnatic succession, the right to partition, and the denial of major inheritance rights to women have combined to produce a characteristic developmental cycle consisting of a series of phases. During some of these phases, the personnel of the domestic group accord with the standard description of the nuclear family while in others they accord with that of the compound or extended family. This means that a mere counting of the number of simple and compound households displayed by rickshawallas or any other grouping would be wholly useless as a basis for ascertaining "modern" influences.

The phases through which the North Indian domestic group passes, therefore, are ultimately a reflection of certain fundamental events: (a) the breaking of the heterosexual sibling tie by the out-marrying of sisters after puberty and their replacement by in-marrying wives; (b) the breaking of fraternal ties through partition of the coparcenary following the death of the father; and (c) usually after a transitional phase during which efforts are made to keep the domestic group together despite the loss of the patriarch. The full developmental cycle arising from these events follows:

Phase I:

The replacement of female siblings by wives in the domestic group.

Subphase A (Nascent Period): From the moment of the first *gauna*, when the first sister leaves for or the first wife comes to her husband's household, until half of the *gaunas* have occurred. During this nascent period, households contain a mingling of brothers, sisters and brothers' wives together with parents who are normally in transition from Young Adulthood (21–35) to Later Adulthood (35-50). The incoming wives are beginning to bear children and the socialization of the next generation is commencing.

Subphase B (Mature Period): From the point where more than half of all potential *gaunas* have occurred until the complete replacement of sisters with brothers' wives, the domestic group is reaching its maximum size and generational depth. All brothers are acquiring conjugal units and members of the parental generation are moving from Later Adulthood to Old Age (above 50) and death.

Phase II:

The death of the patriarch, normally the father of ego but occasionally a father's brother, and a period when the coparcenary unit is a fraternal extended family. This phase is bypassed whenever there is only one surviving son, of course. When present, it can comprise a large, complex domestic group consisting of the brothers' conjugal units and sometimes, in addition, a widowed mother and/or other widowed female kin.

Phase III:

Brothers partition the joint family and establish separate domiciles, thus breaking the fraternal sibling tie as a basis for corporate activities. Frequently, this occurs due to quarrels among brothers in which pulls of loyalty between conjugal and lineal ties become irreconcilable.

Subphase A: From the establishment of separate domestic groups by recently divided brothers until the marriage of the first child. Marriages occur early among traditional Indians and do not lead to immediate cohabitation. *Gaunas* await the onset of puberty. Thus, married children continue living in their natal household but their marriages signify the movement of the domestic group toward repetition of the first phase in the developmental cycle – viz., breaking of the heterosexual sibling tie. Subphase A is normally "nuclear" in structure and must be seen as a normal period in the life cycle of the Indian domestic group and in no sense indicative of structural change.

Subphase B: From the marriage of each brother's first child until the occurrence of the first *gauna*. With this latter event, the developmental cycle has come around full circle and the original domestic group has been replaced by however many new ones arose in the aftermath of the patriarch's death and the partition of the coparcenary among the surviving brothers. In Subphase B, the domestic group is moving from a nuclear toward an extended structure once again. Children of the household have experienced their Childhood (5–11) and are preparing to enter their "social apprenticeship" (Youth, 12–20) where the learning of adult roles commences in earnest.

On the basis of the foregoing, we may see that structural changes are not automatically indicated where families of a specific kind at any given point in time are observed. A certain number of nuclear families will be normal for the kind of kinship system described above. However, the value of determining the temporal characteristics of the kinship system is that it provides us with a basis for determining when events might occur which would fail to lead to a repetition of the normal developmental cycle. Such events would, of course, demand careful scrutiny as possible indicators of true structural change. With these thoughts in mind, then, let us now consider the domestic organization found among the fifty rickshawallas in our sample.

No simple statement can be made, of course, about the domestic organization found among members of this occupational category. Nevertheless, it was found that the domestic groups of thirty-three rickshawallas fitted somewhere in the normal developmental cycle for North India. These were a mingling of Plains Hindus, Nepalis and Muslims, which suggests that the same kinship principles were operating equally for all. In Table 6, the personnel of the domestic groups at each phase in the developmental cycle are given; these are subdivided by generation and status from the standpoint of the rickshawalla as ego. Here we see that most domestic groups are going through those phases in which sheer numerical size and the pulls between conjugal and lineal ties are both at their maximum. That both are indeed subtly interrelated is suggested by the smaller number of rickshawallas whose domestic groups are in Phase IA, where numerical size averages higher than for IB and II, but where the proportionate number of wives cohabiting with their husbands is less. Phase IIIA merely expresses the inevitable consequences of the process at work in the preceeding phase. The domestic groups of ten rickshawallas have broken up into fifteen new units with an average personnel of less than four in each. Not all were the result of partitions among brothers, of course, because in some families there had been only a single son at the time of the father's death. However, all have in common the fact that they emerged as the end-product of the natural series of temporal events which characterize the developmental cycle in North India. Most were nuclear and the only exceptions were the presence of three widowed mothers entitled to maintenance for life in their deceased's husband's kin group. There were no indications that these groups would not repeat the normal cycle as they moved through time.

Among these normally unfolding domestic groups, two basic residential themes prevailed – a dispersed residential pattern and a single-household pattern. Thirteen are of the former type and twelve of these are rural-based. By rural-based is meant that the main body of kin are in a village while ego is in the city, either alone or in company of his conjugal unit and/or some other male sibling, to earn a cash income which is seen as a contribution to the entire kin group's economic well-being. The main criterion of whether a group with a dispersed residential pattern is still definable as a domestic group is, of course, whether they continue to function as a coparcenary unit sharing economic resources. All of the urban-based domestic groups except one maintained a single household regardless of whether nuclear or compound which indicates that even in the city the basic impulse to form corporate kin groups remains strong despite the supposedly atomizing effects of pecuniary standards, inflated costs, congested living, achievement-oriented occupational stratification, etc. In the sole case of a dispersed urban residential pattern where the kin group remained joint, units were located in Lucknow, Kanpur and Allahabad. Just as we said earlier that

Table 6

Personnel of Rickshawallas' Domestic Groups in Different Phases of the Normal North Indian Developmental Cycle

Phase of the Developmental Cycle	*No. of Domestic Groups*	*Average No. in Domestic Groups*	*Male Agnates Ego/BrSo/*			*Female Agnates*		*Wives of Male Agnates Br/Wi/*			*Outmarried Females*		*Total*
			Fa	*Br*	*So*	*Si*	*Da*	*Mo*	*Wi*	*SoWi*	*Si*	*Da*	
IA	5	7.4	4	16	2	1	6	4	4	–	2	1	40
IB	8	7.3	8	17	15	–	2	5	1	–	5	1	64
II	9	6.3	–	23	10	1	6	4	12	1	1	4	62
IIIA	10(15)*	3.5	1	15	13	–	10	3	10	–	5	–	57
IIIB	1	7.0	–	1	2	–	3	–	1	–	–	–	7
Total:	33(38)	6.1	13	72	42	2	27	16	38	1	13	6	230

* Ten respondents' domestic groups had split into fifteen IIIA units.

caste cohesion tends to be preserved in the face of the shift from traditional caste occupations to modern occupations, so we may also say that the shift from traditional occupations and rural living to modern occupations and urban living does not necessarily destroy the corporate kin group. What actually occurs is that the emphasis of caste is shifted to what I have elsewhere (Gould 1963) termed "adaptive functions" while concomitantly the emphasis of the corporate kin group is shifted from a narrower to a broader range of economic diversification. Put another way, the income structure of the domestic group is modified to accommodate the new economic environment in a fashion that preserves its corporate nature.

Corporateness undoubtedly remains a major value in the Indian kinship system because even in the contemporary urban social order it serves useful purposes. Menial occupations such as driving rickshas are very poorly paid which means that dependence upon other kin in an atmosphere of shared economic well-being inevitably has a powerful appeal. A low standard of living seems to impel the members of kin groups to tap all known sources of potential income and to rearrange their occupational commitments pragmatically in response to opportunities as they arise. The truth of this is apparent not only in the persistence of the normal developmental cycle among so many rickshawallas but is equally apparent among many of the seventeen instances of domestic groups which failed to conform to the normal cycle. Among the latter, four general categories of aberrant structure could be differentiated which are called, (1) the isolated individual, (2) arrested conjugality, (3) arrested lineality, and (4) true neolocalism. Each will be considered in turn.

In five cases, individuals were encountered who had simply broken off all ties with their kin groups and were leading an entirely isolated existence in Lucknow. This group included the three older unwed or widower rickshawallas alluded to earlier. It was clear that all, in one respect or another, were examples of severe social maladjustment. They were disturbed individuals who had found it impossible to make satisfactory adjustments to their domestic environment. One had abandoned his conjugal unit in the village and fled to the city; the other four were either unmarried, beyond the marriageable age or else men who had lost their spouses and declined to remarry. One suffered from leucoderma, or "white leprosy", a highly stigmatic disease in India and the other four showed distinct evidence of severe emotional disturbance. As already noted, driving a bicycle ricksha requires no special skills or education; it simply requires ordinary motor skills and reasonable physical stamina. It affords a variable, generally low income, to be sure, but subsistence can be at least minimally maintained through the occupation. It is an occupation that facilitates both spatial mobility and a measure of personal autonomy. The back seat of the ricksha, albeit with considerable discomfort, can be used as a bed at night if necessary and I have seen it used in this fashion in innumerable instances; in addition, the owners of bicycle rickshas frequently have a shed or some other sheltered place where drivers may sleep and attend to other minimal needs. In short, features of the occupation have a ready appeal to certain classes of deviants and misfits, perhaps especially those suffering from strong feelings of alienation.

Another typical domestic situation, found to be characteristic of six subjects, was what may be called "arrested conjugality". In this pattern we have an illustration of how the desire to maintain the domestic group as a corporate body may lead to the almost complete suppression of conjugal ties in favor of solidarity based upon lineal ties alone. This occurs by the simple device of parents deciding to defer indefinately the marriage of their children, particularly sons, so that the resultant domestic group remains a corporate body restricted to lineal kin. Under conditions of severe poverty and hardship, an attempt is made to achieve tight solidarity by foregoing the relationships on which temporal continuity of the kin group depends. This measure holds down the size of the domestic group while simultaneously obviating the necessity of coping with the potentially centrifugal conjugal and affinal relationships. I do not wish to imply that these are the reasons which respondents gave for establishing this type of domestic group, however. The usual explanation was that poverty made the arrangement of suitable marriages for children impossible. In reality, however, the cause has to be deeper because it is easily shown that many domestic groups as bad or worse off than these nevertheless contracted marriages. It is perhaps a matter of not deliberately starting out in the direction of arrested conjugality but of "discovering" at some point that "failure" to find "suitable" marriages for sons is beginning to pay dividends in that their single status renders a greater proportion of their income usable by the parents. One may draw this inference from much of the interview material.

Actually, there were two variations of the above pattern which merely reflected the different points in the developmental cycle where it was begun. Three were cases in which two or more brothers had remainded joint (Phase II) while either themselves failing to marry or failing to arrange marriages for their offspring. The other three were cases of men who had established Phase IIIA of the cycle but had then arrested the process of development by neglecting to arrange marriages for their children. It must be realized, of course, that in both variations we are speaking of heads of domestic groups who range in age between Later Adulthood and Old Age and who are either unwed themselves at this late point in life or who have children in Young or Later Adulthood who are unwed. It is only under these circumstances that we can meaningfully speak of an "arrested" pattern.

Perhaps the strongest proof that corporateness is a cherished value in itself in contemporary Indian domestic organization is contained in the characteristics of the type of group I have called "arrested lineality". This appears to be a pointed effort to enjoy all the functional advantages of the corporate kin group while at the same time overriding traditional unilineal considerations almost completely. What essentially occurred with four domestic groups fitting this category was that, strictly on the basis of economic expediency, three individuals and one entire conjugal unit had broken away from their lineal kin group and attached themselves to the domestic groups of persons who are normally residentially separate from ego. One person had adopted corporate residence with a mother's brother's domestic group in Lucknow, another with a father's sister's, and still another with a wife's brother's household. A fourth had affiliated with his father's younger brother, to be sure, but this had taken place long after the two had partitioned the original coparcenary and adopted separate domiciles in separate communities. Among the rickshawallas, only four subjects displayed arrested lineality; but evidence from other data to be published in the near future makes it plain that this represents an important functional adjustment to Indian urbanization and modernization which must be taken into account by investigators. It bears repeating in this context that the principle of corporateness in the broad sense which implies economic cooperation and the sharing of economic resources among a grouping of kinsmen must be conceptually distinguished from a given formal kinship structure which, under given sets of conditions, has heretofore been the exclusive recognized basis for determining the personnel of corporate kin groups. For the variations in domestic organization that appear possible in Indian cities today suggest that a considerable lattitude exists for compromise structures which both recombine established principles of kinship organization and at times override them completely. All of this being undertaken, of course, in the name of achieving corporate units bound together by kinship ties.

True neolocalism, in which a conjugal unit formally detaches itself from all other kin groups and assumes an entirely autonomous existence, was rare among rickshawallas. Only two cases were reported. In one, ego himself was living jointly in a household consisting of his parents and two adult unwed brothers – i.e., ego's household was an instance of arrested conjugality. However, two elder brothers, who were themselves close in age but about ten years older than their next sibling in the family, had married and established neolocal nuclear families elsewhere. Thus, there appeared to be a tendency toward arrested conjugality which was qualified by the fact that children who adopted conjugal ties were compelled to live completely separate from the lineal group. The functional consequence of the arrangement was to preserve the principle of arrested conjugality within the natal domestic group. The other instance of neolocalism was fairly straightforward. An original set of two male and one female siblings had split into separate units and in turn had experienced further splits as children matured and married. An original nuclear unit had grown into six neolocal nuclear units by the time of the interview. Only one qualification need be mentioned; that is, the aging father of this family complained that his sons were refusing to give him any economic support, which he clearly felt was his traditionally sanctified due.

Summary and Conclusions

A few basic points have emerged from this study of Lucknow rickshawallas that may provide guidelines for subsequent investigations into the impact of industrialization upon Indian social life. These are:

(1) The adoption of achievement-oriented occupations in the context of

the city does not imply the total abandonment of traditional social organization. Features of the latter remain viable both in rural communities and as "adaptive mechanisms" in cities.

(2) Decisions to migrate to cities in search of modern occupations arise from complex motivations that cannot be explained by allusions to simple economic factors like poverty and landlessness. Low caste migrations into Lucknow and Kanpur were proportionately higher before World War II than afterward, whereas high caste migrations displayed opposite characteristics. This was the result of changes which not so much altered economic as political and status relationships in the rural areas. Deprivation was not solely in terms of poverty but relative to particular sets of conditions which any given caste or grouping of castes had enjoyed in the past.

(3) Entry into modern urban occupations does not automatically imply the disintegration of the extended family and its replacement by the neolocal nuclear family. Assumptions that this invariably occurs arise from historical experiences with industrialization in the West, on the one hand, and with failure to distinguish normal processes of transformation in domestic groups from genuine structural change, on the other. The case of the Lucknow rickshawallas indicates that in a country like India, at least, compound kin groups are retained with great frequency in the urban environment regardless of occupation. Nuclear families almost invariably appear to be merely phases in the developmental cycle rather than genuinely new manifestations of kinship structure.

(4) Compound kin groups persist because corporate activities determined and validated by kinship ties continue to enjoy importance in the eyes of those whose life and work are situated in cities. That corporateness is the principal end valued is attested by the variations that occur in domestic organization in order to achieve it. Both lineal and affinal considerations are at times overridden for the purpose of assuring the existence of a grouping of kinsmen who will contribute the fruits of an often wide diversity of occupations to the common lot[1].

BIBLIOGARPHY

Bloch, Marc, 1961, Feudal Society. London: Routledge and Kegan Paul.

Fortes, Meyer, 1958, The Developmental Cycle in Domestic Groups. Cambridge Papers in Social Anthropology, No. 1.

Gould, Harold A., 1959, Family and Kinship in a North Indian Village. Unpublished Ph. D. Dissertation. Washington University (St. Louis).

—, 1960, Castes, Outcastes and the Sociology of Stratification. *International Journal of Comparative Sociology* I: 220–238.

—, 1961, Sanskritization and Westernization; A Dynamic View. *Economic Weekly*, June 24, 1961: 945–950.

1 I am indebted to Professor Leonard Kasdan and Mr. S. Kasdan for a most stimulating conversation which led to the decision to undertake this paper at the present time. Professor Kasdan is also to be thanked for a helpful critical reading of the initial manuscript. Finally, the valuable assistance of Mr. Sudama Prasad Mamgain, then a student of anthropology at Lucknow University, is gratefully acknowledged.

Gould, Harold A., 1962, Sanskritization and Westernization; Further Comments. *Economic Weekly*, January 13, 1962: 48–51.
—, 1963, The Adaptive Functions of Caste in Contemporary Indian Society. *Asian Survey* III: 427–438.
Mukerjee, Radhakamal and Baljit Singh, 1961, *Social Profiles of a Metropolis*. Bombay: Asia Publishing House.
Mulla, D. F., 1952, *The principles of Hindu Law*. Calcutta.
Niehoff, Arthur, 1959, *Factory Workers in India*. Milwaukee Public Museum Publication in Anthropology, No. 5.
Passin, Herbert, 1955, Untouchability in the Far East. *Monumenta Nipponica* X: 27–47.
Piggott, Stuart, 1950, *Prehistoric India*. London: Penguin.
Srinivas, M. N., 1952, *Religion and Society Among the Coorgs*. London: Oxford Press.
Wheeler, Sir Mortimer, 1953, *The Indus Valley Civilization*. Cambridge History of India, Supplement.

African Urbanism, Mobility and the Social Network

PETER C. W. GUTKIND

McGill University, Montreal, Canada

In recent years African urban studies have changed from the survey type,[1] the documentation and description of basic demographic and social characteristics, to a more analytical type of inquiry and presentation. Thus a number of conceptual schemes are now being tested. Southall[2] and Banton[3] have tried to apply basic sociological concepts, such as analysis of role relationships, to African urban systems. Southall,[4] too, has raised questions regarding macro and micro analysis both as to approach and method of investigation. Mayer,[5] and Wilson and Mafeje[6] have used group and social network analysis as has Epstein[7] in a particularly lucid presentation. Both Forde[8] and Mitchell[9] have summarized past approaches and suggested new lines of inquiry. While most of these new studies have been penned by social anthropologists and sociologists, geogra-

---

1 For example: *The Social Implications of Urbanization and Industrialization in Africa South of the Sahara*, Paris, UNESCO, 1956. Acquah, I., *Accra Survey*, London, University of London Press, 1958. Leslie, J. A. K., *A Survey of Dar es Salaam*, Oxford University Press (for East African Institute of Social Research), 1963. Southall, A. W. and Gutkind, P. C. W., *Townsmen in the Making*, East African Studies No. 9, Kampala ,East African Institute, 1957.

2 Southall, A. W., *The Theory of Urban Sociology*, typed Ms., n.d. (about 1956) and "An Operational Theory of Role", *Human Relations*, Vol. 12, No. 1, 1959, pp. 17–34.

3 Banton, M., *Role Congruence and Social Differentiation Under Urban Conditions*, Seminar on Social Structure, Stratification and Mobility With Special Reference to Latin America, Rio de Janeiro, June 1962, Pan American Union, Document 5 and "Role Theory and Urbanization", Paper presented at Symposium 26, Werner-Gren Foundation for Anthropological Research, Burg Wartenstein, Austria, August-September 1964, pp. 14.

4 Southall, A. W., Introductory Summary, in *Social Change in Modern Africa*, A. W. Southall (Ed.), London, Oxford University Press (for International African Institute), 1961, pp. 25–30.

5 Mayer, P., *Townsmen or Tribesmen*, Cape Town, Oxford University Press (for Institute of Social and Economic Research, Rhodes University), 1961.

6 Wilson, M. and Mafeje, A., *Langa : A Study of Social Groups in an African Township*, Cape Town, Oxford University Press, 1963.

7 Epstein, A. L., "The Network and Urban Social Organization", *The Rhodes-Livingstone Journal*, No. 29, June 1961, pp. 29–62.

8 Forde D., "Background and Approaches", in *Urbanization in African Social Change*, Edinburgh, Centre of African Studies, 1963, pp. 1–6.

9 Mitchell, J. C., *Theoretical Orientations in African Urban Studies*, Paper presented at the seminar on The Anthropology of Complex Societies, Association of Social Anthropologists, Cambridge, June 1963, 27 pp.

phers,[1] demographers and planners[2] have also shown an interest in comparative African urban studies.

African urban studies have achieved a place in comparative African sociology in part because an ever larger number of Africans have decided to seek alternative ways of making a living. This almost always means leaving the rural areas for a short or prolonged residence in town. While Africa remains the least urbanized of the continents, an urban environment has become the social and economic habitat for possibly 9% – 11% of the continent's population. In political terms, and as social pace setters, the influence of the larger African urban centers is considerable.[3] The growth of modern facilities in such towns is turning them into the showpieces of the new African nations.

Thus Peter Marris writes:

> "With the approach of independence, the people of Nigeria began to look more critically at their Federal capital, and saw in its congested lanes of ramshackle houses a poor reflection of their aspirations. As the Minister of Lagos Affairs remarked, 'It is the mirror through which foreigners make their initial appraisal of Nigeria'. The condition of central Lagos, he said, was 'humiliating to any person with a sense of national pride'."[4]

While it is not always easy to obtain reliable statistics on urban growth and rural-urban migration, particularly since independence, observers are generally agreed that the annual post-independence increase is considerably above that of previous years. What is also said to be a significant and new development is the larger number of Africans, particularly those with some years of urban residence, even if broken by frequent visits to kin and friends in the rural areas, who are staying for a longer period and will, probably, make the urban areas their permanent home. Thus Plotnicov has shown for his Jos (Northern Nigeria) data that Africans are increasingly reluctant to maintain close rural ties and even more reluctant to retire to the rural areas.[5]

1 Steel, R. W., "The Towns of Tropical Africa", in *Essays on African Population*, Barbour K. M. and Prothero, R. M. (Eds.), London, Routledge and Kegan Paul, 1961, pp. 249–78; Hamdan, G., "Capitals of the New Africa", *Economic Geography*, Vol. 40, No. 3, July 1964, pp. 239–53, "The Growth and Functional Structure of Khartoum", *The Geographical Review*, Vol. 50, No. 1, Jan. 1960, pp. 21–40; De Blij, H. J., "The Functional Structure and Central Business District of Lourenço Marques, Mozambique", *Economic Geography*, Vol. 38, No. 1, Jan. 1962, pp. 56–77; Mabogunje, A. L., "*Yoruba Towns*", Ibadan, University Press, 1962, "The Growth of Residential Districts in Ibadan", *Geographical Review*, Vol. 52, No. 1 Jan. 1962, pp. 56–77; Morgan, W. B., "The 'Grassland Towns' of the Eastern Region of Nigeria", *Transactions and Papers 1957*, Publication 23, Institute of British Geographers, London, Philip, 1957, pp. 213–224.

2 Zaremba, P., "The Urban Development of West and Equatorial Africa", *Africana Bulletin*, No. 1, 1964, pp. 105–134; Georgulas, N., "An Approach To Urban Analysis for East African Towns With Particular Reference to the African Population", *Ekistics*, Vol. 18, No. 109, December 1964, pp. 236–440.

3 Gutkind, P. C. W., "The African Urban Milieu: A Force in Rapid Change", *Civilizations*, Vol. 12, No. 2, 1962, pp. 167–195; Sklar, R. L., "A Note on the Study of Community Power in Nigeria", Paper Presented at the Annual Conference of the African Studies Association, Washington, October 1962, pp. 11.

4 Marris, P., *Family and Social Change in an African City*, London, Routledge, 1961, p. vii.

5 Plotnicov, L., "Modern Urban Population Formation in Nigeria", Paper Presented at the Annual Meeting of the American Anthropological Association, Detroit, 1964, 8 pp.

If this is so then there is clearly developing an African urban way of life – an urban system. It will then have to be approached and studied as such.[1] To do so we have to be mindful of Gluckman's solid guidance:

> "Urban life exhibits sufficient regularities for us to extract systematic inter-connexions which we can arrange to exhibit a structure and we can study how this structure changes".[2]

He goes on to point out that:

> "The starting-point for analysis of urbanization must be an urban system of relations ... We have to start with a theory about urban social systems; but these systems are to be seen as made up of loose, semi-independent, to some extent isolated, sub systems".[3]

While we can expect a considerable increase in urban population,[4] largely of those individuals who are engaged in a futile search for wage employment, it remains to be seen what ties Africans will maintain with the rural areas. Mitchell has pointed out that the cycle of rural-urban-rural migration can perhaps be best understood in terms of centrifugal and centripetal forces.[5] However, what keeps a man in town and what draws him back (*pro tem*) to his rural home will be increasingly determined by economic rather than social ties. Even where cash crops are under cultivation, as in Buganda Province or in Ghana's cocoa belt, providing a steady if uncertain return, it is increasingly the fashion for the owners to employ migrants while they seek additional wage employment.[6] Should an agrarian revolution develop in Africa, i.e. a major shift from subsistence to surplus cropping, cash cropping on small or large units, an ever increasing number of Africans will seek employment in non-agricultural activities. Then for a large number of urban Africans the break with the land and rural traditions is likely to be complete and final.

Of course, it is probably far too early to indicate exactly the salient characteristics of African urban society in the years ahead. At present urban life in Africa is marked by certain well-known characteristics which were shaped in the immediate pre-independence period. In East Africa's urban areas, particularly since the second World War, the population is usually composed of many tribal groups living in either peri-urban areas or on designated housing estates within the towns. Demographically, the urban population is composed primarily of unmarried young men and few women. Africans come as "target workers" to

---

1 Gutkind, P. C. W., "African Urban Family Life and the Urban System", *Journal of Asian and African Studies*, Vol. 1, No. 1, 1965. In press. (About 10 pp.)

2 Gluckman, M., "Anthropological Problems Arising from the African Industrial Revolution", in *Social Change in Modern Africa*, A. W. Southall (Ed.), London, Oxford University Press, 1961, p. 68.

3 Ibid., p. 80.

4 Hance, W. A., "The Economic Location and Functions of Tropical African Cities", *Human Organization*, Vol. 19, No. 3, Fall 1960, pp. 135–136; *The Geography of Modern Africa*, N. Y., Columbia University Press, 1964, pp. 52–57.

5 Mitchell, J. C., "The Causes of Labour Migration", *Inter-African Labour Institute Bulletin*, Vol. 6, No. 1, Jan. 1959, pp. 12–46.

6 Richards, A. I. (Ed.), *Economic Development and Tribal Change*, Cambridge, Heffer, 1954, pp. 119–140, 161–223.

acquire money and perhaps some new skills but return to their rural areas when it suits them or when their agricultural activities demand it. But more stay longer in town and fewer return to the rural areas.

If these characteristics are a correct assessment of the situation, then *urbanism as a way of life* will become an increasingly distinctive feature in the transformation of Africa. I think it is unsatisfactory to use the convenient label of "transitional societies" to describe the present total social system of African societies as passing through an intermediate phase from being less rural to being more urban. Many complex and yet unidentified processes are at work which may occur at different times and in different contexts from one society to another. The key issue is to find out how change and modernization take place. Central to this discussion is the fact that change and modernization often radically alter the patterns of social relations to bring about a different network of individual and group relations. This transformation is viewed by some observers as productive of negative and anomic characteristics. The individual and the group have been lifted out of the matrix of a complex system which was dominated by primary relations shaped by kinship, close interdependence and group reciprocity. The break with rural life is sharp and abrupt. However, this view ignores "how fluid the traditional (tribal) situation was" and that "individuals and groups were constantly on the move, communities dissolving and crystallizing again in new patterns".[1] Thus quite obviously it is false to pose the rural tribal system as a system of clearly understood reciprocal relations marked by maximum integration and the urban system as one of maximum fluidity, amorphousness or unbridled individualism. A closer and more analytical presentation would reveal that an urban society is as integrated as any other type of community but that integration takes place around different variables.

Thus extended kinship is not necessarily incompatible with African urban society; nor does the mobility of Africans invariably weaken *all* traditional kin and group ties. The question really is what aspects of traditional social organization are both useful and adaptable to new conditions? In what follows I hope to indicate some of the characteristics of urban social networks[2] and to suggest how such networks are shaped by the extent and type of rural-urban-rural

---

1 Southall, A. W., *op. cit.*, 1961, p. 2.

2 The concept of network has received considerable attention in recent years by Barnes ("Class and Committees in a Norwegian Island Parish", *Human Relations*, Vol. 7, 1954, pp. 39–58), Bott ("Conjugal Roles and Social Networks", *Human Relations*, Vol. 8, 1955, pp. 345–84), Jay ("The Concepts of 'Field' and 'Network' in Anthropological Research", *Man*, Vol. 64, September-October 1964, pp. 137–39), Srinivas and Béteille ("Networks in Indian Social Structure", *Man*, Vol. 64, Nov.-Dec. 1964, pp. 165–168).
As a model the concept of social networks has been suggested as particularly suitable for the analysis of mixed and complex groupings. The concept of social structure postulates numerous but interdependent enduring groups and highly specific categories, groups and classes. Srinivas and Béteille suggest that the distinction between social structure (enduring groups – those with "a high degree of consistency and constancy") and networks "is primarily one of boundaries. A group is a bounded unit. A network, on the other hand, ramifies

mobility. My data is taken from the all-African parish of Mulago, one of a number of parishes which make up the peri-urban area of Kampala, Uganda, East Africa.[1]

The area from which my data is taken contains an extremely heterogeneous African community representative of some twenty-five tribes. The parish of Mulago, which borders on Kampala, is one of about twelve parishes (*muluka*) which are part of the *kibuga*, the headquarters or capital of the Kingdom of Buganda. The *kibuga* in turn is a sub-county (*gombolola*), a number of which make up a county (*saza*). On the south, Mulago borders on the predominantly non-African and modern commercial capital of Uganda. To the northwest and east, Mulago is part of a larger sub-county. In 1948 the population of the *kibuga* as a whole was 34,337 and the parish of Mulago 2,500 (estimated). That part of the population of Mulago which was surveyed between 1953 and 1958 amounted to 1339 people, i.e. about 53% of the estimated total. Almost 75% of the African residents of the *kibuga* are Ganda while the rest come from other parts of East Africa. Over the years the parish has steadily become more congested with all the characteristics and features of a slum area. Many of those who live in the parish work in Government and business offices in Kampala; others work at the large and nearby Mulago Hospital and others operate shops and services in Mulago itself.

There is considerable mobility in and out of the parish and also from one part of Mulago to another. Firstly, there is a steady stream of Africans settling in the parish from outside Buganda Province. Likewise many people leave

---

in every direction, and for all practical purposes, stretches out indefinitely ... The character of a network ... varies from one individual to another". (p. 166)
Such a formulation allows more adequately for a description and analysis of many semi-independent social situations which result from disturbances and struggles, so much the mark of African urban life. In this sense a network "has a dynamic character. New relations are forged, and old ones discarded or modified. This is particularly true of rapidly changing societies in which individual choice plays an important role". (Srinivas and Béteille, p. 166). The objective, then, of network analysis is to "chart the type and the channels of interaction between persons and the extent of regularities which give a minimum of order and coherence to social life in communities which have no clear structure of discrete groups". (Southall, 1961, p. 25.)
The concept of social structure sprang from the work of social anthropologists working in relatively static and ethnically homogeneous communities. Few such communities are now being studied by anthropologists. As societies change they take on a new and different kind of complexity – a complexity which is increasingly the outcome of the way individuals, as individuals, manipulate a variety of situations and social relations. This in turn is the result of an ever widening field of choices which the individual can make in social, economic and political life. This is the essence of change and modernization which gives rise to new networks which cut across and involve change over the entire system. (See: Mair, L., *New Nations*, London, Weidenfeld and Nicolson, 1963, pp. 11–31).

1 Fieldwork was carried out between April 1953 and July 1955 and August 1956 to August 1958, while on the staff of the East African Institute of Social Research, Kampala, Uganda. For a description of the peri-urban area of Kampala see: Southall, A. W. and Gutkind, P. C. W., *Townsmen in the Making: Kampala and Its Suburbs*, East African Studies No. 9, East African Institute of Social Research, Kampala, 1957. Second Edition.

Mulago to return to the rural areas. Secondly, due to the fact that the parish is part of Buganda Province, many Ganda constantly move in or out of the parish. Thus between November 1953 and March 1954 slightly over 10% had left Mulago while just short of 17% were newcomers and 8% had returned to the parish for the second or third time.

Thirdly, there was a good deal of mobility within the parish. Almost 11% of the residents, most of whom had been in Mulago from 9 to 30 months, had moved once since their first arrival; 6% had moved twice and 4% more than twice. Over 61% of those who moved within the parish were non-Ganda. When further interviews were carried out between November 1957 and March 1958, the intake into the parish amounted to 31% (17% newcomers and 14% returnees), whereas only 12% of those who had been interviewed between November 1953 and March 1954 had left Mulago. This intake into the parish was reflected in an overall increase of the population of the *kibuga* to 52, 673 by 1959 and of Mulago (now enumerated separately in the 1959 Uganda Census) to 3767; an increase in eleven years, over the 1948 estimate, of 66%. The estimated population of the *kibuga* in 1964 is 65,000 (up by 23%) and of Mulago 4,200 (up by 13%).

These broad characteristics of mobility and population growth are closely linked, particularly the former, to the types of social networks in Mulago which are either kin-based networks or association-based networks. This distinction turned out to be useful when analysing certain characteristics of those more permanently resident (i.e. primarily Ganda) in Mulago (although frequently interrupted by *brief* visits to nearby rural areas) and those (primarily non-Ganda) who moved in and out of the parish, often staying away many months before returning to village or town. Thus Table I indicates that non-Ganda, who have been in and out of Mulago over a period of up to 8 years, up to March 1954,

Table I

Frequency of Visits to Rural Areas[1] *(50 miles and further) of non-Ganda Males 18 years and over.*

1953–1954 Sample

Time Span	*After Every 3 Months of Residence*	*After Every 6 Months of Residence*	*After Every 12 Months of Resedince*	*After Every 24 Months of Residence*		*Sample Total*
	41%	49%	8%	2%	100%	100

Table II

1957–1958 Sample

	30%	26%	38%	6%	100%	100

1 Of at least 2 weeks but no more than 3 months.

frequently return to their rural homes. While Ganda can see their kin and friends virtually whenever they wish, and rural kin and friends come to see them in Mulago, non-Ganda must make a special effort to return home. This they do often although Table II indicates that compared with the 1953–54 sample, the 1957/58 group had moved less frequently.

For a Ganda to visiting the rural areas does not mean that he must give up his employment or otherwise, significantly, pulling up his roots. Non-Ganda ties with urban life are thus frequently broken and on each return they must find new lodgings, new jobs and perhaps new friends. While they are not necessarily rural-oriented, the fact that they come without their families continues to tie them to a kin-based network which forces them back to their rural homes. However, while living and working in an urban area they are tied to a non-kin associational network which has resulted from their contact with members of the same tribe, or their work or neighbourhood associations. Each one of these contacts produces a set of network relations which are operative at different times and under different conditions. At times these networks overlap when tribe and composition of the residential neighbourhood are the same,[1] or when members of the same tribe are employed together. However, association-based networks need not be linked to common tribal background.

Perhaps the most outstanding example of a non-tribal network is the beer bar[2]. There are anywhere from six to ten bars in Mulago. At weekends and at the end of the month small rooms are crowded with customers. Various varieties of African beers are brewed by women, a number of whom have developed a reputation for their excellent beer – beer which has body and gives the drinker the feeling that he is consuming more than mere liquid. Each bar may be filled with 5–25 people and on a really crowded day many more sit outside the room on benches placed in the courtyard. On such occasions men and women of every tribe represented in the parish will sit together and jostle and joke with one another. It is a favourite place to pick up a women and make whatever arrangements are desired. Friends made at work or in Mulago will frequent the bar as a group. At the start of an afternoon or an evening out, men can be seen playing a card game or any number of other African games. Some beer sellers set aside a little corner or open place for such regular customers. There is much coming and going, much joking and shouting and occasionally dancing. Europeans and Asians are often mocked in informal and spontaneous mime. Men and women discuss the affairs and personalities of the parish. They make cutting remarks about other tribes; they debate on a high moral plane thieves and prostitutes. Men give money to help out those who plead special needs in casual conversation. Newcomers use the occasion to make contacts, to seek lodgings and jobs.

As the afternoon and evening wears on, and as men and women drift in and out of the bars, the excitement and commotion heightens. Minor fights and

---

1 Gutkind, P. C. W., "Urban Conditions in Africa", *The Town Planning Review*, Vol. 32, No. 1, April 1961, pp. 20–31.

2 Southall, A. W. and Gutkind, P. C. W., 1957, op. cit., pp. 57–63.

bottle smashing occur. Those more sober will try to restrain those more excitable and persuade them to go home. Casual contacts and friendships made earlier will dissolve in anger, accusations and sudden violence. Property might be smashed and heads broken. Thieves and confidence tricksters will then ply their successful trades. Tribal feelings will be expressed more bitterly and factions will line up. But when it is all over the same people will return the next day and the next weekend seeking companionship and friends.

These informal associational networks extend into the community as a whole. Drinking clubs and credit societies are often born in beer bars. They may last for months until they break up to be re-formed at a later date. For the newcomers a beer bar is a central point of contact. For men it is a place to find a woman; for the down and out it is a way to pick up a drink and some money. For many more it is a way of recreation, of showing off and a debating union where personal and group problems are discussed – but never resolved.

Another common feature of Mulago's non-Ganda is to belong to small credit societies, of perhaps 4–8 members, which allows each participant in turn to receive a share of the wages of all other members at the end of each month. As the penalty for absconding with the money is likely to be a severe beating, should the culprit be found, members of such credit societies tend to be linked in mutual aid and close association. The composition of three such groups was based on friendships made at work rather than on tribalism. Yet another non-tribally based form of association are groups of young men who join together to employ a young girl or older woman to cook for them. Towards this end they pool their resources. Such groupings are very loosely knitted types of association. Yet they should be seen as a particularly suitable structure as men can enter and join such groups without complex contractual and obligatory commitments. The existence of such groups is often attractive to newcomers who do not know their way about but through a friend can join a "supper club".

Other networks are based on residence in a tribal enclave whose members, usually non-kin, aid each other in many ways. Such enclaves often give a strong emphasis to a "we-group" feeling which is expressed in the manner in which they refer to other groups. Not infrequently they appoint one among them as a leader and spokesman. In doing so members of such tribal settlements have developed a more structured type of associational network which supports the individual in meeting virtually every contingency he might face. An example of this would be how members of a Luo settlement, comprising 8 men, two of whom had their wives and small children living with them, came to the aid of one of their number who had been arrested and fined in the sub-county court. His fine was paid by others of his settlement. In turn he was asked to find employment for a newly-arrived Luo because he was a minor foreman in the Public Works Department. As this request was made to him during a period of economic recession he was not able to locate employment. The other Luo of his settlement accused him of wanting to be paid for his services. A mock court was established and he was asked to move elsewhere – a step he finally took after having fallen ill and believing this to be due to witchcraft.

This event also illustrates that ethnicity is not always a sufficiently strong bond even under conditions of extreme heterogeneity in urban areas where ethnicity acts as a protective measure *vis-à-vis* the politically and socially dominant Ganda.[1]

Association-based networks are adaptable. They provide the non-Ganda from far away, and resident in a foreign setting, with friendship, mutual aid and support. To stand alone is impossible. The need for a supportive structure for a non-Ganda immigrant is on the mind of many. Out of several hundred interviews, virtually all of which make the same points, the following two are typical examples:

A

"When I first arrived in Mulago I looked for any person of my tribe I knew. I was lucky to find a friend and I stayed with him for three weeks before I found a place for myself. I had a little money when I arrived but after four days in Mulago almost half of it was stolen. My friend introduced me to his friends (not all of whom were of the same tribe) to ask for jobs. Eventually I found work as a sweeper in a big office.

"I now live with a group of young men only one of whom is a member of my tribe but two others work in the same office as messengers. We go to work together because one of them has a bicycle and I can ride with him. We cook for each other because we cannot pay for help. When a member of my tribe goes home I give him messages for my wife and if I have any money I will give some of that too.

"I am now trying to get better work where I can get more money. So I went to see a Ganda friend of mine. He likes me because I can speak his language. But I do not really like the Ganda people because they treat us all with contempt.

"On Sunday I play football. I have joined a club and pay one shilling every three months. There are people from many different tribes in my club but we get on well together. I sometimes get tired of living here and having to buy all my food. If I get tired of work I go home but I always come back."[2]

B

"I have lived in Mulago for almost one year. It is the longest time that I have been away from my country. But I expect to go home for leave next month. The first time I came to Mulago I only stayed two months before I went home. But I came back again and stayed longer. I came back to Mulago because I had friends here and I knew that they would let me sleep with them.

"I sometimes go with women but there are not many here in Mulago. I have never been with a Ganda woman because I do not have money to pay them.

"Not long ago I was beaten up by another man and I took a complaint to the parish chief. I took a friend along with me to help to introduce me to the chief. The Ganda chiefs are not like our chiefs so I knew that he might not listen to me.

"Whenever a friend of mine goes home I give him money for my wife. I get this money from my friends but I always pay them back.

"I have some friends but they are not like the friends at home. They are just friends. You cannot trust your friends because they might spoil your name or beat you. In my home I am not beaten and if that should happen I will go to the chief and he will punish the culprit."[3]

---

1 Gutkind, P. C. W., "Accommodation and Conflict in an African Peri-Urban Area," *Anthropologica*, N. S. Vol. 4, No. 1, 1962, pp. 163–173.

2 From my unpublished field notes, October 1954.

3 *Ibid.*, February 1957.

What appears to be significant about these accounts is the fact that associationally-based networks provide a migrant non-Ganda with the instrumentalities to obtain a home and a job. Some networks are really class networks. As a migrant repeatedly returns to Mulago, or elsewhere in the *kibuga*, he gradually selects his friends according to similar skills, wealth and education. Such relations generally cut right across tribal background. Thus in Mulago there was a "Monday Night Club" composed of 4–10 members representing five different tribes. Most of the members were foremen, on public works, junior medical orderlies, junior clerks or small-scale artisans. When they met, usually on a rotating basis at a member's house, they just talked about anything that came into their minds. They aided each other both financially and with their labour, such as on the occasion when two members had help from the others to build extensions to their houses. When they met, which was irregular, they were always well dressed and in conversation they would debate the failures of other people, their bad habits and manners and the aspirations they had for themselves.

As his field of contacts extends, the migrant shifts from one kind of network to another. Friends become enemies and enemies friends. Much of the internal mobility within Mulago could be traced to acts of violence or accusations of theft or uncertain love affairs which badly disrupted the individual's relations with neighbours, fellow tribesmen or friends.

Participation in many different associations, such as credit clubs, recreational associations or beer drinking clubs, does not provide the individual with a set of clearly defined relationships which have predictability and regularity over time. Such relationships can be broken by all manner of means. Having visited his rural home means, in most cases, that on his return to Mulago he will have to start all over again the complex process of finding a home and a job. His past friends have gone; his job has been taken by another. Under such conditions men latch on to any type of organization and relationship which they consider suitable for their immediate and short-range needs. An associationally-based network in this sense is a particular kind of structure which lacks the formalness and cohesiveness of kin-based networks. Association networks must provide the individual member with concrete benefits of assistance and protection. Yet at the same time the unique feature of these networks is that they are constantly manipulated by their participants; this means that they are ever shifting and possess an amorphous quality which is reduced to a more structured situation only by the fact that such networks always exist. They can best be isolated by means of following the activities of specific individuals rather than by tracing collective activities.

If we now turn to kin-based networks we shall see that they are associated with quite different characteristics. In the first case kin-based networks are only established when either mobility is low or when circumstances favour their establishment, despite rural-urban-rural mobility. The latter is illustrated by the Ganda residents in Mulago, the vast majority of whom move frequently and easily in and out of Mulago. This is clearly indicated in Table III. Thirty-one per cent visited their kin and friends from once to five times per month; 36% up to 8 times every two months and 33% between 2 and 8 times every three months. This is in strong contrast with non-Ganda migrants.

Those Ganda who were married, but had left their wives at home, had frequent visits from them and other kin and friends when they found it difficult or inconvenient to leave Mulago. Weekend visiting in both directions was very common. Food was generally brought to Mulago by a rural visitor or a parish resident brought some back to his urban home. It was also very common for a parish resident to bring back a young child, perhaps his brother's child, to look after for a short or prolonged time. Not infrequently a steady stream of kin and friends would visit a Mulago resident and stay with him for a few days or weeks. Such visitors would expect hospitality which involved the host in considerable extra expenditure. This was, not infrequently, resented and formed the basis of bitterness and strained relations.

Table III

Frequency of Visits to Buganda Rural Areas (within 70 mile radius[1]) of Ganda Men[2]

	1 visit to rural area	*2 visits*	*3–5 visits*	*6–8 visits*	*8 or more visits*	*Totals*
per month	6	11	14	–	–	31
Every 2 months	3	11	16	4	2	36
Every 3 months	1	10	14	4	4	33
	10	32	44	8	6	100

1 Exclusive of those visiting within a 10 mile radius of Kampala.
2 Both single and married men over 18 years.

Most Ganda occupy higher economic and status levels than non-Ganda. This gives them better and more secure employment. In addition many Mulago Ganda own cotton and coffee gardens, looked after by kin or friends or non-Ganda migrants, which give them further incomes. In the parish virtually all shops are owned by Ganda, a fact which is resented by non-Ganda who claim that the former cheat them.

Thus economically and politically the Ganda dominate the parish. Few of them extend their contacts socially to non-Ganda. Most Ganda live on or near the "main street" running north-south through the parish. Non-Ganda live in close proximity but avoid close contact with Ganda. Between December 1953 and July 1954 one Ganda houseowner evicted three non-Ganda tenants to make room for Ganda renters. Ganda women who have too frequent contact with non-Ganda men are criticized and made to feel inferior. At the same time most beer brewers are Ganda women whose clientele are predominantly non-Ganda. In this way and through the authority of the Ganda chief, Ganda and non-Ganda residents are tied into overlapping association-based networks, politically and economically.

Ganda society in Mulago rests on kin-based networks. Although a Ganda lives away from his home he is never far away from its influence. Indeed, the village, via its individuals, extends into Mulago. The basic Ganda social unit in Mulago is, typically, a man and his wife and children or a man and his older children. Numerous other combinations also exist, such as two brothers whose sister cooks for them or a brother and sister, both employed in Kampala, sharing a household. It is less usual for a man to share his household with any of his wife's relatives although there are some cases of an older sister-in-law helping a Ganda shopkeeper. Few Ganda live alone.

When ceremonial and ritual occasions arise, birth, marriage or death, Mulago Ganda invariably return to their rural homes to participate. Shops are then closed and those employed in Kampala seek leave for a day or two. It is true that such easy urban-rural-urban movement is made possible because of the proximity of Mulago to the Ganda rural-interland. But is is also possible because of the substantially greater wealth of the Ganda who can afford to maintain a town house and a country estate. Non-Ganda who generally hold inferior jobs cannot move back and forth as easily although their tribal home may not be substantially further away than that of many Ganda.

In addition the Ganda have imported into the urban areas not only a network of kin-based relations but also those corporate institutions which make up the total structure of Ganda society. Thus in the peri-urban area of Kampala, Ganda own land in exactly the same manner as they do in the rural areas although they use their urban land for different purposes. Some land in the *kibuga* is held by virtue of the official offices held by the owners. The way the land is administered in the urban area has something in common with its administration in the rural area. Land disputes are handled by the judicial institutions of the Ganda.

Furthermore, the fact that most Ganda in Mulago and elsewhere in the *kibuga*, are never far removed from others who are of the same clan (whatever the operational importance of this grouping is at present), reproduces the basic structural categories of Ganda society in town. For Ganda, therefore, urbanism as a new and distinct way of life becomes simply an extension of the structure, operation and the values of Ganda society as a whole. In this sense urban Ganda, while anchored in a kin-based network, are also part of an association-based urban network. Such a network is fashioned by new opportunities and demands, by new forms of differentiation, stratification and competition resulting from economic, political and social transformation.

For the Ganda, urbanization and urbanism as a way of life has not resulted in an abrupt break with the past. For urban Ganda, the model of the desirable society continues to be the traditions of the main features of Ganda life and culture. The urban non-Ganda, however, must construct for himself a pattern of social life and organization designed specifically for urban, and thus non-traditional, conditions. To achieve his ends he must participate in a network of contacts and associations which are radically different from those of his kin-based rural environment. As he progressively stays for longer periods in town, urban life presents itself as a more desirable social model and, presumably, a more clearly structured social order.

In this paper I have tried to point to a distinction between kin-based and association-based networks. These two models of social organization should not, however, be seen as mutually exclusive. They meet and overlap at numerous points. They are designed to meet different conditions. A kin-based network is designed to meet the demands of reciprocal roles; an association-based network is designed to meet, flexibly, new situations to which role responses are yet uncertain. Southall, I believe, is one of the first to attempt an analysis of comparative rural (kin-based) and urban (association-based) role functions. He writes:

> "Our hypothesis is that the empirical, commonsense distribution between town and country life may be given sociological precision by determining certain features of role structure in each case. In general, town life is characterized by role-relationships that are more narrowly defined, more specific, more unequally distributed between persons, more extensively developed in latent role structure, more numerous as a whole in relations to persons who are themselves living at a high spatial density, and more fleeting in their duration over time. In short, the passage from rural to urban conditions is marked by a rise in the density of role texture".[1]

While this might be a fruitful way of analysing a complex system of behaviour, I believe that the social network concept allows for the documentation of how in practice the individual and the group manipulate various roles both simultaneously and separately. In this respect social network analysis points to the way in which role performance is a part of the operation of a system, or a series of systems. To achieve a better understanding of how participation in various types of networks determines and structures specific roles, i.e. ethnic, kin, political, economic or recreational roles, micro-analysis is likely to point the way.[2]

---

1 Southall, A. W., 1959, op. cit., p. 24.
2 Southall, A. W., 1961, op. cit., pp. 25–30. In a forthcoming publication on Neighbourhood Units in Mulago, Kampala, I hope to apply some of the suggestions put forward by Southall.

Kinship and Geographical Mobility in a Sample from a London Middle-Class Area

JANE HUBERT

London School of Economics and Political Science, London, U.K.

THIS paper deals with a small sector of the results of research in progress among a set of middle-class families in London. The object of the study is to analyse the structure and estimate the magnitude and social significance of the kinship systems of British middle-class families; it was conceived as an extension of earlier work in London, and is being carried out in conjunction with a parallel study in Chicago.[1]

The British study, with which I am concerned here, started with a pilot investigation of 30 families living on a private housing estate in North London. This estate, "Greenbanks", is generally considered to be a "good middle-class area", having a high proportion of professional people living on it. Following the pilot survey, a random sample of 60 households was taken of the total population of electors' households on the estate (about 250 in all). This sample was heterogeneous in terms of marital status, family stage, age, religion and occupation, though the majority of individuals are married with children, Protestant, and the occupations of the heads of households fall within the broad band of "middle-class" occupations.

A second random sample was drawn from a population of married couples with dependent children from a delimited area of Highgate village in North London. The sample therefore differs radically from the Greenbanks sample in

1 The London Study, as also that in Chicago, is financed by a Research Grant from the National Science Foundation of the United States, to which grateful acknowledgement is here made. The Principal Investigator in the London Study is Professor Raymond Firth of the London School of Economics and Political Science. The Principal Investigator of the Chicago study is Professor David Schneider, to whom we are indebted for very valuable discussions of the London project. The author is Research Officer and team leader in charge of the project. She wishes here to acknowledge the help given in the preparation of this article by Professor Raymond Firth, Mr. Anthony Forge, Dr. Sutti Ortiz and other members of the team. (A few preliminary results from the London study have been published in: Raymond Firth, "Family and Kinship in Industrial Society", *Sociological Review Monograph*, No. 8, Keele, 1964 and Dorothy Crozier, "Kinship and Occupational Succession", *The Sociological Review*, Vol. 13, No. 1).

that it is homogeneous in terms of family stage, and thus more so in terms of age too. The sample from Highgate was also, for various reasons, more uniform in terms of religion, having far fewer Jewish families than the estate.

All the 167 adult individuals in the two random samples could be said to be middle class by at least some of the criteria generally used to place people. Apart from occupation, their style of life, socio-economic level and general behaviour were distinctly middle class, even if only insofar as they were neither working class nor aristocracy or "plutocracy", although within this general homogeneity there were wide variations of such items as income, class origins and speech patterns.

Since only a small part of the field material collected is relevant to the subject of this article, little need be said about the nature of the methodology or results of the whole study. Briefly, the object was to estimate the importance of *extra-familial* kinship, i.e. the importance of kin outside the immediate family, in everyday life and in times of crisis, in terms of contact, exchange of services, influence in decision-making and on general behaviour patterns. The study was basically anthropological in method, using genealogies as the basic framework, and collecting material over a number of interviews. Although the actual interviews were of an unstructured nature, the material was collected systematically for each household. A comprehensive *aide-memoire* of over 20 pages covered education, occupational and residential history of the informants and all their kin, the nature of contact and services between kin, specific kin relationships, kinship and family ideology, the role of friends and any factors which were thought to bear possible relation to kinship attitudes and behaviour. The bulk of the material was of a qualitative kind, but was collected in such a way that certain quantitative aspects could be abstracted from it for purpose of analysis.

The families of the individuals in the samples varied considerably in terms of size, varying between extremes of one or two known relatives to over 300. Apart from size, they varied too in terms of the degree of corporateness, in "family ideology" and attitudes towards kin and kin obligations, and in general kinship behaviour.

Within the wide scope of the material collected certain areas are relevant to the discussion of kinship and geographical mobility. They are, for example, the origin of the individuals in the samples, the reasons for coming to London (for those informants born elsewhere) and the use made of kin in these circumstances, the location, degree of scatter or corporateness of their kin, the relation between geographical distance and contact patterns between kin, and the importance of actual geographical location.

Since the analysis of our data is still in progress, the discussion of quantitative aspects of the material has been limited for the purpose of this article to the 30 married couples from the second sample area, Highgate Village, though qualitative examples have been drawn from both samples.

Origin of the Informants

The majority of the individuals in the Highgate sample are not born Londoners. 22 out of 60 were born in London, the rest elsewhere. This is not surprising since one might expect a metropolitan population to be drawn from all over the country. But it contrasts with the origins of the working-class informants in Young & Willmott's survey of Bethnal Green, where 83% of men and 85% of women were born in London.[1] Taking very crude geographical areas, a similar number of the Highgate individuals were born in the south (including the south-west) of England, and the north of England – 11 in each; 6 were born in Scotland ,1 in Ireland, and none in either Wales or East Anglia. A surprising number, 9 out of 38 non-Londoners, were born abroad, but only in rare cases were they born of foreign parents – in most cases their parents were living abroad, which itself has some kinship relevance.

Most of the Highgate informants are thus migrants to London, and come from a wide range of different areas. By definition, all 30 married couples now live in London, and over two-thirds of them also first met their spouses in London; of the 21 pairs who met there, in only 5 cases were both born there; only 2 couples first met in any other "home town" of either of them, the rest elsewhere in the country or abroad. Thus there was in nearly every case some degree of mobility before marriage, on the part of both men and women. Spouses were not, on the whole, drawn from a home environment and very few met either directly or indirectly through kin.

The 2 couples who met in their home town first met as children, which may or may not be considered to be meeting through kin. Of the others, only four couples met through relatives of some kind. Eleven couples met through their training, or in connection with their work, the other 13 either socially or in some indeterminate way. The high proportion of couples who met through college and work is perhaps typical of a professional group of people, though Rosser[2] sees this as a general trend in mate selection.

The fact that most informants married spouses from different areas implies that either their parents moved from the place they were born, or that the informants themselves left home before marriage. In fact in most cases both men and women had been living away from home for some time before they married. This is not unexpected in the case of the men, but is so with the high proportion of women. Exactly two !thirds of the wives were living away from home before they married, all of them for over a year, and the majority of them for five or more years.

What emerges from this is that the informants, and in particular the women, are independent of their parents before they married, at least in terms of residence. This contrasts with the working-class situation usually described, in

---

1 Michael Young & Peter Willmott, *Family and Kinship in East London*, London, 1957, p. 169.

2 Colin Rosser and C. C. Harris, "Relationships through Marriage in a Welsh Urban Area" *The Sociological Review*, Vol. 9, No. 3. November 1961; p. 310.

which a girl lives at home until she marries and possibly for some time after she marries, until the couple can afford a place of their own. This early independence of girls from their parents, and especially from their mothers, is significant because it affects the type of relationship they have with their mothers, and attitude towards them, in adult life. Certainly we have not found situations at all like those described by Young and Willmott[1] in Bethnal Green, where married daughters depend on their mothers not only for day-to-day services in the house, but also for emotional support in their daily life. The fact that this does not commonly occur in Highgate does not mean that the young wives do not have strong affective ties with their mothers, but residential independence long before marriage, combined with professional training and general independence of outlook, must lead to at least a different sort of relationship between married daughters and their mothers; one expressed not in terms of daily contact and moral support, but in perhaps maturer ways, with dependence only in times of crisis, e.g. in confinements and illness, not in the daily running of their lives.

Independence from parents is not merely an accidental concomitant of professional life. In most cases there is explicit agreement that children should be independent of their parents. This is manifested in earlier life by the willingness to send children to boarding schools. This attitude is apparent, when their children marry, in the strong preference on both sides for the young couple to set up house on their own, and in order that this should be possible parents will provide money towards a house rather than let them have to move in with them.

This stress on independence is significant as one of the main factors in the formation and development of kin relationships and attitudes. It means that young people can choose to live where they like, or where their work takes them because the sort of relationship they grow up to have with their parents, and thus with their other kin, does not depend on frequent and intense contact of any kind. From childhood onwards there are different attitudes, and expectations of parent-child behaviour; and different ways of expressing emotion.

This fact makes the assessment of relationships with kin somewhat more difficult. It means that frequency of contact cannot be taken in isolation as the criterion of a close relationship, and in fact it may sometimes be misleading as an indication of the strength of an affective tie between two kinsmen.

The relative freedom, in intellectual and emotional terms, of children from their parents, is important in various ways in their subsequent relationships with extra-familial kin in general. In one respect merely being residentially independent, especially in order to get professional training of some kind, enables a person to widen the scope of their contacts, and to meet people with whom they have things in common, e.g. similar training and intellectual disciplines. Young people will be freer to choose as friends people they like, and this may extend to members of the family as well. "Community of interest" is often quoted as one

1 Young & Willmott, *op. cit.*

of the most important things in the choice of friends from within the family. These people, by virtue of their background, education and occupation, have additional criteria to apply in their selection of kin. In fact one might have expected far fewer and less intense relationships with kin than is the case. What is surprising is not the paucity of kin relationships, but the number and richness of them considering the alternatives open to these individuals, and in many cases the lack of common interests between them.

To return to residential independence – it can be seen that it is not only our informants that have moved from their parental home or home area, but the majority of their kin have scattered too, in this and the previous generations.

Dispersion of Kin

The known kin of all the 60 individuals with whom we are concerned are widely dispersed throughout England, and in most cases overseas as well. In none of the cases was there any localised family all of whose members lived within a single area, and this applies to the families of those born in London as well as to those born elsewhere. Although there is a wide scatter of kin – and 50 out of 60 Highgate individuals know of some kin living abroad – the distribution is not necessarily even. In some cases there is a quite even scatter of kin around the country, but in others there are definite groupings of kin in one place, though with some other kin scattered elsewhere.

In the latter case, the informant or his or her parents, have often moved from a rural area, leaving behind a number of kin who form, at least in the view of the individuals who have left, some sort of kin group, and visits to these kin are often referred to and thought of as "going home". In some of these families there is a substantial number of kin actually left behind in this place of origin, and there is said to be a great deal of interchange of visits and services between the households concerned. In other cases there are very few kin actually living there, but those that have left still think of the place as a sort of kin base. Typically these kin nuclei are rural farming families, but others are centred around family businesses, and occasionally there are groupings of kin which have no economic basis at all, though this seems to be more of an exception. The most interesting aspect of kin groupings of this kind is perhaps the attitude towards them of the members of the family who have scattered to other parts of the country. To some extent there are mixed feelings towards them – a mixture of regret at not being part of a close-knit family group, with all the moral support and security it affords, and relief at being independent of it, and reasonably free from the demands and pressures that living within a close group of any kind carries with it. Whatever the ambivalence towards kin groupings of this kind, there is usually a perceptible influence exerted by kin *en masse*, and this has a definite effect on patterns of contact, as will be seen later.

At the other extreme from these families, in which there is a locatable place of origin where some kin at least still live (and to which Ego, though geographically separated, still feels a definite tie) there are families which have scattered over the generations, and have no existing kin "home", nor even clusters of kin living near each other in any one place. In these cases it is not only our informants who have moved, but others in the same generation and in the parental generation too. Members of this sort of family tend to feel that they, as individuals, or as households, are more isolated from the rest of their kin than are members of families that have a kin base somewhere. There may in fact be no difference in the availability of kin in the two cases, but a certain degree of security does seem to be felt if there is a group of kin living in one place, or even a few kin with whom they can identify a particular place that is known and familiar.

In families where kin have scattered, usually more than one – and often very many – nuclear families and individual members of the wider kin universe have moved into London, but this does not mean that a new kin group will necessarily, or even probably, be formed. In London, proximity does not necessitate social contact. Many members of the same wider family may migrate to London, but it is important to note that they come as individuals, or as individual families, not as kin groups. In some cases a parent, or occasionally a sibling, may come to London because a child or sibling is living there. But beyond this, migration to London seems to be an individual affair, and kin coming to London do not expect to become part of, or form, a kinship group of any kind. How far co-residence in London affects or influences contact patterns will be discussed later. Here are two important points: that migration tends to be an individual action, and that proximity in itself does not imply or necessitate intense social relations to any degree.

All the individuals in Highgate gave reasons for moving to London that are in general unrelated to kin or kinship relationships. Of those who were not born in London some, of course, came as children, and thus came for their parents' reasons, not their own. Of the rest, the majority came before they were married, and both men and women came mainly for professional training, or to take up a job. Nine of the 12 husbands who were not born or brought up in London came to take up jobs, but 3 came originally for professional training, and one as a refugee from abroad. A higher proportion of the wives came for training – 8 out of 17 not brought up in London, whereas 7 came for work and one (with her husband) as a refugee from abroad. Five others merely came with their husbands when the latter came, and one came in the war to live with her mother while her husband was abroad, and when he came back they found somewhere to live in London. None of these people, except this last, came to London either with kin or because of kin. The young married couples on Greenbanks show a similar pattern.

In the cases where our informants have moved to London from some other area there is very little evidence that other kin have followed them. It might have been expected that parents would come to London to be near their children, or at least live near one of their children. In fact, of the 12 husbands in the sample who moved to London as adults, not one has a parent living in London; similarly they have only two siblings out of a possible 23 living in London.

(Both these two came for quite independent reasons, and in fact there is no contact at all with one of them.) In the case of the 17 wives who have come to London, 3 have one parent each, in each case widowed, who have moved there since the daughter came, explicitly to be nearer her. This may well be a significant point – that aged or widowed parents tend to turn to their daughters rather than their sons. In the case of their siblings, only 7 out of a possible 37 have moved to London – three of these are from the same family, another came with the informant and the other two with their husbands.

With regard to the parents who have not moved to London, this is not usually because they are already living near some other child. In only about 50% of the cases do they have one or more of their children living anywhere within the same area.

The families of the informants who were born or brought up in London have also scattered. In most cases their parents have remained in London (and thus are living reasonably near at least one of their children), but a large number of siblings have moved out of London. Altogether 62% (excluding the informants from the sibling group) have moved somewhere else. In many cases the sibling group has completely split up.

The Highgate informants then, and also their siblings, have in general been highly mobile and very few sibling groups are located in one place. The most localised sibling group is that of a woman with five living siblings, three of whom farm within the same area of Scotland, another nearby and only one (apart from herself) who has moved altogether. This is an exceptional case, however, and in fact is the result of the conscious attitude of the father, who gave farms to each of his children. At the other extreme from this family is a man with four sisters and two brothers who live as far apart as Sussex, Warwickshire, Yorkshire, Devonshire, Scotland and Bedfordshire; again these are mostly farmers, but there was no desire or attempt to find farms within the same area.

In most cases the informants and their brothers and sisters have moved because of their work and this is a characteristic of middle-class, especially professional, people. The 60 individuals living in Highgate are not the exception in their sibling groups. The latter have also moved around the country though surprisingly few have moved into London, or even within easy "commutable" distance. Thus there seems to be no tendency for siblings to follow each other when they migrate. The high mobility within these families is unrelated in nearly every case to the residence or mobility of other members of the family.

Among the Highgate informants the presence of kin in London was only in one case given as a major reason for moving to the city, but it might have been expected that when they did arrive, or before they actually came, they would have mobilised kin for various purposes. The problems that generally face a working-class migrant to the city are those of where to live, where to look for work, how to live until the first money comes in. In the case of our informants these problems were generally solved before they arrived, and we have no evidence that they made prior arrangements with kin. Those who came for training had this already arranged, and those who came to work also, except in a few cases, had already fixed up jobs before they came. In this way a migrant middle-class population differs from a working-class one. Professional men and women apply for appointments and usually only move when they have accepted a job. An unskilled or even skilled labourer will usually come to London to look for work.

The difference is, then, that middle-class individuals or families will not *have* to mobilise kin or anyone else before or when they arrive. They do not come to London needing, generally, help in finding work, and seldom even in finding somewhere to live. In fact only one husband in Highgate found work through a relative, and this was after working for 18 months in London already. This was not a case of landing in London and depending on other people to find work. The level at which "job-finding" is done among these people is a different one. In this case it was a question of hearing about a job at a party given by his wife's great-aunt, but other examples of help with jobs between kin of the informants (again very few) show that it is not a question of "speaking for" a relative as employee to employer, but using influence and connections at a more elevated level.

This independence from kin with regard to job-finding is not only a question of relative financial security and professional qualifications (although these are obviously important factors), but is also a matter of well-defined attitudes and definite preferences. It is very often stated explicitly that people should not turn to kin to find jobs for them – even the one husband who did have help did not consider this to be an accepted form of behaviour. The fact that in many cases professional people can depend on their own qualifications to get jobs is very relevant, but even in this sphere the more attractive jobs may not always be obtainable, and kin in many cases could be of use.

Although there is a definite disinclination to ask for help from relatives for finding jobs, or getting into colleges and so on, it is interesting that this often co-exists with a willingness to help other relatives. It is not the "done thing" to be on the receiving end of kin help and influence, but to use one's own influence is quite acceptable. Though they do not necessarily see it in these terms, status is conferred by giving, not receiving.

Very few of the informants who came to London to train or work made use of relatives to supply them with places to live. Occasionally kin would be stayed with temporarily, but never for long. In a few cases a young girl coming to London at the age of 17 or 18 shared a flat with a single sister, or lived in the house of a married sister, and in one case a young "deb" lived for a season with her maternal grandmother. Apart from this there is no pattern of coming to London and being provided with somewhere to live. The only help given in this context is occasionally in the form of loans towards buying a house, but this is another question altogether.

In general then it can be seen that these people have not only come to London as individuals, or individual families, but have also remained independent to a great extent even when other kin are living in London.

It has been shown earlier that most informants have kin scattered throughout the British Isles and overseas as well. It can be seen from the Tables that many kin are at some considerable distance from Highgate, and analysis of each individual case shows that in fact nearly every individual has at least some kin living at a good distance from them as well as some closer and others within London. In the context of kin relationships three aspects of kin scatter are of major importance – the distance they are from each other; the actual geographical location of them in terms of e.g. London v. provincial towns, urban v. rural, etc.; and the degree of concentration of kin in one or more places.

Geographical Distance and Maintenance of Contact

Since the main object of the study was to assess the importance of extra-familial kin ties and hence, in general, extra-household ties, we were naturally concerned with discovering the relation between geographical distance and patterns of contact. Obviously distance between two individuals must have a limiting effect on the amount of contact between them, even if only to a minimal degree. If two kinsmen are separated by the distance between London and Edinburgh it is obvious that very frequent contact is ruled out merely for reasons of time and expense, if not any other. On the other hand, if they live in next-door houses, contact must be frequent at least at the level of chance meetings in the street, except in extreme cases of positive avoidance behaviour. To this extent then we would expect to find an inverse relation between distance and frequency of contact, ignoring at this stage any discussion of the quality of the contact. Beyond this extreme limiting effect, however, there is no reason why distance should be a factor of any great importance in the maintenance or frequency of contact with kin, and may be of considerably less importance than other factors such as genealogical distance, personal selectivity, and so on.

In the course of the field work detailed information was collected on the frequency, quality and type of contact between the informants and their kin. Of necessity only occasionally was information gathered about contact between relatives of informants as opposed to contact with Ego. The main part of the material was of a qualitative nature, i.e. every recent form of contact was discussed with the informant with regard to every relative on the genealogy. The emphasis was on contemporary contact, this being interpreted as within the last five years or so, and quantifiable aspects such as frequency of contact were abstracted from the qualitative material. Every type of contact was discussed – face to face, correspondence, telephoning, meeting at ceremonial occasions, and so on. Similarly, all degrees of contact were distinguished, e.g. casual visits, weekend trips, holidays together, incidental contact (e.g. at the house of another relative, or occupationally). Also important to us were reasons for contact or non-contact – the extent to which visits are made for pleasure, for duty, or for "economic" reasons or a combination of some or all of these. Contact patterns were also related to attitudes towards kin and the affective aspect of the relationships.

From the information collected about exchange of visits, a frequency of contact for each informant with every one of his or her relatives was extracted for purposes of tabulation. These were daily, weekly, monthly, quarterly, yearly or less than yearly but within the last five years. Obviously these are very crude measures of contact and can only be used in conjunction with the qualitative material. For example, a relative who comes to stay for two weeks once a year has the same "frequency" as another who is seen at someone else's house once a year. However, as a crude measure this scale serves a purpose, and in fact the information yielded by this method, dealing only with frequency, is supported by the rest of the qualitative data from which it is drawn. All the hypotheses arising from examination of this tabular material were considered in the context of the material.

Similarly a scale of distances from the sample areas was devised. Again this was a crude measure, since it does not take location into account, referring only to actual miles from Highgate; it also does not indicate whether kin at a given distance are concentrated in one place or are scattered at different points. The scale distinguishes an area within three miles of Highgate (or Greenbanks respectively), within Greater London, within 70 miles (which corresponds roughly to the Home Counties), within 200 miles, more than 200 miles but within the British Isles, and abroad. For certain purposes the overseas category was divided into the Commonwealth and the rest of the world.

Tables were drawn up on the basis of these scales to see the relation between distance and frequency of contact. In order to see what differences there were between different genealogical categories of kin with regard to contact frequency and distance, separate tables were drawn for maternal and paternal kin and within these for first, second and third cousins, aunts and uncles, great-aunts and uncles, and various "removes" of cousins. Other tables were drawn up for parents and siblings. The only significant differences were found between members of the family of origin (and their spouses and descendants) on the one hand, and the rest of the kin on the other. Within the wider kin group, i.e. outside the family of origin, no significant differences could be found in the general configuration of the distance/contact tables. For further analysis, therefore, two main Tables were used: *Table I*, which includes all kin of the family of origin, i.e. parents and siblings (including step- and half-siblings and step-parents) and spouses of siblings and descendants of them all. *Table II* includes all other living kin and their spouses. The tables are summary tables of the kin universes of all 60 individuals, and for this reason as well as others cannot be considered in isolation in any final analysis, but can be used to answer a few questions about the gross relation between distance and contact frequency.

Two main questions present themselves. Firstly, how far, if at all, does distance affect or determine the *maintenance* of kin contact? That is, does distance to any degree bring about the dropping of kin ties altogether, or proximity lead to activation of them? Secondly, how far – if at all – does distance affect the *frequency* and *type* of contact? In fact, however, this second question usually makes certain assumptions about the nature of contact in an "ideal" situation;

it implies that if kin were always immediately available then contact would be always maintained at an intense level, i.e. that people will desire to have maximum contact with their kin. This assumption is not justifiable in the case of our informants – a middle-class, professional, independent-minded set of people.

Even if we were to find an inverse relationship between distance and frequency of contact, this would not mean that distance is necessarily the cause of infrequent contact. It is usually assumed that there is a causal relationship between the two, but this aspect may be of less importance than it would at first appear. As discussed earlier, very large distances will obviously mechanically affect the number of times some people see each other in cases where, in other circumstances, they might see each other more often. Apart from this, what emerges from all the qualitative material on contact, and the nature of relationships between kin, is that these people do not expect to have, or want to have, relationships with most of their kin which demand close or frequent contact with them.

Tables showing Residence, (in Terms of Distance from Highgate) and Frequency of Contact with Kin. (Highgate Sample – 60 individuals).

Table I

Parents, Siblings and their spouses and descendants

Distance from Highgate → *Frequency of contact ↓*	*Up to 3 miles*	*Within greater London*	*Up to 70 miles*	70-200 *Miles*	*Over 200 Miles but in U.K.*	*Abroad*	*Location not known*	*Total*
Weekly	19	20	3					42
Monthly	10	45	34	5				94
Quarterly	2	24	49	26	4			105
Yearly	1	10	46	61	33	11	1	163
Less than Yearly		21	33	24	34	26		138
Contact by Letter *only*		2	7	10	1	17		37
Total in Contact	32	122	172	126	72	54	1	579
No. not in Contact		16	10	12	13	52	29	132
Total	32	138	182	138	85	106	30	711

Table II

All kin (& their spouses) except parents and siblings (& their spouses & descendants)

Distance from Highgate → *Frequency of contact ↓*	*Up to 3 Miles*	*Within greater London*	*Up to 70 Miles*	*70–200 Miles*	*Over 200 Miles but in U.K.*	*Abroad*	*Location not known*	*Total*
Weekly	1	2						3
Monthly	2	11	11					24
Quarterly	6	40	19	5	1	1	1	73
Yearly	11	59	87	32	30	5		224
Less than Yearly	1	151	116	99	53	77	4	501
Contact by Letter *only*	3	24	18	20	11	40	3	119
Total in Contact	24	287	251	156	95	123	8	944
No. not in Contact	3	293	240	338	135	373	664	2046
Total	27	580	491	494	230	496	672	2990

The degree of intimacy either preferred or obtained with kin varies mainly according to whether these kin are part of the family of origin, or are more distant kin, and in addition to this, on a variety of "historical" and personal factors. Geographical distance is seldom the sole cause of infrequent contact, though it may be a contributing factor, and is sometimes the reason given for it.

The fact that we have found families scattered all over the country, and around the world, is part of the existing kin situation – an intrinsic part of the general looseness of many kin ties, and is not the "cause" of this looseness. People live apart for a variety of different reasons – professional, financial, idiosyncratic – but also they are *enabled* to do so because the nature of their relationships with kin is not of a kind that demands close proximity or intense contact with them. Some of the probable reasons for this have already been discussed.

From the Tables it can be seen that with regard to maintenance of any kind of contact at all there is an obvious difference between the two sorts of kin – the family of origin (which can be taken here to include their spouses and descendants), and the rest of the kin universe (i.e. all other kin recorded on the genealogy, plus spouses). Of all the kin in the family of origin, some sort of contact is maintained with 81% of them, compared with only 32% of all other kin. Thus it would seem that in the family of origin contact is maintained regardless of where they live. (If one looks at actual full parents and full siblings, ignoring their spouses and descendants, the percentage in contact is much higher still – over 90%). In the general category, which includes the families of the kin in the family of origin, the only kin who seem to be dropped to any significant degree are those living overseas. The fact that a smaller porportion of kin who live abroad are in contact may not be a simple function of distance. Kin who move abroad may do so partly to break away from kin, or if not quite as positively as that must at least be emancipated enough from their kin to be able to leave the country. Many of those now out of contact are families who have emigrated to places like Australia, thus they are people who have chosen to live a "new" life. Apart from this, of course, there is obviously very little chance of contact of a face-to-face kind with someone in the Antipodes. Of actual full siblings and parents, only one of each are out of touch altogether, even those very far away; it is generally the descendants of siblings who have lost contact, thus where the relationship is genealogically close it is only very rarely that geographical distance, however great, will affect the maintenance or non-maintenance of contact.

Outside the family of origin a far higher proportion of kin are not in contact, and to some extent this does vary with distance. Within London and the Home Counties about 50% of kin are in some sort of contact, in the rest of the British Isles about 35%; of kin living overseas only a quarter are in contact, but this is not unexpected. If contact with a cousin in England tends to be of the order of an occasional visit once every year or so, it is not surprising that often there will be no contact at all with others who live abroad.

This is, of course, only a majority pattern. Nearly all our informants have contact with some kinsmen who live far away. What the data does show is the *selective* quality of contact between kin. For example, half the kin (excluding kin of the family of origin), who live in London and the Home Counties are in contact with our informants, the other half are not; genealogical distance at this point does not determine whether contact is maintained, thus other factors must account for the fact that some are seen and others are not. To a great extent who is kept in touch is a matter of personal preferences, with certain elements of duty in the case of older relatives, but even here a certain amount of selection goes on with regard to who is felt responsible for and who is not.

This element of selection of kin with whom a person will keep up contact is very important, and is one of the most significant aspects of the material gathered from this middle-class sample of families. The first stage in selection is of course made by the informants' parents, and the kin about whom the informants have some knowledge, and thus appear on their genealogies, comprise not only their parents' effective kin group, but also other kin of wider range. The majority of relatives an individual has contact with are those whom they have been brought up to know, or have met through their parents; from this group he then selects out the kin that will make up his own effective kin set. This selection at each generation is highly significant for the apparently idiosyncratic nature of an individual's effective kin at any given point.

Thus the kin with whom an individual has no contact are basically of two kinds – those whom he has not met, or at least do not or did not form part of the effective kin set of his parents, and those whom he knows but has dropped either deliberately or merely through lack of interest. The factor of geographical distance is important mainly with regard to the latter category of kin.

All the kin with whom an individual has some sort of contact constitute what we have called his "effective" kin set. So far I have been considering how far geographical distance affects, or is related in any way to, the inclusion or exclusion of kin in this effective set. With regard to parents and siblings and all their descendants there is little difference whether they live in London or 200 miles away; in both cases 85% or more are in contact, and it is only with those living overseas that one finds a "sloughing off" of about half of them, i.e. no contact of any kind at all, even by letter – mainly the descendants of brothers and sisters. Outside this close range of kin there is more dropping of kin the further away they live, and this is probably partly an accumulative effect of geographical separation over the generations.

Frequency of Contact

The relation between distance and *frequency* of contact is of a rather different order. Again it varies in the two major segments of extra-familial kin. As would have been expected, parents and siblings are seen much more often, and contact is of a more "intense" nature, than with other kin, wherever they live. Disregarding for the moment the type of contact, the largest proportion of kin outside the family of origin, in any single distance category, are seen less than once a year. That is, wherever they live the majority are seen very infrequently, whereas parents and siblings and their descendants are seen on the whole far more often than this. Thus, although distance may be a contributing factor, and in extreme cases a limiting factor, genealogically more distant kin are not in frequent contact, whatever the relative distance at which they may live, and living far away does not necessarily mean that any less contact is had with them. With parents and siblings, however, the influence of distance as a limiting factor is in one way more marked. This may at first appear to be contradictory, since it is also clear that wherever they live they are seen more often than other kin, but in one sense the relation between geographical distance and frequency of contact is quite marked. From the table it can be seen that the largest proportion of kin in any one cell varies on the frequency line according to distance. That is, the largest proportion in any one cell of those living in Highgate are seen weekly; those in London – monthly; in the Home Counties – quarterly or yearly; between 70 and 200 miles away – yearly; further away – yearly or less than yearly. This suggests that contact with parents and siblings is generally kept at some sort of maximum, i.e. that these relatives are seen not necessarily as often as possible, but as often as practicable and desirable, in view of the distance between them.

Although some correlation is found between distance and frequency of contact, one thing is also clear – that geographical proximity in itself does not imply, or socially necessitate, *intense* contact between kin. This is particularly true in London, and probably for any large town. Only 8 out of the 60 individuals in Highgate have no kin at all known to live in London, but out of the total of over 770 only 60% are in contact. Excluding parents and siblings and their descendants, only about half are in contact, and only about 1% of these are seen even as often as once a month. As suggested earlier, our informants are selective in their choice of friends from among their kin, wherever they may live. They do not feel that living in the same city means that contact has to be maintained, or if it is that it has to be very often. It is, of course, partly that London is a very big place – travel from one side to the other is as difficult, often more so, than a journey across country; also some areas of London are as unrelated as two separate towns. But apart from this size and heterogeneity of London, there is seldom the attitude that living within the same city necessitates the instigation or maintenance of ties with kinsmen.

People come to London for a variety of reasons; few, as already seen, come primarily for reasons connected with their relationships with kin. This "accidental proximity" as it can be called, is very different from the sort of localisation of kin in e.g. a rural farming area where there will usually be a complex set of social (and often economic) ties, involving frequent interchange of contact and services.

The majority of adults in Highgate have come from areas other than London, and of those born in London most of them have at least one parent who was born somewhere else. Out of all these families there are a number who still have a locatable kin "home" from which they or one of their parents originally came. In these situations, unlike cases where individual kin have scattered to London, this kin situation existed prior to Ego. There is a pattern of kin residence and interrelationships into which Ego (or a parent) was born. By definition, the people we are concerned with are the ones who have migrated from these areas, but this type of place still has an important effect on the nature of kin relationships, not only between the people remaining there, but also between them and the ones who have left (v. also p. 65).

The material suggests that an individual is more likely to maintain contact with relatives who have remained in a place of origin of this kind than with those who have left it too, in spite of probably having more in common with other "migrants", and that the kin remaining in a group of this kind exert more influence on other members of the kin universe than kin elsewhere and that relationships are manifested in more frequent contact in families which do have a kin locus of this kind than in families where there is no identifiable "group".

This difference in contact patterns is obviously in part a difference in the ease with which these kin can be visited. If a number of families are located in the same area then visits made over a long distance to see one can be extended to other kin in the area without any great additional effort or time. When kin are scattered all over the country, particularly in different rural areas, visits to individuals or individual families involve a great deal of time which most people can ill-afford.

There is, however, more to it than just the relative ease with which a number of kin can be combined in one visit. People may talk of visits to these places as going "home", and it is considered to be natural to call on most of the family when visiting the district. Often these visits are expressed in terms of duty, but there is also, at least in some cases, a sense if not of belonging to a family then at least an acceptance of some sort of social relationship between the families or individuals concerned.

One example of this sort is a woman who has over 60 relatives living in one area of Scotland, and she has contact with 40 of them. Twice a year she goes to stay on her father's farm, and while she is there she goes around visiting her other relatives. Although she says, "It's rather a chore having to go round visiting everyone; sometimes I think it would be nice to go home and only see one's parents", she thinks of this *area*, not only her father's own farm, as "home", and apparently would not think of *not* visiting all these relatives in spite of having very little in common with many of them.

This type of family group may of course form in London, and there are one or two families where this has happened, but these are easily distinguishable from the families who, though living near to one another in London, have no sense of belonging to a family "group", nor any feeling that they ought to visit or make friends with each other just because they are kin and happen to live quite close.

From another point of view, however, living in London is significant in the maintenance of some kin ties. London is the capital city of the country and as such is visited by thousands of people every day for a variety of different reasons. Most visits are probably primarily "non-kin" visits, and often a relative is seen only when he comes to town on business. It is not always clear whether ties would be maintained with all these people if our informants did not live in a place frequently visited for so many reasons. We are unable to gauge, since our own samples are drawn only from London, but it would be interesting to know how many kin are in contact, and what proportion this is of the total kin known, in a *similar sample* drawn from *another town*. In a family that has spread all over the country is it the London "branch" that sees the largest number of kin? Do they become "pivotal" kin in any sense? From the material it would seem that contact is sometimes maintained with peripheral kin who, in other situations, would have been dropped. Beyond this, however, there is no evidence that the branch of the family in London, or any individual there, tends to become a pivotal point of the family, or that being in London leads to any function as family base, or gatherer of family information or any other central role.

Type of Contact

So far, discussion of contact has been almost solely in terms of bare frequencies. More important than the frequency is the *type* and *quality* of contact between individuals and their kin. This can obviously not be discussed here in any great detail. Briefly, the intensity of contact varies with different sorts of kin. Relationships with parents generally involve, if not frequent contact, then periods of intense contact at various stages of the year. Nearly all informants spend weekends or holidays with their parent or parents at regular intervals; contact with siblings tends to be slightly less intense, but staying in each others' houses often occurs. Outside this close range of kin, however, contact is usually of the order of day or part-day visits – there is very little sleeping overnight. A lot of contact is also in the nature of "ancillary visiting", i.e. kin are only seen because they live with, or near, some other relative who is visited, or because they happen to come to London for some other reason. Others are only seen at weddings and funerals or other family gatherings.

The ancillary kind of visiting is most evident in the case of kin living far from Highgate. A high proportion of kin live at some distance away. Nearly all the 30 families concerned have at least some kin who live over 70 miles away, with whom they maintain contact. This sort of distance is too great to cover and return from in one day except in unusual circumstances, or in the case of particularly dogged individuals. This means that contact with kin living 100 miles or so away must be of one of three major kinds, or some or all of these kinds. Firstly, they may be seen when they come to London for some reason; secondly, they may be visited for a night or longer; and thirdly, they may be visited while the informants are staying in the area with someone else, kin or non-kin. A certain proportion of kin are seen only in the first situation, i.e. when they come to London, but not very many are seen *only* in these circumstances.

The second alternative is the most common for members of the same family of origin; as discussed before, if parents and siblings live very far away then visits usually involve staying with each other; the third alternative is the most common for other kin. Where there are groupings of kin in any one place, at some distance from London, visits are usually made to stay with the informants' parents, and other kin are visited while they are in the area. It is not possible to assess whether these other kin would be seen, anyway as often, if there were not a close relative living there who forms a focal point for the visiting family. Ties with some members of the older generation may often only be maintained in order to please a parent, or at least in order not to let a parent down by neglecting to visit people who are important to them.

Considering the number of kin who live at a distance it is perhaps surprising that more contact is not maintained solely through correspondence. In fact, however, where contact is maintained, it is generally reinforced, at least sporadically, with some sort of face-to-face contact. Out of all the kin with whom informants have contact, only 10% are written to but never seen. Many of these are abroad, and here there is often the understanding that if the relative concerned returned to England, contact would be resumed; but even with kin living abroad a relatively small number are in correspondence who are not seen at least infrequently. In a few cases people also keep up a correspondence, unsupported by personal contact, with an elderly relative who is not mobile, and towards whom they feel a minimal degree of responsibility but not enough to warrant visits over any distance.

Most of the kin who are indicated in the Table as having only written contact are people with whom Christmas cards are exchanged or at least sent to. Sending a Christmas card is a way of continuing to recognise a kin tie, but it is, at its barest, a very minimal degree of contact. In general, if contact is maintained at all, there is some degree of actual face-to-face contact. Without this, ties with kin tend to atrophy. This may be partly due to the relative mobility of most people, anyway of those at this income level. Very nearly all of the 30 families have at least one car, and have enough money, with a few exceptions, to take advantage of all the modern means of transport available. In this situation, therefore, ties with kin that are maintained can be maintained on a face-to-face level. There is seldom necessity to keep in touch only by correspondence with kin who live in other parts of the country.

Contact then is generally of a face-to-face kind when it is maintained at all, but, as seen earlier, it is very infrequent except in the case of genealogically close kin and a few others chosen from the many possible kinsmen. In addition to this, partly because of geographical separation, and partly because of the level of sociability in these sort of families, very little contact is of an informal nature. There is little "dropping-in" to each other's houses, even in the case of people living within the same neighbourhood. Thus, however close kin live to one another, even if they are on visiting terms, the advantages (and perhaps the disadvantages) of living in proximity are not exploited. Not only is "accidental" proximity not sufficient reason for contact where there was none before, but if there *is* contact there is seldom the need or desire for incessant exchange of visits and services that such proximity makes theoretically possible.

Summary

The total picture given of these Highgate families is a complex one. The individuals come from diverse origins, in geographical, social and occupational terms. Not only have many of them moved to London from other areas, but also most of their siblings and other kin have been equally mobile. In very few cases have kinship ties or obligations entered into decisions to move, either in the case of the informants themselves or their siblings and parents. Mobility in all generations, undictated by kinship ties, has led to a wide scatter of families all over the country and overseas.

This mobility is largely a function of the sort of careers taken up by both the men and the women. Apart from this, however, it can be seen that it is also made easier by the relative independence of children from their parents at an early stage. There are explicit attitudes, held by both children and parents, that they should be independent of one another at least in the daily functioning of their lives. Children often go to boarding schools, later to colleges and universities, and are prepared, for the latter, to live at great distances from their families.

This does *not* mean that relationships are ineffective or necessarily distant between parents and children, or between other sorts of kin. The expected patterns of behaviour are based on strong affective ties which are not, however, expressed in frequent and intense interchange of contact and services or mutual dependence. Just because there is not frequent and intense contact does not mean that the affective tie does not exist. Nor that, in certain circumstances, kin are not called upon for assistance or advice. It is significant that certain services are given regardless of the geographical distance between kin. For example, one of the situations in which mothers are most frequently called in to help is at the birth of a baby. Nearly all the young wives had their mothers to stay in the house at least during one confinement, i.e. when she herself was in hospital. Many mothers travelled from great distances to do this, one or two even from abroad. Thus it can be seen that distance is no barrier to the sort of services these sort of people tend to need. Neither mothers nor daughters expect or want daily exchange of household services in normal circumstances, neither do they generally want constant contact with each other.

The type of relationship between parents and children obviously determines to a large extent the sort of relationships an individual will have with the rest of his or her kin. If a relationship with a parent is not manifested in constant interaction then two things result. Firstly, the ideology and attitudes with which a child is brought up will be of such a kind that he does not expect a close relationship with his extra-familial kin, and secondly, because of relatively infrequent contact with parents and siblings, genealogically more distant kin will enter into his life even less, and ties even with relatives who may be in constant contact with a parent may be dropped or maintained according to individual preferences. In this sense geographical distance may enable ties to be dropped without, generally, upsetting the relationships between other kin.

Considering a wide divergence of occupations and cultural interests and, in some cases, of class background, a great many ties are maintained with relatives. Generally, contact is not frequent, but this seems to bear little direct relation to geographical distance except insofar as the latter acts as an extreme limiting factor. Where people want to see their kin, wide distances are covered relatively often. Expectations of extra-familial kin behaviour do not usually demand frequent contact, even when proximity allows it. With closer kin, specifically parents and siblings, there is more evidence to support the hypothesis (often held for all kin) that as much interaction will take place as possible at all times. Even for parents and siblings this is not entirely so, but here behaviour approximates more to this hypothesis, and this is so in spite of the ideology of independence with which children grow up, and the complex set of circumstances arising out of a wide range of occupations and cultural interests.

Ties with kin outside the family of origin are maintained on a more selective basis, and they are often manifested only in contact of an intermittent nature. Partly this is because these ties are not often of a very strong kind – it is fair to say that to a great extent these people function independently of the majority of their kin. But it is also partly because more overt behaviour patterns of any more intense nature are not expected between members of these families.

Kinship and Distance in Rural India

K. ISHWARAN

York University, Toronto 12, Canada

SHIVAPUR village is a cluster of houses and huts grouped and arranged on lines of religion, caste, kinship and economic status. It is located south-east of Dharwar, Mysore state, India. Fields and orchards surrounding the village indicate the mixed economy of the community. Its population, 3,809 in number distributed among 631 households, occupies a limited space of 62.35 acres of land. They possess 562.25 acres of cultivable land and 1068 livestock. That means, an average villager owns 1½ acre of land and every third person owns just one head of livestock. The houses are built partly of stone and mud, or of mud only, and the huts are made of bamboo, millet stalk or dried grass. The stone houses are a symbol of prosperity and prestige, whereas mud houses generally represent the poor of the village. The low-caste Hindus and the untouchables living on the outskirts of the village invariably have huts.

The material culture of the villagers is simple. This is noticeable in the materials used for the construction of dwellings, in their traditional dress and ornaments and agricultural implements. The local carpenter, blacksmith, mason and potter supply the materials and services necessary for the construction of their houses. The weavers of the villager produce part of the blankets and carpets for their daily use, the artisans supply the indispensable tools and other equipment for agriculture, and the farmers grow the food required for the village. The wooden plough still dominates the agricultural scene, and has successfully rendered the only tractor, bought recently by the cooperative society No. 2, useless. It is now rusting idle and the farmers sarcastically remark that it cannot be sold even as scrap in the nearby market.

The settlement pattern, based on caste, sub-caste, occupation, patrilineage and religion, facilitates understanding of the functioning of kinship in this village. There are thirteen castes and forty sub-castes, each occupying a distinct locality and following a traditional calling. The sub-caste (upajāti) is a real unit which forms the basis of the village social structure. It preserves its identity and individuality by rigidly practising sub-caste endogamy. Each sub-caste believes in continuing with its traditional occupation, handed down from generation to generation, and regards the pursuit of the traditional occupation as a duty enjoined by religion. My informant Mānappa, who happens to be a teacher outside Shivapur, once told me with much emotion how bad he feels whenever he looks at the tools used by his father, who was a carpenter with great devotion to his hereditary occupation. On his father's death, my informant reported, he and his two younger brothers became separated. The property, the tools of his carpenter father and the farm families dependent on him were inherited by the three sons. The youngest brother continued to follow carpentry, while the second brother gave it up entirely in favour of a new job as a teacher. Mānappa, the eldest son, my informant, however, did not feel like giving up this job once and for all. He continues to associate with the traditional occupation and shares work with his youngest brother during summer vacation. This gives him the great satisfaction of being nearer to his deceased father, since he grew up watching his father at work. This bond with the traditional calling is a characteristic feature of the community wherein occupation and kinship are closely related.

The cohesion of caste and kinship is reflected in the layout and the naming of streets. The dwellings of high-caste Hindus and their temples are located in the heart of the village, whereas those of the low-caste Hindus are on its fringes. The untouchables reside farther away on the outskirts of the village. Out of eleven streets, eight are named after caste occupations.

A notable feature of the settlement pattern of the village is that some streets are also named after the patrilineages composed of several households. A street generally represents a localized lineage of minimal depth. Every sixth household in the village belongs to one or other of the twenty patrilineages in the village. A patrilineage usually is composed of a group of males and females tracing descent through the paternal line. A large lineage is normally broken into different smaller units, to grow bigger in size and to break up again. Though the several households of the same lineage live in separate dwellings in the same street, the members of a single lineage continue to cooperate in times of crisis, family rituals and ceremonies and in safeguarding common interests. A lineage may be faction-ridden within itself, but it forgets its differences and unites when there is a threat from outside the lineage. In this respect, physical proximity as manifested in the alignment of residential units of the members of the lineage has great influence in fostering inter-personal relationships amongst them. Their unity is often expressed in public on occasions like weddings, religious festivals and harvests. The two lineages in Shivapur, one, I, belonging to the Lingāyat caste group, the other, M, belonging to the Marāthā group, have been competing for prestige for a long time now. In the bullock race at the time of the Kārahunnive festival, both lineages make such a show of their cattle wealth that the whole atmosphere is charged with tension. Two years ago, the two lineages faced each other on the occasion of the election of the chairman of the statutory panchāyat (village council), each supporting the candidate of its own caste. The Marāthā lineage kidnapped a member of the Lingāyat lineage whose vote was a decisive one in the election. The matter took a serious turn and was about to result in violence. The possible crisis was averted by the timely intervention of the police, who took the leaders of the two lineages to their headquarters for further enquiry.

The kinship solidarity is reinforced by the presence of a large circle of kinsmen having mutual obligations within the village and also outside it. Usually, a person's effective links with relatives outside the village is reckoned in terms of geographical distance, consanguineous and affinal relationships, class differences and kin-mindedness. The physical proximity of kin is an influencing factor in bringing the relatives closer. The greater frequency of interaction amongst them owing to nearness manifests itself in a variety of activities. It is also quite likely that the nearness of kin may also result in tensions and conflicts. But when the distance among kin is relatively great as conceived by the people themselves, it need not necessarily lead to indifference amongst relatives. On the contrary, the relationships may be more obligatory than expected, this depending on the line of descent and the degree of kinship ties and feelings. In this highly kin-oriented, predominantly patrilateral society, the attitudes and obligations of the mother's brother, mother's sister, married sister and daughter and maternal grandparents towards Ego would in all probability outweigh the distance. In this context, the geographical distance is very much conditioned by cultural forces. For instance, the position of the mother's brother in this bilateral kinship system is next to the mother in importance, and he is looked upon as a guardian, a loving and affectionate person, by his sister's children. The values associated with his kinship status affect his contacts with his sister and her children irrespective of distance. Therefore, the assumption that geographical distance results in the weaking of kinship bonds and obligations need not necessarily hold true, as may be seen in the case of Indian villages like Shivapur. Further, it may be pointed out that what constitutes a particular distance to one may not constitute the same to others; these people measure distance not in terms of geography as such, but in terms of social and cultural factors peculiar to their way of life.

2

Kinship is an institution of great strength and vigour in Indian villages. It continues to fulfil various needs of individuals, which are being increasingly met by agencies outside the family and kin-group in industrial societies of the West. Of the several functions of kinship, sex gratification and socialization-economic, religious, protective and political-are the core functions, and there are practically no agencies outside the home to share these responsibilities. This being the situation in the countryside, these needs are served by the system of kinship.

Territorial contiguity is obviously manifested in the distribution of kin and their inter-personal relationships. Consanguineous and affinal relationships normally extend within a radius of twenty miles, as found in Shivapur. Their kinship horizon does not extend beyond this limit owing to the fact that their world-view is conditioned by physical, climatic, dietetic and other cultural factors. The villagers are reluctant to give their daughters in marriage to, and bring daughters-in-law from, hilly areas, and those surrounded by streams and rivers, with a heavier rainfall than Shivapur, and places where jawar, wheat and pulses are not grown, since these people are used to a diet made of such grains. It is customary that married daughters and sisters living outside the village should be personally invited and escorted on important festivals like "Nāga Panchami" (worship of Snakes), "Deepāvali" (the festival of lamps) and Gauri Hunnive (the festival of the Goddess Gouri), and also at family ceremonials like naming of the child, puberty rites, engagements and weddings, rites of pregnancy etc. Failure to honour such kinship expectations and obligations is bound to lower one's status in the eyes of relatives, near and distant, and the community. These festivals and family rituals serve as mechanisms to bring siblings and other relatives together and foster kinship cohesion. These occasions recall one's obligations to one's relatives and thereby induce one to behave in accordance with the norms of kinship. On Nāga Panchami day, which falls in August, brothers and sisters and their children are expected to meet and together pour milk on the Snake God, made of earth, stone or metal, uttering the names of all the members of the family. Presents are given by brothers to their married and unmarried sisters on this occasion. A brother fulfilling these obligations not only earns for himself a good name and honour (maryāde) but also enhances the status and prestige of his sister in her conjugal as well as natal home. Again, the Deepāvali festival, celebrated in October, is centred round brothers and sisters. On this festive day, the sister waves the lamp facing her brother, for which she receives in return a gift in cash and kind. A person avoiding such obligations looks small in the eyes of womenfolk and is sometimes nicknamed a "crow". There is one such crow in Shivapur as far as I know.

People like to avoid such censure at any cost and, on the contrary, would like to earn a good name. These kinship values prompt individuals to contract new alliances within a short distance, which can be covered on foot or in a bullock-cart in and out of the rainy season. The relative physical isolation of Indian villages is still felt during the rainy season owing to lack of all-weather motorable roads.

Shivapur receives an average rainfall of 800 mm. About fifteen miles west of Shivapur lies the forest zone (malenād), running parallel to the coast, which receives an average rainfall favourable to the cultivation of paddy only. Territory north-east and south of Shivapur, in contrast to the forest zone, forms part of the Deccan plateau, where the topography is more or less like that of Shivapur. In forest areas, living and working conditions are different from those in Shivapur, and people are not willing to establish marital relations with people living in the villages west of Shivapur. Once it so happened that during the marriage ceremony of a daughter given in marriage to a youth of the malenād region, the host experienced great difficulty in supplying an adequate amount of rice to the affinals, who were mainly rice-eaters. This incident became a source of misunderstanding between the two parties. The malenād guests commented that the people of the plains are not able to supply enough rice even at a wedding. In return, it was retorted by the local people that the bride would miss her jowar bread hereafter in her conjugal home. In their opinion, jawar is essential in the menu and one should not give one's daughter to a place where it is not available. Also, girls of the plains cannot bear the hardships of working in the fields in knee-deep water, like the belles of the malenād. Such differential environmental conditions restrict marital links with villages outside the plains. No wonder that Shivapur has not established marriage relations with the malenād villages, except the one already mentioned.

Sub-caste endogamy is a very potent force uniting members in different spheres of life. The economic, religious, political and social interests of a sub-caste group merge into one, resulting in kinship solidarity of its members. There are thirteen castes, divided into forty sub-castes, which strictly follow the rules of endogamy. Though the people of Shivapur talk liberally in terms of rapid social change brought about by the modern forces of education, transport, communication, urbanisation etc., they are unable to cite instances of more than one inter-sub-caste marriage in the village, that of its only medical graduate's marriage which took place recently. This single instance of breach of sub-caste endogamy has become the object of criticism of the village folk.

The village school was established as early as 1864. The village is within easy reach of two cities located on either side. Buses and trains connect it with the outside world. The press, radio, movies and educational institutions exist very close to the villagers. Despite these forces, their conservatism and traditional outlook on sub-caste endogamy have remained so strong that they cannot imagine their children marrying outside their sub-caste. Their attitudes towards endogamous marriages are further strengthened by the occupation associated with the sub-caste.

The priest, farmers, weavers, carpenters, washermen, blacksmiths, brrbers etc. in this village have for generations contracted marriages withiu their own occupational groups, There is practically no occupational mobility amongst the people except in the case of a few individuals. The rigid occupational structure has resulted in the delimiting of the geographical boundaries within which marital relations take place. It is evident from the number of marriages that have occurred amongst the occupational sub-caste groups in Shivapur that village endogamy is common to the extent of 7% and about 70% of the marriages take place within the taluka, the next administrative unit, composed of 100 villages, and about 20% of the marriages within the district, with only 3% of the marriages beyond the district, the frontiers of which do not ordinarily extend beyond sixty miles.

Religious and class endogamy have added further strength in favour of kinship ties within a narrow area. The status of individuals in this community is primarily determined by the amount of land and cattle. The Lingāyats, who are in the majority, are also the land-owning group. Not one of these Lingāyats has given his daughters in marriage to those in the nearest cities. During the third year of my investigation in the village, a farmer once spoke to me in confidence about finding a partner for his marriageable daughter. I suggested a boy whom I knew working in the University office. The farmer immediately enquired how much land was owned by the boy's parents. To his disappointment, I said that the boy was a landless graduate. The immediate reaction of the farmer was that he would only give his daughter to anyone, literate or illiterate, possessing a minimum of twenty acres of land. In the same vein he made a query: "All is well while he is in the job. If he loses his job or dies, what about his wife and children?"

Marriage in this society, as illustrated above, is regarded not just as an affair between two individuals but an alliance between two families and kin groups, involving a series of material transactions and counter-transactions. It also results in the re-arrangement of social relationships within the family group. The marriage of a daughter severely affects the fixed pattern of relationships within the natal as well as the conjugal family, in the initial stage at least, especially when she is a stranger to her husband's family. The natal family experiences, in the new marital alliance, loss of a loved member, disturbance of family cohesion, fear and suspicion on account of the daughter's helpless position in the new environment, whereas in the conjugal family some of the members, like the mother-in-law, sisters-in-law, husband's brothers' wives, in fact all except her own husband, look upon her as an outsider and often treat her as an intruder. While I was collecting my field notes about the factors leading to the breaking-up of joint families, I was invariably told by my respondents that the arrival of the new wives was the main cause for it. In their opinion, new wives coming from unrelated families bring new values and new interests which cause tensions and conflicts, finally leading to the breaking of the solidarity of the extended family group. Shivapur villagers, therefore, are reluctant to establish new marital alliances which are beyond their local, regional and cultural horizon.

Such customs as cross-cousin marriages, uncle-niece marriages, exchange marriages and other types of preferential marriages within the kin group prevalent in this society help to explain the occurrence of a greater number of marriages within a limited geographical region wherein relatives are localised.

The kinship diagram (opposite) of a large extended family group of a well-to-do farmer, composed of 36 members, of whom 19 are males and 17 females, characterstically illustrates the bonds of marital relations among the intimate kin within a radius of ten miles, that too inter-linking.

In this family, even though Ego has been adopted by his father's father's brother, No. 3, he is the patriarch and sole trustee of the family property and interests. Ego himself married his father's sister's son's daughter from village M and his third daughter, No. 16, was also given to her father's sister's son, and his fourth daughter, No. 20, is married to her mother's brother's son, No. 20, in the same village. Ego's youngest brother, No. 11, married his father's sister's daughter, again from the same village. That means, within the life-time of Ego four marital ties were established with the same family in the same village. Further, Ego's mother came from village K and, in turn, Ego's sister, No. 9, was given in marriage to her mother's brother's son, his brother, No. 10, married his mother's brother's daughter, and Ego's brother's daughter, No. 23, is already "named" as a prospective bride of her mother's brother's son. Again, Ego's sons, No. 14 and No. 18, secured wives from village H, with which marital relations were already established by the marriage of Ego's father's sister.

From this kinship network we understand that Ego's family created its marital relations between kin, that is, cross-cousin and uncle-niece and other types of inter-kin marriages, all in three villages within a radium of ten miles. The practice of such relationships is very much appreciated in Shivapur, and the inhabitants take the earliest opportunity of contracting marriages of this kind.

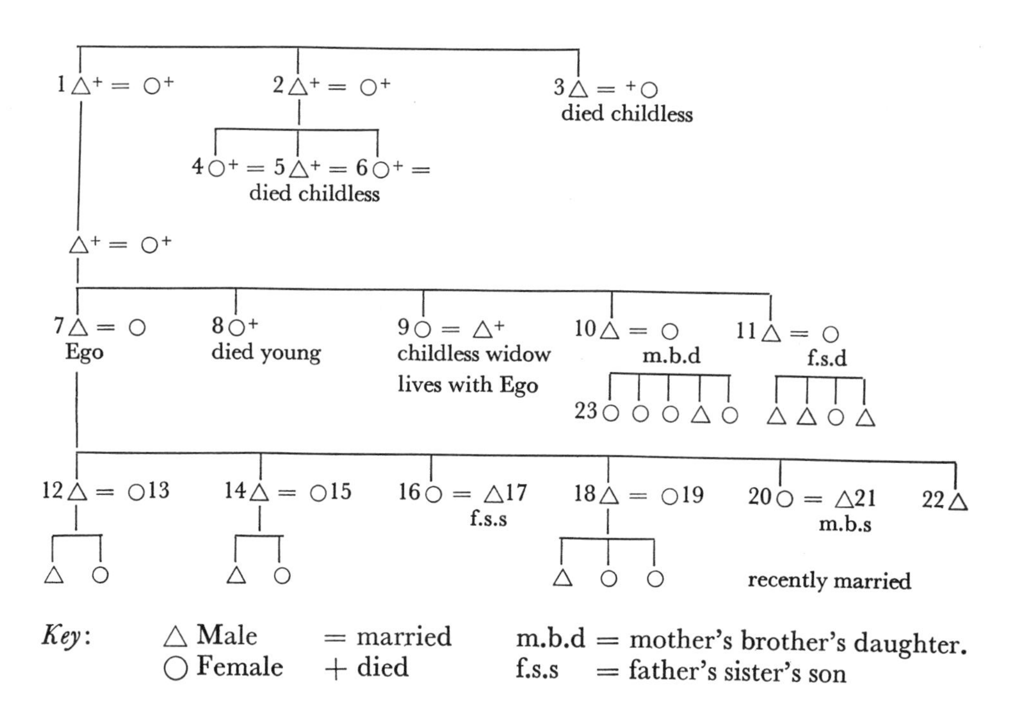

Uncle-niece marriage, exchange marriage and other types of preferential marriages within the kin group are traditionally approved since they renew and reinforce the already existing kinship relationships. Desertion, divorce, death and widowhood do not dislocate the familial relations. The deserted woman takes her children, especially if they are still young, to her natal home, which is ready to provide a place in times of crisis. A young widow generally does not continue to stay in her deceased husband's house and is drawn towards her parental home, unless the widow has grown-up children to look after her. The void created by the wife's death is filled by her younger sister, who occupies the place of mother to her deceased sister's children. When the circumstances do not permit such an arrangement, the young children are generally protected by their mother's brother or by their mother's parents. The functional significance of kinship is felt most during such critical events in life. In order to meet such events, this community has naturally narrowed down the physical boundaries of kinship ties.

3

The economic rights and obligations of kinship are usually performed by agencies outside the family in modern industrial society. Specialized agencies like orphanages, occupational institutes, social insurance corporations and public health organizations do not exist in Shivapur. In the absence of these agencies, kinship has assumed various responsibilities and continues to perform these tasks within its capacity.

The economic interdependence of farmers and their kinsmen can be marked in the dominance of joint families and the favourable attitudes of the people towards them. The Lingāyats and Marāthās are the only two land-owning groups with a large number of joint families. Besides, the artisans too have a greater number of extended families in proportion to their total population. A widowed daughter and her children, or a widowed or deserted sister and her dependents and other near relatives look to the parental family in times of crisis. Such dependents are not treated as an economic burden, and make themselves useful in the economic activities of the family. In the kinship diagram illustrated above, Ego's sister, No. 9, became a widow at 12 and returned to Shivapur to live with her parents. She is now about fifty years of age and an important member in the family. Ego told me that all his brothers jointly bought sixteen acres of land, which was given as a gift to the widow for her maintenance. Several instances could be added to the list showing the role of the joint family as an agency of social security for its members in times of need.

The goldsmith, the carpenter and the washerman, and also the barber families in the village invariably support one or other affected member of their intimate kin group. Four-fifths of the artisan families mentioned above have extended family types. Amongst the dependents in these families are father's mother, mother's mother, mother's brother's children, widowed daughter's children, and married daughter with her husband and children. My informant Somappa, the village barber, told me that, when his daughter's husband could not maintain himself in his village, he invited him to come and settle down in Shivapur. At first, Somappa gave his son-in-law part of his traditional work and later helped him to open a hair-cutting saloon. The three washermen, two goldsmiths, one Lingāyat priest, one carpenter and the owner of the Chandrashila tea-shop are migrants to this village through their wives. Such immigrants are looked upon by the village people as outsiders, though they are incorporated in the community life. It would normally take two generations or more for their assimilation.

There are about 30 households in this village which are named after the villages from which they came to Shivapur. People make a distinction between the local inhabitants and the migrants, between those who have migrated through fathers, and mothers and wives, the former being superior to the latter. For instance, the local goldsmith and leather-worker are considered superior to the migrant in their respective areas of work. This evaluation in terms of superiority and inferiority is not merely due to local patriotism but also, primarily, to the value system attached to patri-locality and the subordination of women to men. From the practical point of view, the outsider is viewed as one who has encroached upon the limited opportunities shared by the local inhabitants. It is also likely that the migrant may build up economic and political strength, which is not appreciated since it threatens their own power and prestige in the village.

The village political life is not so simple as it appears. As one begins to understand it intimately, one realises how intrigues and factions, rivalries and conflicts sometimes create tensions within this quiet-looking community. Troubles normally come to the fore during elections, religious ceremonies and festivals, litigation over land and the like.

The panchāyat elections since 1949 have been a major source of conflict and tension in the village. Elections are fought more on the basis of caste, kinship and locality than on any ideological basis. A study of election results reveals that the Lingāyats in a non-Lingayāt locality and the Marāthās in a non-Marāthā area were defeated, mainly on the basis of caste. The candidates contesting the election were mostly dependent on their kinsmen for their votes and also, through them, the votes of others.

A Muslim candidate took full advantage of his father's elder brother who lives in Dharwar and runs a big grocery shop. Many Muslims of the village and other low-caste people purchase grocery at his shop on a credit basis. Moreover, he wields influence as one of the leaders of the Muslim community of Dharwar and Shivapur. This person visited the village on the eve of the election and enlisted the support of his people against non-Muslims and was responsible for giving strength to Muslims to maintain the balance of power.

Another instance may be cited to illustrate the role of locality in village politics. A Marāthā contesting the chairmanship of the panchāyat needed the support of a woman belonging to the Lingāyat weaver caste, a nominee of the Government on the panchāyat committee. He managed to secure her vote in favour of his candidature though there was another contestant for the same position belonging to her own caste.

Territorial alignment of kin, as already explained, ensures massive support of the kinsmen during elections. Kinship solidarity asserts itself against others in the village during festivals and religious ceremonies, by display of pomp and largesse leading to rivalries and conflicts. Mention may be made here of the conflict during the recent "Holi"festival involving kinsmen and non-kinsmen, Lingāyats as against Marāthās, which took a violent turn, with injuries to some members of both parties. Political interests were the motivating forces, as I came to know later on, behind this criminal offence. Group conflicts in this village, it may be observed, generally centre around kinship and locality. The nearer the distance between kinsmen, the greater the cooperation in times of need.

A knowledge of the narrow geographical distribution of kin and their role helps one better to understand the political life of the village. In the traditional political structure of the village, the headmanship of the village was vested in a single Lingāyat family belonging to a large patrilineage called by the name of Pātil. The office of headman had been for generations within the same lineage, but on the basis of rotation from one family to the other. The headman, in the execution of the various functions of his office, had the support of his kinsmen, besides that of the officers of the state and the religious dignitaries of his caste. With the breaking-up of the patrilineage, jealousies and rivalries started amongst the several households of the lineage. This created a split in the kin group as well as in the group of the priests. The priest living close to the headman's household joined the party of one of the officiating headmen, while the other priest joined the rival group within the same patrilineage. The solidarity as well as the conflicts as found within the same patrilineage were maintained for a long time by the support of kinsmen.

The modern political system introduced by the statutory village panchāyat, to which members are elected by the adults of the village, has affected the position and authority of the traditional headman. This has also reduced to some extent the political status of kinsmen, who in the past used to exercise influence in the village life through the headman. The political office of headman is now no longer inherited, but is open to every individual in the community for contest. In addition to caste and kinship as determining factors in the election of members of the panchāyat, new factors such as education and political ideologies are influencing the political scene within the village. Any individual in the village can now contest not only the local election but also the taluka and district elections of the panchāyat machinery. This has made possible the functioning of kinship in a wider geographical area. The former president of the Shivapur panchāyat is now a member of the taluka Development Board, representing the members of the panchāyats of all villages in the taluka, and got support from the members of his own caste and kinship groups spread over the region. This obviously indicates that geographical mobility in the political structure is again regulated by the geographical distribution of one's relatives and castemen.

The continuity of the kinship system as revealed in the worship of ancestors (pitris), in the preservation of the family property and in the desire for the continuation of the family line through adoption in case of lack of a male child, institutionally prescribes in some way the range of kinship relationships and the geographical limits within which relations should occur. The various rules of marriage, like caste and occupational endogamy and intra-kin marriage, are rigidly followed, that too within a limited region, and have effectively circumscribed the range of kinship relations. The prevalence of joking and avoidance relationshipsi n the village speaks of the degree of closeness and integration of kinsmen, their rights and obligations to one another and their relative physical proximity.

In the past, the strength and stability of kinship were manifested by such joking and avoidance relationships amongst certain categories of kin. The joking relationship between mother's brother and sister's son and between maternal grandparents and grandchildren, and avoidance relationships between mother-in-law and son-in-law, for instance, which are common in Shivapur, indicate the intimate contact and cooperation of relatives, which is made possible by shorter distance. In a changing society, however, these relationships cannot remain unaffected. Some of the old men in the village told me that the former relations among grandparents and grandchildren, and the obligations between kinsmen, are weakening in the towns and cities and the wind of change is gradually blowing in their direction too.

4

The foregoing account of Shivapur can be fruitfully compared with the data on kinship collected in the city of Dharwar.[1] Two miles north-west of Shivapur is Dharwar, the administrative headquarters of the district, an educational centre and seat of a University. Its population of about eighty thousand is composed of the Hindu, Muslim and Christian religious groups. The Hindus, who form the majority, are divided into twenty castes, and each of these is again divided into sub-castes varying from ten to fifteen in number. Of the several castes, the Brāhman and Lingāyat castes are prominent in various spheres of life. The two suburbs, Kalyan and Gokul, so named for the sake of anonymity, represent the localisation of the Lingāyat and Brāhman castes respectively.

Since 1817, when the British conquered this part of India and made Dharwar their headquarters for the administration of the region, it has grown, slowly and steadily, from a small town of about eighteen thousand to one of eighty thousand. This non-industrial city has modern means of transport and communication, and modern urban values have been influencing the attitudes and behaviour patterns of its population.

The Lingāyats of Kalyan are mostly illiterate and dependent on agriculture. In terms of Redfield's concepts, Kalyan can mainly, if not wholly, be described as a "folk society", although some of them are educated and employed in the city. The people of Shivapur and Kalyan resemble each other to a greater extent in their caste and kinship values, beliefs and behaviour. The pattern of settlement is based on sub-caste and patrilineage. Kalyan is mainly a cluster of twelve large patrilineages, and several households of the same lineage usually form a neighbourhood, and some streets are named after the patrilineages. People are very conscious of their patrilineage and kin group. In this community, practically everybody is related to everybody else. There is not only sub-caste endogamy but there appears to be local endogamy as well. Kinship in this suburb is the basis of a territorial group. The close proximity of kin is conditioned by the alignment of residential units belonging to the same kin group. The presence of a large circle of kin in the suburb facilitates reinforcement of kinship solidarity.

---

1 The author is indebted to Mr. D. A. Chekki, Karnatak University, Dharwar, for the following data which he has collected for his doctoral thesis, under the author's supervision.

Filial piety and strong kinship loyalty are manifested in their ancestor-worship and high frequency of mutual visits, aid and cooperation, inter-kin marriage, naming habits, exchange of presents and the like. The spatial distribution of kin within limited geographical limits is an important factor in the cohesion of kinship.

A study of 303 marriages in Kalyan reveals a geographical distribution of marital ties in the same suburb to the extent of 39.61%, 16.72% in other suburbs of Dharwar city, 28.05% within the same taluk and district, and 15.84% in the neighbouring districts, all within a radius of 60 miles. There is a single instance of a marital link outside the state. Moreover, more than 30% of the marriages are amongst kin. All this demonstrates the fact that more than half of the relatives of Kalyan are either in the same suburb or in the same city and the majority of them are in any case within a radius of 15 miles.

Such a limited geographical horizon of kinship is due to sub-caste endogamy, physical proximity and knowledge of each other's family background, possibilities of increased personal visits and mutual help among kin, and preference for inter-kin marriages and suspicion and fear of conflicts in marital links with distant and unknown people with strange customs.

Apart from emigration and immigration of women on their marriage, eighty per cent of the men have been residing in the same suburb, 17% have migrated to or from the nearby villages, and only 2% have migrated to other places in the same or adjacent districts because of economic exigencies or demands of government service. Not even a dozen persons have migrated to another state in the country. This very limited geographical mobility, owing to the increased dependence on land, illiteracy and traditionalism, is kinship-oriented. Migrants maintain close contacts with their kin in their native place and are bound together by kinship and economic ties. Kinship values offset the spatial distance in the persistance of mutual rights and obligations of kinship.

The Brāhmans of Gokul, however, are educated, and urban occupations are the main source of their livelihood. In this suburb, both traditional and modern values pervade the atmosphere. Brāhman kinship values emphasize performance of "Shraddha" (propitiation of ancestors), filial piety and other kinship obligations. But in the last century or so, during the British rule and after Independence, the process of modernisation has been influencing the life of these people in more ways than one. Modern education, industrialisation, urbanization, modern means of transport and communication, modern economy and occupations, new values and new aspirations have accelerated the pace of modernisation and are bringing about modifications in attitudes and patterns of behaviour.

During the last few decades, the social and geographical mobility of Brāhmans has been on the increase. Unlike Lingāyats in Kalyan, kinship among the Brāhmans of Gokul is not territorial. There are hardly four patrilineages, each with a limited number of households, in the entire suburb, although they have a number of kin residing elsewhere in the city.

An analysis of 266 Brāhman marriages indicates a wider geographical distribution of marital relationships. In sharp contrast to the higher frequency of marriage alliances in Kalyan, hardly 3.88% of marital ties are found in Gokul itself, 31.95% in other parts of the city, 24.5% in the same taluk and district, 31.95% outside the district, and 8.27% outside the state but within the country. Matrimonial relationships stretch far and wide, relatively speaking, among Brahmans because of rigid adherence to Gotra exogamy, the difficulty of finding a suitable mate for the daughter in the vicinity, and less liking for marriage among preferential kin.

Educational achievements in specialised skills and occupational mobility between generations and within the same generation, so characteristic of the Brāhmans of Gokul, has been responsible for increased geographical mobility of relatives. Economic and kinship roles often coincide among the urban peasants of Kalyan, but economic and kinship activities outside the household differ in Gokul as the nature and place of work are different between father and sons and even amongst male siblings.

Fifty per cent of the people have migrated from and to Gokul within the same district, and thirty per cent of them have migrated to places outside the district but within the state, and nineteen per cent of the people have migrated to different cities and towns of India outside Mysore state, for education and employment in the case of males, and in the case of females on their marriage. Moreover, a little less than one per cent of the relatives have also migrated to some countries outside India. The unit of migration is an adult male or married couple with or without children.

Migration within the state shows kin-oriented tendencies. That is, people migrate to places where their relatives have already gone and settled. The newcomers to the towns and cities receive help in the initial stages for education and/or employment. The wider distribution of kin among Brāhmans and the relatively greater geographical distance have affected to a certain extent the frequency of mutual visits, help and cooperation. But despite social mobility and spatial distance, the migrants maintain contacts with their native kinsfolk by attending family rituals and ceremonies and rush to their place of origin in times of crisis and share the expenses too.

Geography, to however a limited degree, will have its influence on kinship. But the degree of kinship relationship, intimacies and other personal factors may overcome the geographical barriers. In case of the Brāhmans of Gokul, in spite of the wider geographical distribution of their kin, it is observed that they maintain contacts through visits, correspondence, mutual aid and exchange of presents. These communication channels unite relatives and make them conscious of kinship obligations and the importance of kinship solidarity. It appears that physical separation of kin among Brāhmans has not to any great extent led to the weakening of kinship sentiments or other adverse consequences.

The study of kinship among two caste groups in the two suburbs of Dharwar city suggests that the process of modernisation will have differential effects on the kinship system of different groups belonging to different castes, with different educational standards, occupations and degrees of assimilation of new values.

The above comparative review of kinship in rural and urban India suggests that, with urban influence on the peasants as in the case of Kalyan, one might expect the degree of change in the kinship system of villages like that of Shivapur to be similar to that of the people of Kalyan in Dharwar city. When the people of Shivapur and Kalyan receive increasing education and change their occupation from agricultural to urban and assimilate modern values more and more, one can reasonably expect an increase in the geographical mobility of the urbanised villagers, and its impact on kinship could be similar to that found in Gokul, the Brāhman suburb of Dharwar city. However, it is difficult to ignore caste and other factors which may set in motion varied changes in the kinship system of different caste groups of rural India.

Kinship, Succession, and the Migration of Young People in a Canadian Agricultural Community[1]

SEENA KOHL and JOHN W. BENNETT

Washington University, St. Louis, U.S.A.

1. Introduction

THIS paper presents our findings of a study of the influence ot kinship upon the migration[2] of the sons and daughters of ranchers in an agricultural region of the Canadian section of the North American Great Plains. Succession to the ownership of ranches, or marriage to local men, are the alternatives to emigration for the young men and women, respectively. However, we have found that kinship and family structure play quite different roles in emigration for men and women.

The genealogical patterns of kinship in this region, and its terminological features, do not differ significantly from those described by various writers for Anglo-American society in general (e.g., Parsons 1943; Firth 1956). Similarly, we find that the functions of kinship in this agricultural society have the flexibility and variability noted by observers. Since Anglo-American kinship is lacking in specific rules governing inheritance, association of kin, and the choice of occupations, considerable variability in the role of kinship in such processes is found from case to case. Moreover, we find that kinship can be "opted" according to the demands of particular situations. As Freeman (1961, p. 210) notes in his discussion of this optative aspect of kinship relations, the degree of recognition of such relationships varies

1 Data used in this paper were obtained in the second of three field seasons of work in southern portions of the Province of Saskatchewan. Since additional data will be collected during the season of 1964, our report is preliminary and incomplete. The research has been supported by the National Science Foundation of the U.S. Government, and administered by the Social Science Institute of Washington University at St. Louis. The paper has benefited from the criticism of Anthony Lauria, Jr.

2 Since we feature the out-migration of young people, we do not consider emigration of adults due, for example, to drought or economic failure. In any case, kinship has less influence upon emigration of this and other types. (For a brief study of the impact of climatic-economic hazard on migration in the Canadian Plains, see Alty 1939.)

"...from one society to another, and within a society, even from individual to individual. Thus in the observance of arbitrary demarcation it is merely the cessation of inter-communication,... that tends to terminate kindred relations and the moral obligations associated with them. It is, in other words, a *de facto* and not a *de jure* termination. Indeed-it is always possible where circumstances make it advantageous, for a dormant relationship to be revived if those concerned are ready to recognize it."

We find in the ranching community studied that kinship serves routinely as a means to enter the ranching occupation. The "developmental cycle" (Goody 1962) of the nuclear family and its associated ranching enterprise involves the takeover of a ranch by the son from his father, and the eventual retirement of the father and mother. The successor then prepares his own son for a similar succession. Entrance into the ranching occupation in this region is possible only through this cyclical transition[1] from family of orientation to family of procreation.[2] For the ranch son, the nuclear family and the kin ties in the region are means to an end which keep him within the region. Emigration out of the community is discouraged. The ranch daughter's situation is different: while her affective ties with the family of orientation are strong, entrance into adult status, *i.e.* marriage or an occupation, does not depend upon the aid given by her parents. Since women do not, except in rare cases, succeed to the enterprise, there is agreement on the part of both mother and father that she must find training and career elsewhere. Thus she is encouraged to emigrate.

Migration of young people from rural areas into urban centers is increasing throughout the Canadian Province in which the region lies, in keeping with a similar trend throughout North America and most of the world. However, the population of this ranching community has remained stable: its out-migration of young people has not been so great as to result in a reduction of numbers over the past generation. Emigration of ranch women is greater than for the men, and during the past 15 years, emigration by ranch sons has actually decreased, creating additional pressure on the land. (See Table 1). The reasons for relatively

Table 1

Permanent Emigration of Young Men and Women

Time Period	*Total No. Women, Age 18 and Older, Born on Ranches in Region*	*Total No. Women, Age 18 and Older, Who Leave Region*	*% Women Who Leave Region*	*Total No. Men, Age 18 and Older, Born on Ranches in Region*	*Total No. Men, Age 18 and Older, Who Leave Region*	*% Men Who Leave Region*
1900–1915	14	7	50%	18	6	33%
1916–1930	25	14	56%	21	9	43%
1931–1945	30	20	67%	28	13	46%
1946–1960	30	25	83%	25	4	16%

1 See J. C. Gilson 1958, for a conceptualization of the "family farm cycle" on Canadian family farms and ranches.

2 For a comparative case from Norway, see Park 1962.

low outmigration in this community are to be found in its current prosperity,[1] and in its devotion to a cultural tradition.

In studying intimate forms of social organization in modern rural communities, it is always necessary to remember that the people are members of the larger community of the nation, and even of the world. The ranchers speak the Midwestern variety of English; they possess the familiar traditions and myths of Anglo-American society; they look at the same television programs as city people, and have learned the value, or the lack of value, of the almighty dollar. At the same time, they possess a local social system of considerable solidarity, kinship connectedness, with its own folklore and historical mythology. In many North American rural communities, the external pull of the national cultures is extremely strong, stronger than local attractions.[2] However, the local social system in our ranching community has been strong enough to encourage ranch sons to view city life with considerable disdain; to resist the blandishments of the mass media, and to prefer to be a rancher with all its hard work, but also with its identity and solidarity.[3] Our task is to determine the role that kinship plays in maintaining this solidarity and ideology, while at the same time, affording possibilities for establishing ties with the outside world if they are so desired.

2. Setting

This research on the kinship system of the ranching community is one part of a larger regional study (Bennett 1962, 1963) devoted to the historical ecology of settlement and economic enterprise. The region is part of the semiarid northern Great Plains, subject to extremely variable climate and soil, the adaptation to which entailed great hardships and concomitant changes in technology and way of life on the part of the settlers who came from a humid environment. Within the region there is wide variation in habitat which has resulted in the juxtaposition of various forms of farming and livestock production. Some of these possess cultural styles of relative distinctiveness. This paper deals primarily with the ranching population although it will delineate points of contrast between ranchers and farmers.[4]

---

1 See: Royal Commission on Agriculture and Rural Life, Rep. No. 10, p. 81, where prosperity of the agricultural enterprise is seen to be closely related to family-enterprise continuity.

2 This "pull" is almost universally assumed by rural sociologists (*e.g.*, Royal Commission, Saskatchewan, Report No. 7, p. 123).

3 It is suggested that this may be one key to the curiosity and abiding interest shown in ranching culture by city people. Ranchers have, with urbanites, the majority values of the urban middle class, but at the same time they differ in their ability to obtain lasting satisfaction and identity in bucolic settings, surrounded by scenery and history. In the view of the many nostalgic urbanites, the rancher enjoys the best of all possible worlds.

4 Some observations on our methods of research: due to the distances involved in travel to the ranches, and as one result of the "Code of the West" (you always offer hospitality to the traveller), the interviewing pattern usually included dinner or supper. This gave the

Settlement

Since the settlement of this region began in the late 1870's, the historical period of the pioneer frontier is recent enough to afford ample documentation for the investigator as well as to provide an ideological focus for the regional resident. The sequence of historical changes from a relatively isolated[1] frontier to a rural society very much involved in the wider world, is telescoped within the lifetime of the aging first- and early second-generation residents of the region.

The modern settlement of the region began with the movement of sheep and cattle ranchers from Montana. Following these came single young men who drifted west with the frontier. Many arrived with the Royal Northwest Mounted Police and stayed to establish a cattle enterprise. The completion of the railroad in 1883 opened the area to migrants from eastern Canada and the U.S., and by 1900, the ranching community was well established. The community distinguishes carefully between those families who arrived before 1900 and those who arrived after 1900. The pre-1900 arrivals – mostly ranchers – are "old-timers," and this term denotes respect, admiration and nostalgia for the "real" pioneer.

Encouraged by the active settlement policy of the Canadian Pacific Railroad and the Canadian government, most farmers arrived between the years 1904

---

interviewers the opportunity to put notebook aside and "just visit" while washing dishes or peeling potatoes, or in the case of the men, just sitting and talking. Needless to say, these occasions afforded the greatest insight into the community and permitted observation of the entire family group in a relaxed situation. Fathers always came home for dinner (the noon meal), and where there were hired hands, they were present too. Often neighbors (male) would be present; either they were on their way to town and had stopped to visit – or were helping out. If they were present at the dinner hour, they were also fed. Often visiting continued past the dinner hour since the men had no time clock to punch, and enjoyed the opportunity to socialize with the investigators.

The history of each family was obtained by writing the family genealogy, beginning with the entrance of the first member into the region. We collected the history of the family's movements into and out of the community for two, and in some cases three, generations as well as information about the informant's attitudes toward and knowledge of his family members. This device served another purpose in that the interviewer was able to get information about the values the informants held towards occupational choices other than ranching, as well as informants' attitudes towards the outside community and towards other family members in the region.

The use of genealogies as a way of exploring the community's values and actions proved to be a fruitful means of collecting and organizing data. There is much local interest in the history of settlement which our anthropological interests were able to tap without being viewed as threatening. Since there are marriage connections among almost all the ranchers, the genealogies enabled us to map the whole ranching population in terms of its kinship connection and their social connections as well as its geographical distribution.

1 The frontier isolation of the region should not be overstressed. This part of Canada has been called the "last best West" (Sharp, 1948), which means it was settled a generation or more later than comparable portions of the U.S. northern plains. Its settlement, except for a brief period in the late 1870's, was created by the railroad, and rail contacts with Eastern Canada were available from the beginning. However, in comparison with the situation today, the early years were lived out in relative isolation and frontier individualism.

and 1916. The farming population designates as pioneers those farm families who came as part of the big tide of homesteaders.[1] However, the ranch population designates as pioneer farmers, those farmers who came prior to the 1910 homesteader group. Many of the pre-1910 farm settlers were as much rancher as farmer, and there was less distinction between the two occupational cultures than exists today.

With the arrival of increasing numbers of farmers as competitors for land and the closing of the open range, a sharper distinction arose between ranch and farm. After 1905, the influx of farmers and new legislation led to the establishment of fenced agricultural properties, and from this time on, differences in life style, traditions, and attitudes between ranchers and farmers become important. These differences have persisted, reinforced by the mass media and commercial exploitation. In some respects, the region sees itself as more "old Western" today than it actually was in its "Old Days," and this percept is related to the insistence on the ranching community as the original and authentic settlement of the region.

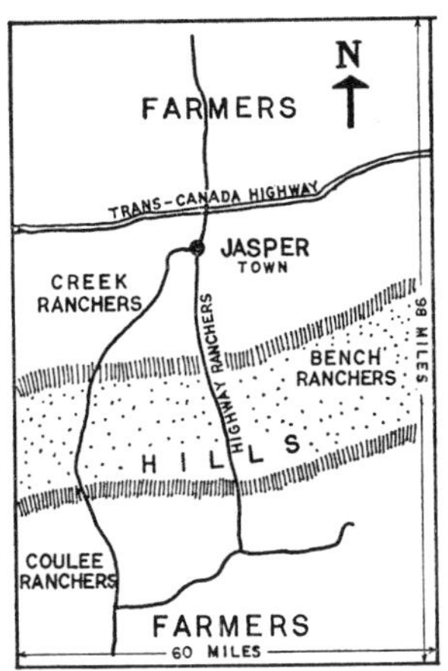

The Community

The region is sparsely populated (1.7 persons per square mile).[2] Often one must drive from one to seven miles in from the main road to get to the ranch house. The topography is varied, the vistas endless: rolling hills and plains, cut through by small creeks along which the ranchers settled. The farmers, who arrived later in time, homesteaded in the flat plains north and south of the range of forested hills which constitute the region's most prominent natural feature. The town of "Jasper," population 2,400, is a few miles off the major east-west Trans-Canada highway and is the chief trading center and railhead for the region, although not its geographical center.

Since 1952, school children have been bussed from the surrounding area (in some cases up to 30 miles) to the central schools in Jasper. There is one district, "Happydale," which still maintains two original one-room schools

1 See Morton, 1938; and Sharp, 1948.
2 The density for the ranching district is even less – about 1 person per sq. mile.

when it is able to get a teacher. However, most of the original school houses have been abandoned. In a few instances, the farmers and ranchers in the area have taken them over to use as a social hall, partly for nostalgic reasons, partly as a serious effort to revive community social life.

The accepted conveniences such as plumbing, electricity, phones and passable roads are still in the process of entering some districts, so that where they are available, the occupants make special note of them. Electricity was introduced in most districts in 1958, thus all ranch houses with one exception have electric power. With the introduction of electricity, freezers and other electric appliances appeared, which may be present even in the absence of running water. The style of living (house and interior furnishings) vary greatly from ranch to ranch, from the modern suburban picture-window style to the original log cabin.

The ranching community is divided into four distinct geographical districts. Most of the ranchers studied live between 2 and 28 miles from the town along a partially paved (for 20 miles) highway leading up to the Hills and a small Provincial park. These people are known in the region as the "Highway ranchers' or "the ranchers south of town" (as opposed to "the farmers north of town"). This road is kept open at all times and is, for the region, heavily traveled.[1] The second group, the "Creek ranchers," live within a 10 mile range along a gravel road extending west of the town. This road is often impassable by car in rain or snow. A third group, the "Bench ranchers," on or near the crest of the hills, are relatively isolated from other ranchers and from the town. They live on several sides of an Indian reservation, and for the most part are regarded as "rough" by the ranchers close to town. The fourth group, the "Coulee ranchers," live about 30 miles from the town, have their own school (to 8th grade) and are part of a tightly knit social community which includes the farmers who live on a nearby agricultural plain known as "Happydale."

3. Kinship and household

Kinship Connections

The great majority of ranch households are related by marriage. In the household survey, only 3 out of 42 households have no kin ties in the region. Often two groups of kin will have more than one affinal tie. There are cases of brothers marrying sisters; brothers marrying cousins; sisters marrying cousins and an uncle and nephew marrying a mother and daughter. Some of these marriages resulted from the family contacts and friendships created by dele

1 At most hours of the day there are usually at least two or three cars heading into or away from town. Ranchers or their wives who live along this road think nothing of driving the 10 or 15 miles two and three times a day. During haying, when machinery is constantly breaking down, a rancher or his wife can make as many as six trips into town. By heavily traveled we mean that there is a good deal of local traffic back and forth; however this cannot be compared to a busy urban street.

prior marriages. Often, too, a visit by a relative (usually female) from outside the region results in marriage to a neighbor, thus extending the ties.

The most numerous connections are between families who had been early settlers and who have been able to keep their sons in the region. This is a direct result of the fact that they are able to provide land for their sons which, in itself, is a result of early settlement. In the past, more marriages were a result of propinquity: we were able to map several local nuclei of intermarrying kin groups in the first generation of settlement. Today the brides come from a wider geographic area. In our sample, 24 of the wives of ranchers came from the region, half from farms, half from ranches; 14 came from outside the region; and the origins of 4 were unknown. Although one-third of the marriages in the sample were with farm girls in the region, the links to the farming population had not been extended outside of the girl's particular nuclear family. Thus, the kinship network "dead-ends." (Schneider n.d.) The ranch son-ranch daughter marriages act as interconnecting links which extend beyond the immediate nuclear families involved. In part this is due to the fact that there already existed more than the one marriage link between the ranching families. In part, it is due to similar occupational roles and sentiments of solidarity among ranchers.

There were two groups of ranchers who had intermarried extensively: the "Highway" group, near the town of Jasper, and the "Coulee" ranchers, isolated from town by relatively poor roads. In the former group, the ties are considered distant ones, *i.e.*, cousin-cousin connections, a product of marriages of the past generation. In the latter, the connections are between nuclear family members and thought of as "closer." The large number of marriage ties are regarded as one reason why the ranching community has maintained its social cohesion. The fact that "everyone out here is all mixed up" is regarded as "good."

Among the Highway and Creek ranchers, the family relationships that were acknowledged and/or emphasized are usually perceived by the informant as prestigious. Those that were not acknowledged or emphasized are usually perceived as destructive to one's status in the community. Thus, a marriage connection to one of the bigger ranchers in the region would be stressed, while a marriage connection to a marginal rancher was described by the term "shirt-tail relative," or not mentioned. Mention of extra-legal connections, *i.e.*, common-law marriages, were avoided where they were felt that such connections would downgrade the status of the informant, although they were common knowledge in the community. As a consequence, in the taking of genealogies, we found some relationships stressed and others passed over quickly depending upon the status attitudes of the person being interviewed.

Emphasis was placed upon the patrilineal line, unless the matrilineal relatives had also been ranchers and early settlers. This is understandable in view of the high prestige that ranchers as pioneers have in the region. The women from surrounding farms who had married ranchers (with 2 exceptions),[1] when

1 One woman was hostile to any questions which were asked about her or her husband's family. It was difficult to even get the names of her children. A possible reason is that she married her husband's nephew, after her husband's death, and did not want the interviewer

asked to tell about their own family's entrance into the region showed surprise that anyone could be interested since they were neither early pioneers nor ranchers.[1] The stress placed upon the family as ranchers, functions to perpetuate the ranching traditions and also to prevent alternative occupations from appearing acceptable to the ranch son. This is discussed further in a later section.

The Household

The nuclear family is definitive in teaching the ranching trade and in acquiring land, and it is these which are requisite for entrance into the occupation. As can be seen on Table 2, the household most commonly consists of the nuclear family, a man, his wife, and their unmarried children. However, most ranch enterprises have included at some point in the family cycle more than one nuclear family.

Table 2
*Household Composition of Ranch Enterprises**
(August 1963)

	Number
Married pairs, no children	7
Nuclear Families	18
Families with Added Kin	3
Nuclear Family Units in Separate Houses on the Same Ranch	12
With the husband's parents	12
With the wife's parents	0
Nuclear Family Units in the Same House	
With the husband's parents	0
With the wife's parents	1
Individual Occupants	
Male	4
Female	0
Total Number of Households Sampled	45
Nuclear Families, Now Living Alone, Who Lived With the Husband's Parents on the Same Ranch or in the Same House at a Prior Period	7
Nuclear Families, now Living Alone, who Lived With the Wife's Parents on the Same Ranch or in the Same House at a Prior Period	2

* A ho usehold is defined as a unit which has separate cooking facilities.

to possess this information. A second reason may have been that while her present husband was a respected rancher (due to the size of his herd, not to his personality), her family were poor itinerant farmers, and were supported by her husband. The second woman came from one of the more prosperous and well established farms in the area. Her family raised purebred cattle and were beginning to talk about the farm as a ranch. Her parents were highly regarded in the community. This woman felt it was "natural" and expected to be asked about her family.

1 The most common response is typified in the words of an informant: "You really want to talk to Joe about his family... my family aren't "Old Timers." They came late (about 1914). It's Joe's family who are the interesting ones."

The ideal is to have your "own place" but few newly married couples do, and here farm-ranch differences become important. It is possible for a young man who desires to farm to do so by renting or purchasing (with the help of his father) ½ or 1 section (1 section = 1 square mile). A ranch operation requires much more land and a larger capital outlay. The usual pattern for the farm son starting out is to rent an additional ½ or 1 section of land and work with his father, sharing equipment and labor. If he is married, he will build a house on his own land, creating a separate household. On the other hand, an accepted pattern for the ranch son and his wife is to live with the young man's family with the implicit or explicit aim of taking over the ranch when his parents retire. In some situations they move into the same house, in other cases a smaller house is made available for them, or the older couple retire to a smaller house on the place or in town.

The society is *de facto* patrilocal, since upon succession the young rancher brings his bride to the home place, where his parents may still live.[1] There were no instances of the *ranch* son moving to his wife's parent's place, be it ranch or farm. There were, however, two cases in which there was no ranch son to inherit, so the succession to the ranches went to son-in-laws raised on farms. In both of these cases, the son-in-law had his own farm, but assumed the purchase of his father-in-law's ranch so the latter could retire. The sons-in-law decided to take over the ranches because the arrangement was financially advantageous.

The Grandparents: Residence and Retirement

The patrilocal residence patterns, and the greater functional involvement of the paternal grandparents in the lives of their sons and spouses, help to maintain ranching cultural traditions[2] and the continuity of ties between the son and his family of orientation.

Slightly under one-third of the women married to ranchers came from outside the immediate region. In families where the wife was from the outside,

1 Flexible inheritance patterns, frequent disputes between parents and sons, and between sons, the vicissitudes of the economy, competition for land, and other factors influence succession so as to prevent strong tendencies toward primogeniture, or any other fixed form. Local people view the choice of son for succession as subject to idiosyncratic factors and "historical accidents," and regard it as not subject to any rule. What seems to be a major factor determining the successor is the degree of investment in the enterprise (in terms of time and labor), made by the son at the point that the father is aging and is considering retirement. In any case, the *de facto* patrilocality and its related "bound-dependency," afford a contrast to the strong normative emphasis on individualism, independence, and "going it alone." It is an instructive demonstration in not trusting statements of values as guides to social behavior. (By "bound-dependency" we mean the relationship of dependency of a young man on either his father or an established rancher for help in starting out, and the tendency for the dependent relationship to be prolonged indefinitely (Bennett and Kohl, 1964).

2 That is, the traditions are maintained in two ways: the role of the paternal grandparents is emphasized and potential dissidents leave.

her parents were much less involved in the life of her family of procreation than the parents of her husband who lived in the region. Children whose parents were from the immediate region generally had both sets of grandparents living in the area.

In these cases where both sets of grandparents were available, the intentions and desires for contact, and the affectual ties between them and the married couple appeared to be about equally divided between maternal and paternal sides. However, as noted previously, patrilocality is dominant, due to the functional necessity for the son to remain on the ranch after succession. As a consequence, the son's parents would see more of the new family than the wife's. The wife was simply accepted into an established household: a pattern structurally identical to patrilineal-patrilocal households in agricultural societies around the world.[1]

Aged ranchers typically prolong their control over their enterprise (and their succeeding sons) even when they are physically unable to perform many routine tasks. The father who refused to retire is a common figure in the region: almost a folk figure, judging by the many anecdotes told about such men. The maintenance of control (which is in contrast to the farmers, who are more inclined to retire into towns which are outside of the region, and rent or sell the place outright) is due not only to the father's desire to guard the establishment, but also to the fact that ranchers dislike town life. As one retired rancher said, "it's (living in town) like being caged." There is a genuine attachment to the country and an abhorrence of crowds, cramped spaces, and close social interaction.

One ranch which had been taken over by a son-in-law was still referred to locally by the name of the father-in-law, and the leased grazing land also remained in his name. Another rancher whose father had retired into Jasper owned 49% of the cattle, deeded property and "improvements"; his father retained control with 51%. The son stated that he was unable to make the innovations in management he desired until he could obtain majority ownership after his father's death. He indicated considerable envy of three of his peers who had complete control of their ranches and opportunities to try new methods of pasture and livestock management. In these three cases, the fathers were deceased.

The reciprocal of this continuity of parental control was the aid given the new family of procreation. The most common form of succession is purchase of the ranch in installments by the son, and terms are usually arranged so as to make it relatively easy for him to do so. In light of the steadily increasing value of land, acquisition of a ranch is usually impossible or very difficult without this type of arrangement. The "bound-dependent" features associated with the

---

1 And one which, in the Japanese case, for example, has been accompanied by considerable difficulty for the young bride, who is at the mercy of her husband's relatives, especially the mother-in-law. Definite tendencies in this direction were noted in the Jasper ranching families, but were relatively weak as compared to Japan and varied greatly from family to family.

takeover, as described above, are viewed locally as the price one must pay in order to obtain a ranch, and the young couple are expected to cope with it and not complain too much. As one young wife put it, "Sure, I get mad at my father- and mother-in-law, but what can I do? ... After all, without their help we would never be where we are."

The favorable prices for beef cattle in the decade preceding our study have meant greater financial possibility of savings for retirement, and there seems to be a larger number of town retirements on the part of the rancher fathers than in the previous generation – although it is still less marked than in the case of the farmers. However, the retirement of the older couple to town does not break the ties with the younger family on the ranch, because the town house of the paternal grandparents provides opportunities for temporary residence of school-age children.

In past decades, when roads were even poorer and automobiles less available, schooling often was provided at the ranch in the form of a hired, live-in teacher (we have data on 6 cases – all in the families owning large ranches). In other cases the children would be boarded in town for the entire winter, or even for the entire school year. The country district schools served many, but even down into the 1950's several of the ranching districts lacked such schools, or the schools would be in locations so difficult of access for certain families that town would be the easier alternative. The consolidation of regional schools in the larger towns in the past decade has meant a more standardized educational curriculum than that given in the district schools and tutorial arrangements.

However, since roads are still relatively poor, and winters severe, the town grandparent[1] emerges as a key figure for the school age child. The grandparental home offers the child a place to stay in town overnight. During severe winters, it is common for the grandchildren to spend the school week at the grandparent's town home and come home to the ranch on weekends. The opportunity for the child to remain in town means that he can participate in the local activities, and experience a world quite different from that on the ranch. Where grandparents or other relatives are not available in town, the child has to leave school early to catch the bus home. His dependence upon the bus means that he has little chance to visit his peers in the locality, and is completely dependent upon his parents and the family car or truck if he wishes to leave the ranch. The parents' willingness to transport children the considerable distances depends on their sanction of his activities. Such approval is dependent, in part, upon the parents' orientation to the town and its affairs. A child who has grandparents living in town has an advantage over one who does not and greater opportunity for independence from his parents. Hence the degree to which a child begins to achieve an orientation to the town and social independence are not only a function of parental attitudes, but are also related to the availability of town residence.

We have noted that retirement patterns differ between ranchers and farmers:

---

1 In 8 cases out of a total of 14, the retired people were parents of the ranch husband.

that the elderly ranchers are more inclined to stay on the ranch or at least in the ocality. We found that while farmers outnumber ranchers in the region by about 4 to 1, there were about 10 times as many ranchers in proportion to their total number who had retired locally, than farmers. We have noted that the reasons for these differences lie in the tradition-boundedness of the rancher, and his dislike of urban environments. Of equal importance is the fact that livestock demand year-round attention, and the ability of the grain farmers to take long winter vacations is not found among ranchers, or among the emerging diversified-farmer class;[1] thus the rancher has few opportunities to visit other areas which could prove attractive to him at retirement.

4. Succession and emigration

In the introduction we noted that in contrast with many rural regions of North America, out-migration of young men from the Jasper ranching community was reduced to a minimum; that the great majority of ranches remained in the hands of their founding families; and that the ranch sons preferred to remain in the region to succeed or to start a ranch of their own if possible. The basic reasons for this relative stability of population can be found in the profitable status of livestock production in recent decades, and in the existence of a ranching cultural tradition of considerable depth. We may begin our analysis of emigration and succession with a brief account of this culture and its effect on the ranch sons.

Ranching Traditions

The ranching occupation[2] carries within it distinctive myths and traditions which effectively serve to root its practitioners to the land, insulate them against the pressures of the wider world, and function to maintain solidarity within the occupation and the social group associated with it. There is persistence of a "frontier" or "Western" ideology which valued self-reliance and initiative, both of which are defined as the traits of a "man." The rancher ideal of a "man" includes strength, independence, self-reliance and similar values. Sonnichsen writing about the U.S. West says: "the rancher's code involved courage, cheerfulness, and a willingness to settle problems through one's own powers

1 These farmers incidentally tend to develop rancher attitudes as their herds increase in number. We are obligated to our colleague, Charles Thomas, for this observation. He is studying a district in the region which is undergoing a shift from grain to cattle.

2 As in most parts of the North American West, the term "ranching" has a dual meaning: economic and cultural. In the former sense, it refers to the raising of commercial beef cattle on extensive tracts of grazing land. All or nearly all of the income of a particular enterprise is obtained from the sale of cattle. In the second, or cultural sense, "ranching" is a particular style of life, involving a certain type of clothing, attitudes, and hobbies. In the community studied here, all of the families were "ranchers" in the cultural sense, and nearly all of them were likewise in the economic sense. A very few derived more than 15% of their income from the sale of crops and forage.

and without undue recourse to others."[1] Perhaps of even greater importance was the emphasis placed upon practicality and "getting the job done." A good rancher "knows cow," and the only way you learn is by doing. This ideology has adaptive as well as symbolic significance. In this specialized habitat, the ideology of "knowing cow" is not only myth, but can mean the difference between "making it" and not; between a good operator and a poor one.

However, a consequence of this pragmatic philosophy is a basic ambivalence on the part of the rancher towards the value of formal education for himself and for his sons. There is a deep-seated disdain for the educated man (who for the most part is also city-bred, or at least city-oriented). Most ranchers will say that education is important, and they agree with their better-educated wives that children should finish school, but at the same time, they "know damn well" that education doesn't make a good rancher or a good "man."

In addition to the rancher's ambivalence towards education, there is the social fact that the education the male child gets has little to do with his role expectations. For the most part, the boy has been trained from early childhood to ranch; formal education plays no part in this training or the ambition. Where the son has the opportunity to enter the occupation, *i.e.*, has hopes of buying or inheriting his father's place, this process of apprenticeship and the accompanying ambivalence toward education is not altogether maladaptive. However it does not favor innovation in ranching techniques, and may, as technology changes, prove self-defeating. For the sons who do not succeed to a ranch enterprise, the lack of formal education *is* maladaptive, particularly when they migrate to urban centers, and discover their schooling equips them for menial jobs only.

Farmer fathers are not so insistent that agriculture is the only possible career for their sons, and they are more willing to help the son explore alternatives. They are almost universally favorable toward higher education, and will encourage their sons and daughters to go to college even if it means permanent loss of contact with agriculture and the community. Farming is not bound up with the special traditions of the "man" and the frontier, and is not a profession with automatic connotations of prestige. It is simply one way of earning a living – "a good honest way, mind you," but not the only way. On the Regional Schedule,[2] very few farmers stated that they would never consider any other occupation. Almost all ranchers, or at least all men representing the second or third ranching generation, did say so.

Ranching remains the preferred occupation goal of the sons of ranchers.[3] It is considered a prestigious occupation (as well as romantic) and as such is supported by the community as well as family traditions. The majority of

---

1 Sonnichsen 1950, quoted in Atherton 1961, p. 11.

2 This is a lengthy questionnaire containing items on all aspects of the research, administered to a sample of farmers and ranchers of the region.

3 Ranching often appeals as well to the farm son, creating conflicts between him and his father, who likely as not dislikes ranching and ranchers. The local rodeo entrants number among them farm sons whose main aim is to ranch, who left their father's farm and are working for neighboring ranches to the dismay of their father.

ranches in our region are succeeded to by sons or by close relatives in cases where there are no sons; a minority are sold to non-relatives. When an old ranching family sells the place to an outsider, or to a local farmer bent upon expansion, the ranching community regards it as a "shame"; that is, the separation of the enterprise from the family name is considered a break with tradition.

Succession

Apprenticeship is the preferred means of introducing the neophyte to the occupation of rancher. It starts early in childhood when the child, at the age of 2½ to 3 years, rides in the truck with his father to put out salt for the cattle, or to town for the mail or to get machinery fixed. The child will also sit quietly at the table, eyes wide, while the father and the ranch hands discuss the work for the day: that fascinating work out in the open, with animals and big spaces and lots of movement. Apprenticeship is vital for basic ecological reasons: successful management and development of a particular ranch property requires the most intimate possible knowledge of the terrain and its resources, and this knowledge can be acquired only by lengthy experience. There is a genuine question as to whether agricultural college really is of any great value in training a future rancher, although business school might well benefit him. In any case, the need and the fact of apprenticeship, plus the factor of attachment to the locality and the "place," and, of course, the high cost of "starting out," all combine to keep the ranch son, or at least one, at home. This paves the way for an inevitable succession.

The ideal for the young men is to "start out with your own place"; that is, to buy a ranch on his own and begin management without interference. The strong individualistic values or norms of the culture are manifest here. However, the opportunities for doing this are extremely few, as already noted, due to the high cost of ranching properties. Where family help is non-existent, and the young man is determined to ranch, or has no alternative due to limited education, it may take as long as 15 years to "work off" an ownership in a ranch by becoming a hired man to a rancher without heirs, who is willing to permit such an arrangement. Thus family help, however it may be given, is quietly accepted as the only reasonable way to acquire a ranch. "Starting out" usually involves working for the father in the position of hired hand,[1] then gradually investing the wages in cattle, working toward joint leaseholding, and so on – in other words, gradually accumulating equity. By the time of the father's death, the ranch would be in the hands of the son or other relative, or the final properties could be transferred by inheritance. In some cases, especially where troubles between the father and sons, and between the sons, make succession ambiguous,

1 As a matter of fact, it is very difficult for the observer to tell the difference between the son and the hired man. They are treated in the same way by the father, dress the same, and usually "pal around" together. Often it is the young hired man who introduces the ranch son to social opportunites, *i.e.*, drinking, dancing and women. The mothers worry about such relationships, while the fathers laugh at her worries. (Bennett and Kohl 1964, p. 13),

the property is left to the widow, who then gets one of the sons to operate it until her death. In such cases the operator might be well into his 30's before he was sole manager and proprietor. In other cases, the father would demand continual and repeated proofs of the son's capability before turning over the ranch and going into definite retirement. Such delay could go on for years, as can the financial indebtedness incurred in taking over the place from the father or his estate.

Our current data on succession are given in the following table:

Table 3

Succession Pattern of Contemporary Generation in Control, (August 1963)*
(Total Sample 45 households)

Original Settlers	Father-son agreement Father alive		Father-Son succession Father dead	Succession via marriage	New Purchase	Operation of Enterprise on Shares No kin Connection
	Father lives on Place	Father lives in town				
4	7	2	17	4	11	1

* By "contemporary generation in control" we mean those men who were (August 1964) operating the enterprise. This category cuts across generations and dates of settlement. It does not include those men who were working for their father but who had no agreement with him as to succession. The count is by enterprise rather than individual, and where there were two or more brothers in partnership, they are counted as one.

If we examine the category of "New Purchase," we find that there are 4 cases which can be called "bootstrap," operations, in the sense that the operator bought his own place without the aid of family or others. 2 of these 4 are marginal operations. In 5 other instances of the "New Purchase" category, family help in the form of financial backing was important in obtaining the enterprise. 2 of these cases are really expansions of the existing enterprise, in that the father lent his son cash to buy a small, usually adjoining ranch property, which was then operated jointly with the original ranch. There are only 2 instances where we find assistance given the operator by non-kin. In one case the man had been assisted financially by a large rancher in the district; in the other, the man worked as a ranch hand for 15 years, and then bought his present enterprise with the help of a business man who remains as his partner.

The point is that in all cases of direct succession, and in several of the "new purchase" cases, the financial help of the family, or its indirect influence, was paramount in making it possible for the son or son-in-law to succeed. Thus the importance of the kinship tie of the nuclear family in keeping the son or son-in-law in the region is evident. At the same time, this nuclear family had, in many of these same cases, to choose between several sons, and make it possible for some of those who did not succeed to find work elsewhere. The kin outside the nuclear family had little to do with any of these matters; we did not find a single case of financial or other help extended to the young men from outside relatives, nor did we find cases where, other than the in-law type, a man inherited a ranch from a relative other than parents. However, the extended kin group does sometimes offer help *after* establishment, in the form of lending machinery, favored options for additional land purchase, and the like.

Let us consider the question of alternatives for sons who wished to stay in the region but where the ranch was large enough for only one to succeed. One possibility is for the father to attempt to build up the ranch by improving pasture and water resources, and hence enlarging the herd, to permit the support of more than one family. Another is to attempt to buy more land for the same purpose – a course of action which will involve him in competitive relationships over a scarce commodity with his neighbors, and in general, with other ranchers in the region.[1] These situations also have their ramifications in the land bureau of the Provincial Government, since joint operation of separate lease tracts, with father pasturing son's cattle or vice versa, or with special cultivation of lease land, are all hedged about with careful regulations. In our work on the sociology of lease land, we have found that the Provincial land bureau permits the nuclear family members – father and son – to pasture each other's cattle on respective leases, but it forbids other relatives (e.g., uncle and nephew) to do so. The bureau encourages what it calls "natural succession" (father-son) and the "primary family" (nuclear family). Thus the nuclear kin role in maintaining tradition and in cementing the succession system is reinforced by the role of the government bureau in administering the rancher's most vital resource: grazing land.

In many cases the procedures noted above could not be followed, and the surplus sons would have to leave the ranch and/or community. If their education had stopped before 12th grade, as it did for a large number, their choices were very limited. Ranch labor was one possibility – with the remote chance of buying the place if there was no heir. Another was to migrate further West, into upper British Columbia and Alberta, where pioneer ranches are still available. About half of the emigrations of sons out of the region were to areas where they could establish new ranches. (See Table 4, next page.)

The Role of Kinship in Emigration

Kinship ties with family living outside the region do not carry with them claims for assistance in starting a new enterprise elsewhere. However, the choice of destination for the emigrating son appeared to be influenced by kinship connections. Four of the men (three families are involved) who managed to

1 Some farmers have access to a relatively new type of facility: the cooperative grazing organization, which can drain off competitive rivalries for grazing land. This partial solution is unacceptable to the ranchers. Incidentally, nearly all auchland in the region is leased from the government, but since each lease has a small owned piece, this is bought, and the lease transferred with it - providing the land bureau approves.

Table 4

Migration of Male Siblings of Contemporary Generation in Control (26 Enterprises)

	Outside Region								Within Region			
Total No. Siblings	Total Migrants		Working on a Ranch		Working in a Non-ranch job		Killed in War		Working on a Ranch		Working in a Non-Ranch job	
	No.	%	No.	%	No.	%	No.	%	No.	%	No.	%
63	22	35	11	18	9	13	2	3	34*	54	7	11

* This number includes men who are not only on the family ranch.

establish themselves on ranches outside the region (usually borrowing money from the father) were encouraged to do so by brothers who had previously migrated. In the cases of men who had acquired non-ranching jobs outside the region, there was only one in which a brother followed a brother. In two other cases, the pull to a particular area was exercised by the wife's family.

However, this "pull" to a new community need not be made only by relatives. Former neighbors and friends can exert the same force. We found little attraction exerted by the initial migrants to the region on other relatives remaining in the homeland, during the earlier settlement periods. In only two cases out of a total of 34 examined did a member of the same family come to the region because another was already there.[1] We did find friends and extended families (by this term we mean a nuclear family unit and an unmarried brother or nephew) arriving together – the pull being that of adventure, or hope for a better life on the new frontier. We also found one or two members of the nuclear family (usually father and oldest son) coming out earlier, and after a year or so returning and bringing their wives and younger children. The data for the farm population indicates that relatives exerted a much stronger pull than for the ranchers.

It is fairly common for some ranch sons to leave, try their hands at various semi-skilled or skilled urban trades, and then return to take over the ranch, or buy another with help, in an effort to resume the satisfying identity of "rancher." Often, they are unsuccessful, and leave after a period of work on the home place or in the region. In some of these cases the coming and going was part of the decision-making process of succession. It could be a long-drawn out affair lasting a decade or more. In our sample there are 9 enterprises which had sons between the ages of 18 and 24. The pattern of departure and return was observed for 4 of these. These young men made use of their skills acquired on the ranch, and joined construction crews, oil rigging outfits, machinery repair establishments, or simply worked as ranch hands. Work of this type does not require a lifelong

1 This is in direct contrast to the aid and pull exerted by family members on each other in the process of migrating to the New World from their European homeland. See Kosa 1957, where he notes that 3 out of 4 immigrants came to Canada with the help received from relatives.

committment. In most cases the absence served to resolve some of the difficulties between themselves and their fathers or siblings, or to permit them to resolve their own doubts as to whether they should assume the dependent relationship required of them in succession. All 4 of these young men as of August 1963 had returned to take over the family enterprise and "settle down."

That most of the ranches were in the hands of second-generation successors indicated that there was a close fit between the expectation of lineal succession and the actual behavior. This close fit is due in part to the fact that so few alternatives other than ranching are presented to the ranch son. The educational system is a standard Provincial curriculum with academic emphasis, in which vocational information is not presented effectively. Also, other occupations would involve leaving the region, due to the limited opportunities available locally (Jasper, with its 2400 people, is relatively undeveloped and controlled by a conservative clique interested mainly in preserving the frontier, cow-town flavor). As we have noted, ranchers do not regard cities as offering much in the way of excitement or interest, except for short stays. The "good life" is the ranching life, and while a son might wish to escape from his father's control, permanent departure from the region was not perceived as a desirable solution.

The Ranch Daughter

The role expectations for the daughter differ from those for the son. Ranching is defined as a man's occupation, and the rancher's daughter who desired to manage a ranch; who might ride as well or better than her brothers; who perhaps was more interested in the enterprise and more competent as a manager, knows from early childhood that her chances of doing this are remote. Women might marry ranchers, and in the past most of the ranch daughters who remained in the region, did so. Women can also take part in horse shows and riding competitions, they can participate in "cattle talk," run the picnic lunches at the cooperative brandings and the rodeos, and keep books for their husband – but they are not considered fit to run a ranch.[1]

The ranch daughter, as in other societies, regarded marriage as her primary objective in life. Before marriage she was expected, and in most cases wanted, to receive vocational training in the fields of teaching, nursing, clerical, or more recently, the "glamor" occupations like airline stewardesses. Many of these occupational goals had been introduced to the region by the wives of ranchers and by the home visits of the paternal aunts. The number of in-migrant women who enter as teachers or nurses has been constant through the years, as can be noted from the following summary of our data:

1 Three women in the region *had* run ranches. Two were regarded as examples of "what happens to a woman when she tries to do a man's job." That is: masculine in manner, or, in violation of the norms by living with the hired man. The third was able to run her ranch "only because she is lucky enough to have a special kind of hired help" (*i.e.*, a man who accepted the direction of the woman and did not demand sexual satisfaction). In these three cases the women had undertaken to run the ranches since there were no male heirs.

Table 5

Women in-Migrants

	Came as Individual Teachers or Nurses	*Entered as Relative*	*Total No. of in-Migrants*	*% of Total No. of Married Women in Ranching Community*
1900–1915	3	2	5	29
1916–1930	7	1	8	20
1931–1945	6	2	8	19
1946–1960	5	3	8	20

This fairly consistent flow of trained women has resulted in a pattern of higher educational expectations for the ranch daughters, since the mothers are more successful in communicating their experiences to the daughters than to their sons – for obvious reasons. These aspirations are such as virtually to ensure emigration, and actually their only alternative is marriage in the region.[1] In recent decades all of the ranch daughters who have remained in the region have done so because of their marriage to a local man.[2] Those who left to obtain vocational training have in the majority of cases remained away, since they found husbands in the towns and cities where they did their work. The following table illustrates the trends:

Table 6

Emigration Patterns for Ranch Women

	Number of ranch daughters, over 18, who stay in region			*Number of ranch daughters, over 18, who leave the region*		
	Total stay	*Marry farmer*	*Marry rancher*	*Total leave*	*Married a man from the Region, who left*	*Left to Work outside of the Region*
1900–1915	7*	1	4	5	5	0
1916–1930	19*	3	13	14	11	3
1931–1945	11	2	9	24	15	9
1946–1960	9*	5	3	24	9	15

* The apparent discrepency between the total number who stay, and those who marry a farmer or rancher is due to the number of unmarried women who remained with their family. The reduction in the number of unmarried women in the region today is due to the fact that career opportunities are accepted as the norm.

1 The urban migration by unmarried women is in direct contrast with that of some peasant societies (see Butterworth 1962, p. 271). It is a case in point which highlights the lack of "peasant-like" characteristics of this relatively isolated and rather "traditional" region.

2 Tabulations indicate that among 13 teen-age girls, 11 plan to leave the region to secure further training. One plans to get married, and the remaining girl was uncertain. We may also note that our protocols contain references to ranch wives who actively discourage their daughters from staying on ranches and in the region, and push them toward urban life and vocations. There are local sayings: "ranches are no places for women"; "a rancher is a man who beats his women and doesn't feed his cattle." These remarks should

The role of kinship in female migration

The ways in which kinship support is opted by the daughter may be seen as consequences of certain cultural norms. Thus, where expectations require the daughter to get specialized training for a particular occupation, family involvement constitutes a willingness to support her, and, in effect pushes her out of the region. We have seen that for the son, family aid given him to prepare him for his adulthood, functions to keep him within the region.

The extended kin group, particularly those members outside the ranching occupation, became important elements in the girl's occupational choice, and as agents to help her realize this choice. For example, a girl's stay with her urban relatives while taking nursing or secretarial training. In fact, in some situations, a girl is permitted to go to a particular urban center precisely because there are relatives present. The data indicate that the presence or absence of urban relatives becomes an important factor in the ranch daughter's decision to migrate to a particular area, and in presenting the ranch daughter with examples of occupations which are perceived by her as potential roles.

The community presents to its male children a well defined ranching role with little variation. This is noticeable in dress, speech and by a vigorous and universal feeling that town living is the worst thing that could happen to a man. On the other hand the woman's role is not clearly defined, and there is wide variation in the attitudes and roles a ranch wife can play. For the ranch son, we suggest that the ranching tradition and the failure of the family and the community to present alternative roles, precludes some of the necessary skills for successful participation in the outside world and reinforces the role of rancher. For the ranch daughter, there is no ideological factor which precludes her learning of new roles.[1]

---

be taken lightly, however – they do not represent strong negative reactions to ranching life on the part of the majority of women.

1 Louise Spindler in her monograph, *Menomini Women and Culture Change*, (1962) notes the degree of flexibility and acculturative continuity of perceptual structure for the Menomini women as compared with Menomini men. She writes:

> "Menomini women have always played spectator roles in the Male oriented Menomini society. They have been able to assume roles with a relatively great degree of flexibility, since there were no cultural emphases on prescriptions for female role-taking behaviors." (p. 98)

In the acculturative setting in which they now find themselves, there are no pressing demands similar to those demands made upon the man who must adapt to the white world to earn his living. She relates this fact of cultural retention to the hypotheses made by others (Vogt 1951:93) that women seem to be a force for conservatism. She indicates that the bases of such conservatism may be found in the differential role behavior of men and women, *i.e.* men are charged with "instrumental" roles and women with "expressive" roles – the instrumental roles carrying with them rigid prescriptions for behavior.

Our material suggests a different situation: role flexibility is found for the women as well as the men, but such flexibility act as a factor for change rather than for conservatism. It is the prescribed male role which serves as a conservative force.

Contacts with Kin

Since the region was settled recently, almost all of the ranchers maintain contact with their relatives in the old home place. The women who have entered the region as wives maintain contact with kin outside of the region through letters, visits and the ritual occasions of funerals and weddings. The outside kin group serves a variety of needs of the ranching members. Thus, one ranch wife always visits her mother in the Provincial capital twice a year: in November in time to do the Christmas shopping, and in the Spring for clothes.

Summer is a time of relatives visiting, particularly for the younger members of the family who come to spend a week or so on the ranch. Young house guests are common throughout the summer. They often come in the guise of "helping Uncle George" (Uncle George could do very well without their help and often makes this clearly known.)[1] In addition to house guests, families "drop in" on their way east or west, or more rarely make the ranch their vacation destination. Thus, ties are established between the young ranch generation and their extended kin out of the region, and hospitality is extended by the ranch family so that at a future time when they call on their urban relatives for reciprocity, it can be accepted freely.

Summary

The nuclear family, and kin connections within the community, are extremely important means of keeping the ranch son in the area, while the extended kin who have moved out into the wider community rarely provide incentive or aid for the ranch son to leave the region. The wider kin network outside of the region operates differentially for the ranch son and the ranch daughter. The wider kin network functions for the girl not only as a source of models, but also as a means of making the outside community accessible.[2] For the ranch son, the wider kin network offers little in the way of an alternative to local ranching. However, these kin connections become important for the ranch son at the time *his* daughter is of age to emigrate.

REFERENCES

Alty, S. W., 1939, "The Influence of Climate and other Geographic Factors on the Growth and Distribution of Population in Saskatchewan", *Geography*, 24; 10–33.

Atherton, Lewis, 1961, *The Cattle Kings*, Indiana Univ. Press.

1 There are many stories about the tricks played on unsuspecting city cousins. The adult men often instigate and aid in the trick. A common one is to place a city "dude" on a horse, reassure him that the horse is a quiet one, and then slap the horse as hard as possible so he bucks the rider off. Obviously the best place to do this is near a mud hole.

2 Friedl 1959, notes the important role of the extended kin in acting as an agent of change and as a means of bringing the outside world into the rural community.

Bennett, John W., 1962, "Habitat, Economy, and Society in the Canadian Plains, with Special Reference to Saskatchewan." Mimeographed, Social Science Institute, Washington University.

—, 1963, "Synopsis of a Cultural Ecology Research Program in Saskatchewan," *Plains Anthropologist:* 8; No. 20.

Bennett, John W. and Seena Kohl, 1964, "Two Memoranda on Social Organization and Adaptive Selection in a Northern Plains Region," *Plains Anthropologist:* 8; No. 22.

Butterworth, Douglas S., 1962, "A Study of the Urbanization Process Among Mixtex Migrants from Tilatongo in Mexico City," *America Indigena;* XXII: No. 3; 250–274.

Freeman, J. D., 1961, "On the Concept of the Kindred," *Journal of the Royal Anthropological Institute;* 91; 192–220.

Firth, Raymond, 1956, *Two Studies of Kinship in London.* University of London, The Athlone Press.

Friedl, Ernestine, 1959, "The Role of Kinship in the Transmission of National Culture to Rural Villages in Mainland Greece," *American Anthropologist;* 61; 30–38.

Gilson, J. D., 1958, "The Nature and Implications of Sub-marginal Farms." *Agricultural Institute Review;* 13; No. 5; 19-21.

—, 1959, *Family Farm Business Arrangements.* Univ. of Manitoba, Agricultural Economics Bulletin No. 1.

Goody, Jack, 1962, *The Developmental Cycle in Domestic Groups.* Cambridge: University Press.

Kosa, John, 1957, *Land of Choice.* Toronto: University of Toronto Press.

Morton, Arthur S., 1938, *History of Prairie Settlement.* Vol. 11 of *Canadian Frontiers of Settlement.* Toronto, Macmillan.

Park, George, 1962, "Sons and Lovers: Characterological Requisites of the Roles in a Peasant Society," *Ethnology;* 1; 412–423.

Parsons, Talcott, 1943, "The Kinship System of the Contemporary United States," *American Anthropologist;* 45; 22–38.

Royal Commission on Agriculture and Rural Life (Saskatchewan) Report No. 7, 1956, *Movement of Farm People.* Regina, Sask.

Royal Commission on Agriculture and Rural Life (Saskatchewan) Report No. 10, 1956, *The Home and Family in Rural Saskatchewan.* Regina, Sask.

Schneider, David, n.d., Personal communication.

Sharp, Paul, 1948, "The American Farmer and the Last Best West," *Agricultural History;* 1; 18–20.

Sonnichsen, Chas. L., 1950, *Cowboys and Cattle Kings: Life on the Range Today.* Univ. of Oklahoma Press.

Spindler, Louise, 1962, *Menomini Women and Culture Change,* Memoir 91, American Anthropological Association.

A Study of Mobility among the Ibos of Southern Nigeria

IKENNA NZIMIRO

Formely 7th University of Lagos, Lagos, Nigeria

1. Introductory

THIS paper is divided into two sections. The first part discusses mobility during the historical stage of the formation of different Ibo communities. This mobility was a result of the efforts of various kinship groups to find permanent settlements. This search for permanent places of abode led to some Ibo kinship groups migrating at various historical stages, and founding their own settlements. It led either to such groups being absorbed by a permanent group that had already settled before the arrival of the new group, or to the new group conquering and absorbing the already existing groups.

The second part discusses a new pattern of geographical mobility whereby men move to the new towns in the country quite removed from their places of origin, and settle as traders and craftsmen bringing from time to time members of their kinship groups, and eventually creating at a particular point in time a cluster of kinsmen who become organised into kinship associations which are projections of the traditional forms of social organisation in the places of origin. In both sections we shall explain the causes of the migration and its direction, and show from empirical studies of particular kinship groups the relationship between these migrants and those at home.

II. Cultural Area

The Ibos with whom we are concerned in this paper are those persons who have been grouped into the Kwa linguistic stock, but with variations of dialects and possibility of a common understanding of each other's dialect throughout the whole of Ibo territory.

Their territorial division covers the whole area stretching from the coastline of the Bight of Benin, and continuing to the outskirts of the Ibibio and Efik territories in the East with its Eastern boundary being formed by the Cross River. On the Southern and Western sides it stretches to the borders of the Ijaw,

Jekri, Igado and other ethnic groups, and then spreads across the Niger to the confines of Benin. After passing 6°. 31e North Latitude, it narrows in once more, and extends in wedgelike formation until its utmost Northern limits reach the boundary between Southern and Northern Nigeria where the Akpoto and Munshin are the nearest neighbours.[1]

They have similar cultural features, possessing an agricultural economy, fishing being undertaken in the riverain areas, particularly those along the River Niger. Their physical environments vary very slightly – thick vegetation in most areas with distributed heavy rainfall during the rainy periods.

Because they have a common outlook and share a common cultural life, they could be said to be homogenous in this respect.

Their religious philosophy is essentially based on the ideology of ancestor worship overlaid by the common belief in one God. Society and morality are bound together by their cosmological concepts, and the social organisation of their institutions is sustained by their metaphysical views about life and the universe. Law, order and morality are related to the powers of the great deities, and land is the foundation of justice. Land is of supreme importance in their social existence. As they are an agricultural people, it is the basis of their material life, hence the deities of the land are given an important place in their moral values and conceptions of society and humanity. Territorial communities are essential in that they are defined by the ownership of land which is governed by three cardinal principles:

a) "That land belongs to the community and cannot be alienated from it without its consent,
b) that within the community the individual shall have security of tenure for the land he requires for his compound, his gardens, and his farms and
c) that no member of the community shall be without land."[2]

These wide-spread people have been classified by Forde and Jones into five cultural groups, a classification that is based in some cases on geographical criteria, but nevertheless brings out clearly the importance of a people hitherto neglected in anthropological studies.

III. Social Structure

Since kinship is the fundamental basis of African societies, Ibo social structure is basically built on the family unit which extends to wider groups, members of who constitute the lineage, tracing their genealogy to a founding ancestor.

The three main units of Ibo social structure are the village, the "town" and the clan.

1 Nzimiro, I., Article in Afrika Heute, Bonn 1965, 7–8.
2 G. I. Jones, Africa Vol. XIX, London 1949, page 313.

The Village: Ogboe

The village is made up of persons who claim descent from a common ancestor, the group that we call the maximal lineage. It has a locality and the ritual cult of the earth deity. Thus, ancestor cult and earth deity and the fact that it is an exogamous unit, tend to hold the group together. Authority rests with the head of the village known as the Okpala who is a ritual and political figure and the most senior male of the group in many cases. Outsiders are absorbed into the group and they become citizens observing the rules of the members of the group.

The Town – Obodo, Ikporo

The "town" or the "village-group" is the federation of those patrilineages all of whom claim to be descended from one great remote ancestor. This is not altogether true, but fictions and myths reinforce the belief of belongingness, and among the population of the "town" are persons who are accepted as citizens when they accept membership of one of the lineage groups, and therefore trace their lineage genealogies to the founder of the group that has absorbed them.

The Clan

Where groups of towns claim that they were founded by a distant common ancestor, they constitute themselves as a clan. Ibos in this sense are made up of several clans. The size and population of Ibo clans vary, and also the degree of relationship between one clan and another.

When we talk of Ibo clans, we are treating the term clan in its general usage, but if we break our definition into specific indices for determining a clan organisation – e.g. exogamous units, common cults and ritual collaboration, facts of totemic observances, notions of unity based on descent from a founding ancestor and political ritual offices, we find that the clans vary. Three different types appear in Ibo society.

1) *Localised Clans*
These are clans that occupy one territorial area, e.g. Ngwa, Iheme and Nri Clans.

2) *Localised and Intimate Clans*
Within a town or a village group, clan features appear in terms of group location. We can, for example, call a town a clan in the classical sense that all the component units claim that they are children of a founding ancestor, this feeling being reinforced by common residence and ritual unity.

3) *Dispersed Clans*
Dispersed clans develop from historical processes. The clan units are dispersed and settle in different territorial areas so that the bond of this

feeling of common ideology of their ancestor becomes weaker than in the two other types. The Umuezechima, Ameshi and Ukwu clans are good examples.

Matriclans: Double Descent

The above discussion of the clan system is primarily based on the patrilineal system which predominates among the Ibos, but as we move further to the Cross River Ibos, the influence of another structural system becomes manifest in that we find a double descent system which has been described by Prof. S. Ottenberg. He found that among the Afikpo Ibos, "there are 32 matriclans and 35 major patrilineages. These 32 matriclans are corporate, exogamous, non-residential groupings which vary in size from several hundred to several thousand members. Each has a female founder and a traditional history. However, no precise genealogy, except of its individual lineage segments, can be given and here relationships are traced back about four or five generations.

Members of a clan are dispersed in many villages often throughout Afikpo. Nevertheless they are generally known to one another, greet fellow members by clan names, and take part in activities together. Each clan has a central meeting place where its only shrine is located in the compound of its priest. The spirit of the shrine is an impersonal one and is not an ancestor. Its priest selected by the clan elders, often with the aid of a diviner or the Arochukwu oracle, does not necessarily come from one particular lineage of the clan.

Membership in a matriclan, unlike that in a patrilineage cannot be changed by an individual from Afikpo, but a person from outside Afikpo may be adopted into the clan by touching the breast of a woman member whose child he is then said to become. It is customary for persons captured in warfare to be so adopted because they increase the size and strength of the clan, and they are quickly given full rights as citizens. Afikpo matriclans are not ranked in any special order, though the larger ones are more influential, and they do not join together as clans for any activity. They have no place in the village organisation and they do not act as distinct units in the elders groupings in the village group level, though their elders take part in Afikpo affairs.

A clan is sub-divided into numerous small lineages, called Ikwuera, which seem to average between 15 and 30 members... No matrilineal group intermediate in size between these lineages and the clan exists. Though the matrilineage is not a residential unit its members tend to live in neighbouring villages, its women most commonly marrying within a local area. In several neighbouring villages they trace their relationship back to four or five generations to a female founder whose sisters are often founders of other lineages, or at least most members of them. The eldest male of the matrilineage is the head, and is in charge of, and responsible for, many of its activities. If the members of a lineage become dispersed, or it is growing in size, the head may permit an older member in a distant area to take charge of the members there, thus forming sub-lineage.

As its sub-lineage developes, its members may move further away from the original lineage area through marriage, and it may continue to grow in size, until it breaks its original ties to become a separate matrilineage. The process of fission is a continual one, and has apparently not been affected by culture contact."[1]

Part I

MOBILITY DURING THE HISTORICAL STAGE: PRE-COLONIAL ERA

By the historical stage we mean the period in the history of a particular kinship groud when they were forced by circumstances to migrate and find a new settlement. Such migrations were caused by war of conquest, but in most cases were a result of finding a better farming area to feed an expanding kinship group.

In the case of migration resulting from wars, the important Ibo communities along the River Niger, consisting of more than seventeen kingdoms, migrated in about the 15th to 16th centuries, originally from Benin and Igala kingdoms of West and Northern Nigeria respectively. These migrations were the result of the despotic rule of several Obas (kings). Some of the cruel activities were the excessive collection of taxes from the subjects not only by the Obas, but also by most of their officials who doubled and even trebled the amount of tribute required by law. Some of the officials waged war against recalcitrant subjects, who then migrated. One such wave of migrants were the Umuezechima group cited as a dispersed clan. Other dispersed clans that migrated as a result of despotism were the Ameshi and Ukwu clans of which the important Ibo communities today are Oguta, in Eastern Nigeria and Abo and Inyi in the Mid-Western Region. The Ukwu clan comprises of Abo, Usoro, Ashaka, Afor and Usisa in the Mid-West. Coming further East we find scattered clans like Ogwu comprising Ogwu-Ikpele osimili (near the Niger) and Ogwu-aniocha (outside the bank of the Niger). We find also the Akiri clan split into three groups of which one group belongs to the Mid-Western Region while the other, Akiri-agidi and Akiri-uno are found in the Eastern part of Nigeria. All these communities are today Ibo, and have assimilated Ibo culture in many respects but retain a different political system typical of the areas from where they migrated.

The Igala stock in our sample includes Ossomari, Odelye and Oko and their oral traditions of origin explain the cause of their migration from Ida, the capital of Igala kingdom, in terms of conditions similar to those which obtained

---

1 Ottenberg, Simon: Double Descent in 160 Village Group, Pennsylvania Press, 1950, pages 74–76. I have quoted at lenght Prof. Ottenberg's article to bring out clearly the clan structure as he described it. This is the first real study of a double descent system in Ibo land and this makes the full quotation necessary.

in Benin and caused the migration of Benin people to the East some distance away from the kingdom. All these communities have absorbed into their fold other kinship groups that migrated from other areas.

Migration again occurred also from the Eastern Ibos to the Mid-Western part of Nigeria, that is, across the River Niger. The communities of Asaba, Ibuzor, Ogwashi-Ukwu and some of the mixed communities among the Western Ibos comprise mostly persons who originally crossed the Niger and settled. They were later joined by groups of Benin conquerors who established the Benin pattern of political organisation. In these communities, they have kings who are crowned by the Oba of Benin, and they therefore receive the sword of authority from him which is known as Ada. I call these men Ada kings.

Migration of Ibos towards this part of the country was dictated mostly by economic reasons, the search for land, and not by political conquest of any particular group. However, when we examine their oral tradition, they state that the original kinship group that migrated were the children of a particular distant ancestor who committed a breach of the law and was therefore expelled from the community. Such an example is the town of Ogwashi-Ukwu whose founder was one of the sons of the Eze(king) of Nri and committed incest with his father's wife. Since this was punishable by death, he was advised to migrate because his father loved him dearly and did not want him to be killed.

Nri migrants feature again in some of the traditional history of migration in some of the communities. At Ossomari, we find again Umuchi who claim that their original founder came from Nri, and also the Inwala group in the same Ossomari claim also some distant relationship with Nri. The dispersal of the Nri clan is a result of territorial expansion in keeping with the Ibo system of acquiring land for farming and later for permanent settlement. This sort of gradual expansion has been described by Bridge as the "colonial stage".

This brings us to a final discussion of patterns of migration under this heading. This form of migration should rather be termed expansion into other areas and the acquisition of virgin areas of land which become occupied permanently by the kinship groups. In this way, the founding group acquired and owned the land.

In this respect, the principle which we find among the Yorubas also obtains among the Ibos. Ward Price, writing about the Yorubas, argued that Yoruba land ownership and therefore settlement were based on the following principles:

1) Strong, independent-minded men left their homes with their families and friends to seek out places suitable for founding a community.

2) A man banished from his home for anti-social conduct (as in the case mentioned above) would do the same thing if he escaped sale into slavery.

3) A man who acquired wealth and power over others might deem it advisable to migrate – the Ibo is ever resentful of tyranny.

4) When communications developed, settlement took place at the more

frequent cross-roads. This development can be seen in many areas today and is rapidly raising the value of land in those areas.

5) Hunters, being regarded as the guardians of a community's rather nebulous boundaries might settle in remote forest areas.

6) War refugees might found a settlement on a new site.[1]

The second stage of the acquisition of land by a founding migrant group is called by Bridges the "community stage". Here a growing community founded by a distant ancestor whose descendants are then original owners of a land come into contact with a similar expanding community in its farming and hunting activities, resulting in both communities agreeing to preserve the area by their accepting joint community of interest in the preservation of the land.

The third stage known as the "suburb stage" is where, according to Bridges, "increase in population has made it more or less impossible for one central authority to control individual land tenure and at the same time has been driven away from farming to seek fortunes abroad".[2] This comes within the discussion under part two of this paper.

In all these stages discussed, we have shown how mobility from one geographical area of the country to another has been undertaken by Ibos at a particular period which we call the historical period in that we find it difficult to state the exact stage; but these movements occurred and are remembered in the people's history of tradition of origin.

Part II

THE MODERN PHASE

We shall discuss the modern forms of geographical mobility which fits into the stage styled by Bridges as the "Suburb phase".

Migration into urban areas in Nigeria has become the common feature of Ibo geographical mobility in Nigeria. The rate of Ibo mobility has exceeded that of any of other ethnic group in Nigeria, and this has led to sociological problems which will be discussed at the end of this section, since these immigrants face problems of adjustment in their new situations.

The migration has been caused by four important factors. First is the consideration of "land hunger" arising as a result of density of population which exceeds in some Ibo areas – Onitsha, Awka, Okigwi and Orlu that of any area in other parts of the country. They therefore migrate in search of new areas for farming as in the case of many Awka migrants who go as squatters to farm in distant lands. Some migrate, as we find among those from Owerri, to obtain independent employment or to trade.

Secondly, migration can also be a result of lack of fertility of land for farming.

1 Ward Price, H. L., *Land Tenure in the Yoruba Provinces*, Lagos, 1939, page 5.
2 Chubb, L. H., *Ibo Land Tenure*, Ibadan, 1961, page 10.

Many Nnewi people near Onitsha have deserted traditional farming for trade in distant lands due to the fact that the soil is very poor for agricultural purposes. There are some areas where poverty of land has caused this form of geographical mobility.

The third consideration is migration due to the rising cost of farming, particularly in areas where farming is of great economic benefit and the surplus yams are sold. Farming in these communities is essentially for marketing. This occurs in the Oguta area, and here migration is caused by the rise in the cost of farming leading to farmers deserting their farms for other employments. A survey of adult farming population in five villages in Oguta showed that of a population of 429,178 about 41.5 per cent migrated. Of 369 occupied males engaged in economic activities, 269 were farmers but 100 changed occupation. The changes vary from village to village and in one small village over 50 per cent of the occupied males have changed their occupation. Cost of farming in this community increased to about 300 per cent in the period between 1950 and 1960. This figure was arrived at by comparing the various items of cost in cultivating an area of land which could hold 400 yams, a unit that an averagely poor farmer is supposed to cultivate.[1]

The fourth cause of geographical mobility among Ibos is the desire to seek for a new occupation among the educated elite. For several years, many Ibos began to move outside their own areas to various parts of the country. In about 1934 there developed a Pan-Ibo consciousness in the new urban areas as a result of the expansion of the railways, roads and telegraphic systems, the growth and expansion of trading activities of European and later African firms, and the development and expansion of the Civil Service in the Federation with the subsequent recruitment of clerical white collar workers in these expanding state institutions. Industrial growth in the form of old and modern industries have accelerated the rate of urban development, and Ibos have taken advantage of this growth to move to these new labour pools to seek all sorts of employment which unlike some other ethnic groups' they never consider too low or too undignified. The growing number of immigrants have felt a sort of social distance from their homes, and in order to adjust in their new situations, new Ibo elite groups have organised the Ibo Federal Union. It was conceived as a Federal body which would cater for all Ibo social and kinship groups scattered throughout the country. By this period, the population pressures of Ibos in the urban area of Nigeria was mounting high, and there was a feeling of group solidarity among people who found themselves as minority groups in their new places of abode. They felt uprooted from their social background, and the new organisation was to provide an avenue for new social adjustment.

The founders of this organisation were members of the new Ibo middle class, the professionals, the business class, and the educated white collar workers in the Civil Service. The competitive spirit of an immigrant element is always a factor in their aspirations towards the achievement of status and position on

1 Nzimiro, I., *Family and kinship in Ibo Land*, Cologne, 1963, page 127.

the social ladder. The first generation of immigrants have often improved the social conditions of the second generation. Moreover, the new elite found that in the urban centres adjustment was based not only on their new relations with other ethnic groups, but also on loyalty to the kinship group.

Various factors combined to consolidate this solidarity. Political awakening found expression in the appeal to different ethnic groups by political leaders. By 1948 political tension between the Ibos and another important ethnic group, the Yorubas, mounted high. In this year, the Ibo Union took a new form and constituted itself into the Ibo State Union since the two important southern ethnic groups – Ibos and Yorubas – actuated by the selfish emotional sentiment of their elite considered that each was an in-group and an out-group to the other, and that political statehood should accord each separate group a sort of political independence and consciousness. In article 2 of the Union's constitution it stated that

> "The aims of this organisation shall be:
>
> 1) To devise ways and means whereby all sons and daughters of Ibo land, at home and abroad, shall be brought together under the Union.
>
> 2) To promote cultural understanding among the various groups in Ibo land at home and abroad..."[1]

The cardinal point here is that the Union inspired the organisation of numerous "town unions" most of which followed the pattern of Ibo social organisation as described under the heading on social organisation. Here therefore one finds a different pattern, which is absent in highly industrialised societies, where in most cases kinship groups play a less important role in the cities. Though current research shows the emergence of kinship groups in East London, and also the existence of ethnic areas as subcultural groups in the big cities of America, the pattern of Ibo organisation in these urban centres in the country follows closely the indigenous system of Ibo social organisation based on the village, town and clan.

What the Ibo State Union represents is an urban replica of the structure of Ibo society in rural areas for this union affiliates the numerous village, town and clan unions formed by these migrants in all urban towns. The Union therefore is a pulling together of all Ibo heterogeneous subcultural groups in the urban setting, and these constitute as we find in the United States, one of the subcultural ethnic groups in urban subcultures of Nigerian cities. Official statistics of the Union show that in 1960, the State Union had two hundred and sixtyfive branches distributed in the Regions as follows: Western Nigeria 56, North 94, East 74, Cameroons 26 and Ghana 15. The extent of this organisation illustrates the migratory character of the Ibos.

1 Constitution of the Ibo State Union, P.H.

Sociological problems arising from mobility

How do these Ibos adjust in their places of abode in the new urban settings? What is the attitude of the receiving populations of the indigenous ethnic groups that own and dominate these urban centres? What sort of conflicts have arisen between these people and the migrant Ibos and how do these Ibos ensure that members of their own group do not lose their ethnic identity? These are the questions to be answered in this concluding section of the article.

The first important sociological observation is the existence of conflicts between Ibos and the members of the ethnic groups who own the area to which the Ibos have migrated. This has led to the development of ethnic prejudice against the Ibos, most of the prejudice emanating from the fact that Ibos dominate some aspects of the economic life of these communities. Urban societies are like open-class systems, which tolerate and even encourage mobility up and down the power-prestige scale. Such flexibility fosters intense competition and personal rivalry[1]. In such situations Ibos have in some aspects of economic competition such as distributive trade, sale of merchandise, foodstuffs and other commodities, proved very successful. This has inspired a sort of ethnic prejudice against them since prejudice often reflects the very instability of urban open societies, and the struggle for higher status tends to heighten the sense of frustration, anxiety, and insecurity both for those who have reached a certain social position and those who are seeking to reach it. One can say that in such a situation, the ethnic group constituting a sort of class tends to become a tight in-group which resents intruders.[2]

A case of such conflict is between Ibos as an immigrant group, and Efik people who are the dominant group in their own town of Calabar, one of the ports of Nigeria which has become urban. It was reported on by the Commissioners appointed to enquire into the fears of minority groups in the Regions that constitute the Federation of Nigeria that in this town, Ibos control the bulk of the merchandise trade, the market shades and stalls, and all distributive trade and import commodities pass through them. The Efiks who are the indigenous settlers have not acquired any experience in such economic activities.

The Commissioners examined cases of accusation against the Ibos by some Efik leaders who regard Ibos as an out-group. According to the Commissioners, it was reported that "the Ibos did not observe local customs in the markets, that they expected their own religion to be treated with respect, but did not accord this to those of Efiks and Ibibios, and finally, that where an Ibo interest was threatened, they resorted to a boycott to punish the offender." Commenting on these reports, the Commissioners asserted that "according to the first of these charges, we formed the impression that jealousy of Ibo success in the markets was the main factor, as to the second, we heard evidence of both sides and it

---

1 Young, Kimball, *Handbook of Social Psychology*, London 1953, p. 262.
2 *Ibid.*, page 263.

seemed that charges of this kind could be proved against either party. The third, however, was sustained and, indeed, counsel for the Ibo State Union clearly thought that such action was justifiable."

The Commissioners went on to describe another case of evidence of Ibo solidarity in the community as a means of warding off any attack against their members. According to them, "there was a dispute about a piece of land, which had been bought – so it was alleged – by a group of Ibos in order to build a church; the sale was contested by a non-Ibo who claimed to have a prior claim to the land which rendered the sale invalid. While this question was *sub judice*, the Ibo State Union in Calabar issued instructions for a boycott of the other claimant..."[1]

These examples pointed out by the Commissioners and several others which have occurred in many of the urban areas where the Ibos have constituted themselves through the Union into strong solidarity groups as a defence mechanism against the out-group indigenous inhabitants of the areas to which they have migrated, indicate the sociological problems involved in this Ibo migration.

During the last Federal campaign for the 1964 Federal elections in Northern Nigeria, open speeches were made in the Parliament attacking the Ibos, and some members of the Northern Parliament defying the principles of common citizenship for all, requested the confiscation of the property of Ibo residents in the Region. The Ibos have countered by using various pressure groups of their members to halt such methods. In some areas, they had again to resort to economic sanctions through the boycott of local markets thus compelling the authorities to relax such laws as threatened their trading activities. Our argument is that where a minority group is threatened by the majority, the migrant minority constitute themselves into a strong group to protect themselves against attacks on their members. Such ethnic unity has become the nature of the Ibo mechanism in the face of continuous threats against their persons and property in the open urban societies in Nigeria. The arrival of the Ibos in the occupational world in the country has heightened the anti-Ibo feelings by the elite of the non-Ibo groups particularly the Yoruba elite who held the jobs and status positions for several decades at the time when education had not penetrated into the Ibo interior. By 1937 Ibos had one lawyer and within this decade over two hundred have attained this position. Today there are Ibo lawyers, magistrates, and judges at all levels of the judicial hierarchy of the country. Ibos are University lecturers, medical doctors, engineers, permanent Secretaries, chairmen of government corporations and the bulk of them have proved successful merchants, company directors, transport owners, and in fact, there is no kind of high position in the country in which one cannot find them. It is sociologically true that this new Ibo elite class stand in constant competition with the elite class of other non-Ibo groups notably the Yoruba elite who cannot understand this new Ibo status-seeking concept Ibo elite, even though they may not attend some

1 Nigeria, *Report of the Commission appointed to enquire into the fears of Minorities and the means of allaying them*, London, 1958, page 43.

of the Ibo State Union meetings, subscribe in one form or the other to the principles of the Union, since at all levels, these Ibo elite and the numerous others on the lower rungs of the social ladder find the State Union the only avenue for defending their position in the new situation. It is important to observe that since most of the leaders of the Union constitute the groups mostly attacked by the out-group opposing leaders, the tendency has been for leaders of both groups to convert attacks against their persons into attacks against members of their group However, to the Ibo migrant into a city, the State Union ensures that as a member of this cultural group, his position in the community cannot be undermined without questioning. The examples given by the Commissioners at Calabar justify this assertion.

Ethnic Associations, another Level of Cultural Resocialization

Studies made by some sociologists point to the conclusion that ethnic associations which abound in many African urban towns are agents of re-socialization and serve to fit the new immigrant to the city into the new situation... By this re-socialization process Wallerstein states that the "problem of instructing large numbers of persons in new normative patterns is a key one for a nation undergoing rapid social change". According to him, there are few institutions which can perform this task. The formal educational system is limited in that it is a long-range process with small impact on the contemporary adult population. The occupational system touches a small proportion of the population, and a certain amount of re-socialization is a prerequisite to entry into it. Ethnic organisation through group membership touches all sectors of the urban community and therefore can be said to be a major means of re-socialization. Ethnic groups, Wallerstein contends, offer the individual a wide network of persons, often of very varying skill and positions, who are under some obligation to retain him and guide him in the ways of urban life. Further, he shows that members of the ethnic group seek to raise the status of the whole group, which in turn makes it more possible for individual members to have the mobility and social contact which will speed the process of re-socialization.[1]

Professor James Coleman, in his study of "The Role of Tribal Associations in Nigeria", reveals the same pattern of organisation and functions as Wallerstein. These associations perform important social functions such as:

1. Mutual aid and protection in the urban centres of temporary residence and employment. This normally includes sustenance during unemployment, solicitude and financial assistance in case of illness, and the responsibility for obsequies and repatriation of the family of the deceased in the event of death.

---

1 Wallerstein, "*Ethnicity and National Integration in West Africa*" in *Sociologie Politique de L'Afrique Noire*, page 135.

2. A medium for reintegrating the individual employed in an impersonal city by permitting him to have the essential "feeling of belonging"[1].

In my study of two Ibo migrant groups Onitsha and Oguta, the evidence was conclusive that migrants retain in the cities a sort of kinship unity that enables the members to feel integrated in the new community. Members of these communities have their Town Unions in various parts of the urban centres where more than ten members are found. Union constitutions stipulate the aims and rules binding members, and what benefits should accrue to those who join these unions. Members receive social benefits like conveying the corpse of a member to the home town if he dies; asisting the relatives in the expenses of funeral rites; assistance to members who are in need, such as the lending of money, or assisting unemployed members to get employment; giving legal aid to those who are in any way involved in a court case; settling disputes among members and helping to ensure that no member is left defenceless in the urban centre. It goes further to ensure that no member is left out of the fold by stipulating that when a member continuously abstains from the meetings of the union, he is sent a letter of warning, followed by a deputation to inquire the cause of abstention should no explanation come forth from this letter. When these methods have failed, the union constitutes itself as the guardian of the member in the town by writing to the member's kinship group at home to come and check the straying life of their kin.

A constitution of the Onitsha Improvement Union drawn up to bind all members stipulated that the objects of the union shall be:

1. To promote love and unity among the members.
2. To help any member as may be necessary in times of distress or need.

Like the Oguta Union, it does not allow its members the freedom to misbehave in the urban community and the constitution stipulates in clause 32 that any member who is proved guilty of becoming notorious or a public nuisance shall be severely reprimanded or suspended, and if he fails to amend his faults within three months, he shall be dismissed. This is a different disciplinary action from that of Oguta. Security of members for employment is clearly stated in clause 39, captioned "Unemployment":

> "It shall be the duty of every member to assist any unemployed member in obtaining employment. Any such unemployed member who is proved to be without means of livelihood, may be granted a monthly subsistence of 7s. 6d. for a period not exceeding six months, within which period he may be repatriated or sent to a station where he may obtain employment".[2]

Here the Union serves as an unemployment social insurance policy for

---

1 Coleman, James, *The Role of Tribal Associations in Nigeria*, West Africa Institute of Social and Economic Research, Ibadan, 1959, page 63.

2 Constitution of Onitsha Improvement Union Kano Branch 1935.

its members, and 7s. 6d. in 1935 when this rule was made, was a substantial amount.

Again, dead members are accorded burial, and sympathy is extended to the kinsmen at home. Under funerals, the constitution states that "in the event of death of a member, or a member's wife, the union shall be responsible for the following:

(a) Telegraphic communications not exceeding ten shillings.
(b) Coffin not exceeding £5 5s.
(c) Necessary transport.
(d) Drinkables not exceeding £2 in value.

The family of the deceased shall be repatriated if his late employer refuses to do so...[1]

Ibos have developed more of these associations than any other ethnic group, and the nature of their urban activities makes the formation of these associations important for their life in the towns; These ethnic associations constitute the Ibo Union branches in the urban towns, so that at both supra-Ibo organisation in the Urban towns down to the clan and village associations, the Ibos reassure themselves of adequate socializing agencies for adjustment in their places of temporary abode.

Conclusion

In this article, we have shown that geographical mobility has become a general feature of Ibo history even dating as far back as their oral traditional history can show. This mobility took a new turn during the modern era, and we have pointed out the nature of this sort of mobility and how the Ibos have tried to adjust in the fast changing environment of a country in which they constitute the second largest cultural group, and how also, like other groups they feel the need to protect and defend themselves. Their organisational system in the towns reflects the indigenous social structure based on kinship and lineage systems.

1 Nzimiro, I., Cologne 1963, pages 322–327.

Geographical Mobility and Kinship: a Canadian Example[1]

HELGI OSTERREICH

McGill University, Montreal, Canada

MOST recent theorists in the United States have denied that relatives are of any importance in North American society, and have stressed the isolation of the nuclear family, basing these statements on the demands of a democratic, urbanized and highly industrialized society. It is agreed that social classes differ in the extent and nature of their relations with kin; it is the middle class and upwardly mobile individuals who are considered characteristic of American society and thought to have least awareness of kinship.[2]

The argument is presented that the dominant value orientation of American society emphasizes functional achievement, and that particularistic ties, such as those of kinship, would undermine the universalistic orientation of this social system. "The isolation of the conjugal family... as a primary characteristic of the American system is the mechanism for freeing the occupation-bearing and competing member of the family from hampering ties which would both inhibit his chances and interfere with the functioning of the system."[3] Parsons and Shils concede that there is an irreducible minimum of particularistic, diffuse and ascriptive commitments, and that the nature of the personality system and the nature of the roles of child-parent relationship make affective expression more likely in the kinship situation than elsewhere.[4] The individual, however, is required to transfer such ties from his family of orientation to his family of procreation upon marriage.

It has been pointed out that there is no necessary causal relationship between the nuclear family form of kinship and industrialization.[5] In North American

---

1 This paper is based on the author's M.A. thesis *Geographical Mobility and the Extended Family*, typewritten ms., McGill University, August 1964.

2 R. Cavan, *The American Family* (New York: Thomas Y. Crowell Co., 1953); A. B. Hollingshead, "Class and Kinship in a Middle Western Community", *American Sociological Review*, 14:469–475, 1949; T. Parsons, "The Social Structure of the Family". In: Ruth N. Asnhen, ed., *The Family: Its Function and Destiny* (New York: Harper and Brothers, 1949); L. Warner, *American Life, Dream and Reality* (Chicago: University of Chicago Press, 1953).

3 T. Parsons, op. cit., p. 262.

4 T. Parsons and E. A. Shils, *Toward a General Theory of Action* (Cambridge: Harvard University Press, 1951).

5 S. M. Greenfield, "Industrialization and the Family in Sociological Theory", *America- Journal of Sociology*, 67:312–322, 1961; J. Bennett and L. Despres, "Kinship and Instrun

society, extended kinship ties become theoretically possible when these types of value patterns – universalistic and particularistic – are not seen as a continuum pervading all systems, but as applicable to different systems of the society independently of each other. There is every indication that there is a psychological limitation of the spread of universalistic patterns to the exclusion of particularistic ones. The fact that socialization of children takes place in family groups oriented about particularistic considerations, and that there are, in North American society, very few other groups or systems where particularistic attachments can form, points to the conclusion that such ties will exist between kin even after they have left their families of orientation.[1] These commitments to kin can be made on bases which enable the individual to keep the worlds of achieved and ascribed status apart.

Such theoretical considerations and his own empirical studies have led Litwak to formulate a theory of family structure for North American society which he calls the *modified extended family*. "By modified extended family structure is meant a family relation consisting of a series of nuclear families joined together on an equalitarian basis for mutual aid. Furthermore, these nuclear families are not bound together by demands for geographical propinquity or occupational similarity."[2] Geographical mobility is not disruptive of kin relations because the extended family[3] legitimizes such moves, and modern communication techniques have minimized the socially disruptive effects of geographical distance. Because relationships that an individual has can easily be kept separate from each other, he can achieve status both by deference and by association, and agreement on the value of independent achievement in the occupational sphere lessens the likelihood of nepotism and of authority conflict. The extended family can provide aid in non-occupational areas, and can provide a "sense of belonging" and security on a wider basis than that of the nuclear family. "Theoretically the most efficient organization combines the ability of large-scale bureaucracy to handle uniform situations with the primary group's ability to deal with idiosyncratic situations."[4] This suggests that there is both a need and a capacity for extended families to exist in modern society.

There is empirical evidence from the United States that nuclear families

---

mental Activities: A Theoretical Inquiry", *American Anthropologist*, 62:254–267, 1960; M. F. Nimkoff, "Is the Joint Family an Obstacle to Industrialization?", *International Journal of Comparative Sociology*, 1:109–118, 1960.

1 A. D. Coult and R. W. Habenstein, "The Study of Extended Kinship in Urban Society", *The Sociological Quarterly*, 3:141–145, 1962.

2 E. Litwak, "The Use of Extended Family Groups in the Achievement of Social Goals: Some Policy Implications", *Social Problems*, 7:177–187, 1960, p. 178.

3 The term *extended family* here refers to a social grouping (from Ego's viewpoint) of bilaterally linked nuclear families. Cf. P. Bohannan, *Social Anthropology*, (New York: Holt, Rinehart & Winston, Inc., 1963), p. 100 ff.

4 E. Litwak, "Geographical Mobility and Extended Family Cohesion", *American Sociological Review*, 25:385–394, 1960, p. 394.

feel obligations toward kin[1] and have fairly extensive contact with them[2], and that relatives rely on each other for aid of many kinds.[3] These obligations and activities persist despite geographical and occupational mobility. In the study reported here the concern is with the relationship between geographical mobility and relations with relatives outside the family of procreation. The study sought to test Litwak's formulation, which implies that while geographical mobility may affect the types of interaction patterns found, it should not result in a lessening of ideological and emotional commitment to kin nor should it disrupt relations between relatives. It sought to do so by selecting a sample of middle class English-speaking Canadians homogeneous in all other respects and by comparing those who were geographically mobile with those who were not.

The Method and the Sample

A questionnaire was administered to 45 respondents.[4] Genealogies were obtained, eliciting place of residence, occupation, frequency of contact and types of mutual aid carried on, for each relative.[5] Questions designed to elicit emotional and ideological commitment to relatives, attitudes or feelings about the advantages of having kin and whether respondents saw changes for any reason in their relations with kin were asked. The sample was homogeneous with respect to ethnic origin (Anglo-Saxon descent), social class (middle and lower-middle class), birthplace (Canada) and age (24–50, mean 33.4 years). Religion of the respondents was Protestant (26 respondents) or Roman Catholic (19 respondents); the sample consisted of 22 males and 23 females, all married except one (widow) and all with children living at home except one couple

1 J. Kosa, L. D. Rachiele and C. O. Schommer, "Sharing the Home with Relatives", *Marriage and Family Living*, 22:129–131, 1960; P. J. Reiss, "The Extended Kinship System: Correlates of and Attitudes on Frequency of Interaction", *Marriage and Family Living*, 24:333–339, 1962.

2 M. Axelrod, "Urban Structure and Social Participation", *American Sociological Review*, 21:13–18, 1956; W. Bell and M. D. Boat, "Urban Neighborhoods and Informal Social Relations", *American Journal of Sociology*, 62:391–398, 1957; S. Greer, "Urbanism Reconsidered", *American Sociological Review*, 21:19–25, 1956; T. T. Jitodai, "Migration and Kinship Contacts", *Pacific Sociological Review*, 6:49–55, 1963; E. Litwak, "Occupational Mobility and Extended Family Cohesion", *American Sociological Review*, 25:9–21, 1960; E. Litwak, "Geographical Mobility and Extended Family Cohesion", *American Sociological Review*, 25:385–394, 1960.

3 H. Sharp and M. Axelrod, "Mutual Aid Among Relatives in an Urban Population". In: Ronald Freedman et al., eds., *Principles of Sociology* (New York: Holt, 1956); M. B. Sussman, "The Isolated Nuclear Family: Fact or Fiction?", *Social Problems*, 6:333–340, 1959; M. B. Sussman and L. Burchinal, "Parental Aid to Married Children: Implications for Family Functioning", *Marriage and Family Living*, 24:320–332, 1962.

4 Sample questionnaires are available from author by mail.

5 A complete genealogy was not obtained, as the focus was on the quality of behavior rather than on the extensiveness of knowledge. Dead kin were not included, nor were respondents pressed for information about kin with whom they were not in touch at all.

(2 respondents) who had no children. The respondents all lived in a residential suburb of Montreal and most males worked in the city centre. The Metropolitan Area of Montreal, which includes this suburb, had in 1961 a population of 2,110,000; ethnically the Area was 64% French-Canadian and 18% of Anglo-Saxon origin. The suburb where the study was done was in 1961 76% French-Canadian and 19% of Anglo-Saxon origin.

For the study, the most important variable was that of geographical mobility. A respondent was defined as geographically mobile if he had no relatives in the Metropolitan Area (17 respondents) and non-mobile if he had at least two consanguine kin in the area (28 respondents). Religion and sex varied independently of geographical mobility; however, significantly more mobility occurred in the middle class than in the lower-middle class group.[1] The occurrence of class differences with respect to the characteristics discussed will therefore be pointed out where they occur.

Kin Universe

The number of people recognized as relatives often gives a fair indication of the importance of kinship in a society. Although in North American society the kin universe has been found to be relatively small, it is by no means negligible. The same situation prevails in regard to this sample. In Table I is shown the size of the kin universe of the total sample, and of geographically mobile and non-mobile respondents. The relatives included in the kin universe comprise all consanguines and their spouses, but not deceased relatives. It is clear from these figures that the kin universes of mobile and non-mobile respondents were very similar.

Table I

The Kin Universes of Mobile and Non-Mobile Respondents

Mobility	*N*	*Range*	*Median*	*Mean*
Not mobile	26	14–135	49.5	57.6
Mobile	17	11–140	64.0	62.9
Total sample	43*	11–140	52.0	59.7

* In the case of 2 respondents, information was obtained only about relatives with whom they were in touch.

The most significant relatives in terms of potential or actual contact are adult consanguines. It is through them that other connections are formed – connections with their spouses and children. In North American middle class

1 Social class was determined according to Warner's method of classification. Cf. L. Warner, *Social Class in America* (New York: Harper Torchbooks, 1960). The difference in mobility was significant ($P < .05$).

society, the nuclear family acts as a unit. That this was the case in this study was borne out by the fact that nearly all visiting was done by the nuclear family together and that when speaking about their relationships the informants used "we" and "them" more frequently than they used "I" and "him". It is inconvenient and somewhat meaningless to treat as separate "visitors" every individual in a family that visits, or is visited. Children still living in the parental household are seen, but interaction with them may be minimal. The adults are the focal points of interaction. Which particular adult is interacted with is apparently not fully determined by kinship nearness, the affinal adult sometimes being more important than the consanguine adult. In ten cases the visiting was carried on with the spouse and children of a deceased adult consanguine. The families are the units for contacts or visits. For analytical purposes it becomes important, then, to classify whole families rather than individuals. The procedure adopted was to categorize each "family" in terms of the adult consanguine connecting relative. All further discussion will be concerned with adult consanguines, although this person may represent a single adult, a marital pair and children, or the spouse and children of a deceased consanguine.

The number of adult consanguines known is shown in Table II. Again, the figures are similar for mobile and non-mobile respondents. It may be of interest in illustrating the emphasis on collaterality and the narrow range of kinship in this sample (attested also for the United States) to point out that collaterals comprised 48.5% of all adult consanguines mentioned, the first ascending generation 45.5% and the second ascending and first descending generations only 6% in all. The majority of the genealogies did not include adult consanguines beyond the third degree – the remotest relative mentioned in any genealogy was fifth degree.

The relatives of these respondents were found to be widely scattered geographically and there were differences between mobiles and non-mobiles. It was not merely that non-mobile respondents had relatives living in Montreal, but their out-of-town relatives were located nearer to Montreal than were those of non-mobiles.

Table II

The Known Adult Consanguines of Mobile and Non-mobile Respondents

Mobility	*N*	*Range*	*Median*	*Mean*
Mobile	17	8–37	20	20.6
Not mobile	26	4–34	16	18.3
Total	43	4–37	23	19.2

Contact

Contact can be discussed in two basic ways – its existence and its frequency. It is obvious that *a priori* geographical mobility need not have any bearing on the existence of contact, but it certainly can be expected to influence frequency. These expectations are supported by the analysis of contact with kin among these respondents.

Kin with whom respondents are in touch will be called *effective* kin.[1] "In touch with" is defined as anywhere from seeing daily to sending and receiving Christmas cards. In the ensuing analysis the existence of contact will be measured both in terms of numbers of effective kin and in terms of the *contact ratio* or the percentage of *known* kin who are kept in touch with as effective kin. The effective kin of mobile and non-mobile respondents is shown in Table III. The difference between the two groups is too small to draw any conclusions. However, referring back to the number of known adult consanguines (Table II), we find that the contact ratio is 59% among non-mobile respondents and 46% among mobiles. This difference, although not statistically significant for this sample, is in the expected direction: the greater ease of communication between people who live in the same city may increase the likelihood that contact will exist. The fact that both mobiles and non-mobiles have almost the same number of effective kin is the net effect of two opposing tendencies – non-mobiles have a higher contact ratio but mobiles know about more kinsmen.

Table III

Number of Effective Adult Consanguines, by Mobility

Mobility	*N*	*Range*	*Median*	*Mean*
Mobile	17	3–19	9.0	9.5
Not mobile	28	2–22	10.5	10.7
Total	45	2–22	9.0	10.2

Biological and geographical distance of relatives were found to affect the contact ratio. The respondents were in touch with all available parents and grandparents, and almost all siblings (96.8%). The contact ratio for mother's siblings was 61.2% and for siblings' children 63.6%, while for father's siblings it was 48.3% and for grandparents' siblings 46.7%. For first cousins the contact ratio was only 24.4%. The contact ratio was higher for relatives who lived in Montreal or within two hundred miles of the city than for others. However, beyond this radius there was no necessary correlation between actual distance in miles and contact ratio.

The nature of contacts was very different for mobile and non-mobile respondents. Face-to-face contact occurred with much greater frequency among people who have relatives in Montreal. However, the relatively high incidence of face-to-face contact even among mobile respondents was evident in that only one respondent reported seeing relatives less than once a year. Four respondents reported seeing no relatives more often than once a year. In these four cases

1 This usage of "effective" follows that of R. Firth, *Two Studies of Kinship in London* (London: University of London, The Athlone Press, 1956).

actual occasions of face-to-face contact might be more frequent, since two or more relatives living in different localities were reported as being seen once a year. All other mobiles reported seeing at least one relative twice a year or more. Writing as a form of contact was predictably more important for mobile respondents. Non-mobiles wrote letters to one relative on the average, mobiles to four. In both groups, with more than half of the relatives living geographically distant, only cards were exchanged. None of the mobile respondents reported writing no letters at all. Non-mobiles talked regularly on the telephone to 2.8 relatives on the average, mobiles to 0.9.

Table IV

Index of Frequency of Contact, by Mobility

	Index of frequency	
Type of contact	*Mobile respondents*	*Non-mobile respondents*
Face-to-face	13.5	111.4
Writing	52.8	5.0
Telephoning	12.8	300.6

A combined index of frequencies of face-to-face contact, writing and telephoning can be computed by multiplying the mean number of relatives contacted in each way in each time period by the number of times that time period occurs in a year, and adding the results.[1] Table IV shows the indices for geographically mobile and geographically non-mobile respondents. These indices emphasize the differences, both absolute and relative, between mobile and non-mobile respondents in the types of contact. Seeing is ten times and telephoning twenty-five times more important for non-mobiles than for mobiles. The opposite is true for writing – it is ten times more important for mobiles than for non-mobiles.

Contact with relatives is, then, kept up by both mobile and non-mobile people. The number of effective kin in both groups is similar. However, the frequency of contact is many times greater among non-mobiles than mobiles. Geographical mobility evidently does not terminate interaction with relatives – it merely reduces the frequency.

Mutual Aid

All respondents were engaged in some mutual aid with relatives. There was no attempt in this study to determine the frequency of aid – the focus was on

1 Time periods for face-to-face contact: weekly, monthly, semi-annually, annually, less (counted as ½). For writing: weekly, monthly, semi-annually, annually, cards only (counted as ½). For telephoning: daily, semi-weekly, weekly, monthly, semi-annually. The author is indebted to Professor R. F. Salisbury for the idea of the index.

Table V

Proportion of Respondents Reporting Different Forms of Aid

	Mobile		*Non-mobile*		*Total*	
Form of Aid	*Received*	*Given*	*Received*	*Given*	*Received*	*Given*
Any aid	100.0%	100.0%	100.0%	100.0%	100.0%	100.0%
Caring for children	52.9*	17.6	85.7	50.0	73.3	37.8
Residence during stay in city	100.0	100.0	42.9	46.4	64.4	66.7
Help during illness	11.8	23.5	75.0	60.7	51.1	46.7
Help with odd jobs	35.3	41.2	57.1	57.1	48.9	51.1
Taking care of the house	17.6	17.6	60.7	39.3	44.4	31.1
Advice on personal matters	5.9	17.6	42.9	39.3	28.9	31.1
Valuable gifts	23.5	0.0	32.1	7.1	28.9	4.4
Advice on business or money matters	23.5	17.6	21.4	42.9	22.2	33.3
Help in getting a job	5.9	0.0	28.6	17.9	20.0	11.1
Lending money	11.8	0.0	25.0	17.9	20.0	11.1
Financial help or large money gifts	0.0	11.8	17.9	28.6	11.1	22.2
Long-term residence	0.0	11.8	10.7	32.1	6.7	24.4

* This should be read: 52.9% of mobile respondents reported that they had received care for children from relatives.

incidence of different types. Table V shows the kinds of aid being exchanged between respondents and their relatives.[1] These figures reflect the differential opportunities for interaction that exist for mobile and non-mobile respondents. For almost all types of aid, more non-mobile people than mobile people reported exchanging services with relatives. However, residence during a stay in the city was reported by all mobile respondents but by less than half of the non-mobile respondents. The greatest differences are seen in caring for children, help during illness, taking care of the house and advice on personal matters. These forms of aid, more than the other types, depend on availability on short notice and/or physical presence; physical proximity of relatives then greatly increases the likelihood that these services will be exchanged.

But physical proximity is not necessary for the giving of financial aid (valuable gifts, lending money and financial help or large money gifts). It cannot explain why, for these categories of aid, non-mobiles show a greater incidence than mobiles. True, the difference is not as marked as for services requiring proximity, but there is a difference. A second factor would seem to be relevant – a differential effect of geographical mobility itself. It would seem that the act of moving to a locality where no kin are living has the effect of somewhat *reducing reliance* on relatives for services of various kinds.

Parents and siblings were found to be most important for all types of aid;

1 All aid reported was being carried on while respondents were domiciled as at time of interview, except long-term residence, which refers to sharing a household with an adult consanguine at any time after leaving the parental home.

however, other relatives were mentioned almost as frequently as parents and siblings for residence during a stay in the city. In addition, for some respondents other relatives were as important as parents and siblings in exchanging all forms of aid, and for a few even more important. It should be pointed out that there were many combinations of types of aid and classes of relatives such aid was exchanged with among these respondents, ranging from solely exchanging short visits with parents and one or two siblings (3 respondents) to exchanging nine or ten forms of help with parents, siblings and others (4 respondents). The sample size does not permit fuller discussion of mutual aid. In conclusion, dependence on relatives for help was not general among these respondents; some forms of help were much more common than others; and, moreover, geographical mobility reduced dependence on relatives for aid.[1]

Attitudes

On the basis of exploratory work by Reiss and others[2] a limited number of structured questions was asked, to classify respondents in three ways – regarding their kin-orientation, their ideological commitment and their perception of the "advantages" of kinsmen.

Table VI

Extended Family Orientation

"Blood is thicker than water"	*Is there something "special" about kin?*			
	Yes	*Undecided*	*No*	*Total*
Agree	31	...	3	34 (75.6%)
Undecided	1	2	1	4 (8.9%)
Disagree	5	1	1	7 (15.5%)
Total	37 (82.2%)	3 (6.7%)	5 (11.1%)	45 (100.0%)

The not kin-oriented respondents are boxed in by non-continuous lines.

Kin-orientation

The attitude towards relatives can be kin-oriented in the sense that people consider relatives a special category of people, or it can be not kin-oriented, in that relatives are seen as similar to any other acquaintances. Respondents were

1 Comparing the two social classes, there were indications that some differences in forms of mutual aid reported may reflect class differences. However, since this was relevant for only a few forms, it has no immediate bearing on the analysis of mutual aid in general.

2 P. J. Reiss, *The Extended Kinship System of the Urban American Middle Class* (Unpublished Ph. D. thesis, Harvard University, 1960); J. Kosa, L. D. Rachiele and C. O. Schommer, "Sharing the Home with Relatives," *Marriage and Family Living*, 22:129–131, 1960.

asked whether they agreed or disagreed with the statement "blood is thicker than water" and whether they felt there is anything special about relatives. All those (40 or 88.9%) who answered yes to one or both questions were classified as kin-oriented, the remaining (5 or 11.1%) were classified as not kin-oriented. The answers to these questions are presented in Table VI. Of the 37 respondents who felt there was something special about relatives, 15 or 40.5% could not define this "special" quality, 11 or 29.7% mentioned common descent, 6 or 16.2% permanence of relationship, 6 or 16.2% security and help when needed, and 5 or 13.5% interest and "acceptance" on the part of kin. Geographical mobility was not found to correlate with kin-orientation (Table VII).[1]

Table VII

Mobility and Extended Family Orientation

Mobility	*Kin-oriented*	*Not kin-oriented*	*Total*
Not mobile	89.3% (25)	10.7% (3)	100.0% (28)
Mobile	88.2% (15)	11.8% (2)	100.0% (17)

Ideological commitment

"What is basic is the fact that relations between kindred are governed by a special morality arising from the recognition of common descent... Thus it is usual for kindred to admit a special obligation toward one another: an obligation to give help and support in culturally determined ways."[2] The "culturally determined obligations" in North America were taken to be the five obligations obtained from open-ended questions in the study by Reiss.[3] Respondents were asked how far they agreed in principle with this ideology. Taking each "obligation" separately, Table VIII shows the proportions of respondents who stressed each obligation. The overall pattern is similar for both mobiles and non-mobiles. But for the first four obligations slightly more mobiles stress the cultural ideology. Only the obligation to support aged relatives is more stressed by non-mobiles. The difference between these obligations would seem to be that supporting aged relatives almost necessarily implies geographical proximity and frequent contact. Mobiles know they could not fulfill this (unpleasant?) obligation and some therefore deny that it is an obligation.[4] By contrast the type of

1 Lower-middle class respondents were slightly less likely to say that "blood is thicker than water" than were middle class respondents.

2 J. D. Freeman, "On the Concept of the Kindred," *Journal of the Royal Anthropological Institute*, 91:192–220, 1961, p. 209.

3 P. J. Reiss, *The Extended Kinship System of the Urban American Middle Class*, (Unpublished Ph.D. thesis, Harvard University, 1960).

4 Supporting an aged relative in most cases would mean (or be taken to mean) taking such a relative into the household. The preference of older people to remain in a familiar locality might be the factor which was being taken into consideration by mobile respondents. Note that class differences were not in evidence for this obligation. However

behavior which actually occurs most often and which is presumably enjoyed (being in contact) is least stressed as an obligation; the type which occurs least (help in need) but would be most important for the respondent is stressed most often.

Table VIII

Obligations Towards Relatives

Obligation	*Mobility*	*Yes*		*No*		*Undecided*		*Total*	
A. Obligation to keep in touch	Not mobile	53.6%	(15)	42.8%	(12)	3.6%	(1)	100.0%	(28)
	Mobile	64.7	(11)	35.3	(6)	—	—	100.0	(17)
	Total	57.8	(26)	40.0	(18)	2.2	(1)	100.0	(45)
B. Obligation to be friendly	Not mobile	71.4	(20)	25.0	(7)	3.6	(1)	100.0	(28)
	Mobile	82.4	(14)	11.8	(2)	5.8	(1)	100.0	(17)
	Total	75.6	(34)	20.0	(9)	4.4	(2)	100.0	(45)
C. Obligation to be loyal	Not mobile	71.4	(20)	10.8	(3)	17.8	(5)	100.0	(28)
	Mobile	82.4	(14)	17.6	(3)	—	—	100.0	(17)
	Total	75.6	(34)	13.3	(6)	11.1	(5)	100.0	(45)
D. Obligation to help in time of need	Not mobile	92.8	(26)	—	—	7.2	(2)	100.0	(28)
	Mobile	94.2	(16)	5.8	(1)	—	—	100.0	(17)
	Total	93.4	(42)	2.2	(1)	4.4	(2)	100.0	(45)
E. Obligation to support aged relatives*	Not mobile	92.8	(26)	3.6	(1)	3.6	(1)	100.0	(28)
	Mobile	76.4	(13)	11.8	(2)	11.8	(2)	100.0	(17)
	Total	86.6	(39)	6.7	(3)	6.7	(3)	100.0	(45)

* $P < .10$. For all other parts $P > .10$. The figures in brackets indicate absolute numbers.

Advantages

The perception of advantages differs from the recognition of a cultural ideology of obligation in that respondents' answers are likely to much more directly reflect their actual behavior. Even though both mobiles and non-mobiles accept the same ideology of obligations, those who have gained advantages from actual interaction – the non-mobiles – would be expected to make more mention of these advantages. This is largely borne out by Table IX. A sense of belonging, feeling of security and help and advice are easier to get when relatives are nearby – the proportion of non-mobiles reporting these is slightly greater than that of mobiles. But "affection and companionship" are seen as

lower-middle class respondents were found to stress the obligation to be friendly more than middle class ones ($P < .05$).

Table IX
Advantages of Having Relatives

Advantage	*Mobility*	*Agree*		*Disagree*		*Undecided*		*Total*	
A. Sense of belonging	Not mobile	78.5%	(22)	17.9%	(5)	3.6%	(1)	100.0%	(28)
	Mobile	70.6	(12)	17.6	(3)	11.8	(2)	100.0	(17)
	Total	75.6	(34)	17.7	(8)	6.7	(3)	100.0	(45)
B. Feeling of security	Not mobile	57.1	(16)	39.3	(11)	3.6	(1)	100.0	(28)
	Mobile	47.1	(8)	23.5	(4)	29.4	(5)	100.0	(17)
	Total	53.4	(24)	33.3	(15)	13.3	(6)	100.0	(45)
C. Affection and companionship	Not mobile	35.7	(10)	46.4	(13)	17.9	(5)	100.0	(28)
	Mobile	41.2	(7)	35.3	(6)	23.5	(4)	100.0	(17)
	Total	37.8	(17)	42.2	(19)	20.0	(9)	100.0	(45)
D. Help and advice	Not mobile	46.4	(13)	35.7	(10)	17.9	(5)	100.0	(28)
	Mobile	29.4	(5)	58.5	(10)	11.8	(2)	100.0	(17)
	Total	40.0	(18)	44.4	(20)	15.6	(7)	100.0	(45)

advantages of relatives by more mobiles. Here it would seem that physical proximity also increases the chances for stress and disagreements. Mobile respondents, then, might well stress the positive side, since they derive affection and companionship on special short visits and the chances for friction are small, while non-mobiles might be remembering disagreements as well. The differences between mobiles and non-mobiles here, as in contact, seem to depend on physical proximity, not on the fact of mobility. A small minority of the respondents (8.9%) did not feel that they derived any advantages from having relatives at all.

In conclusion, the similarity in attitudes between mobiles and non-mobiles shown by the questions on kin-orientation, appears in the other questions. The small differences found for ideological commitment and "advantages" result from the factor of physical proximity and concomitant behavior rather than from any attitudinal change associated with geographical mobility.

Conclusion

This study cannot be regarded other than as exploratory, due mainly to the size of the sample. The figures showing means and percentages should be regarded as indicating possibly significant characteristics of Canadian kinship and possibly significant similarities and differences between groups.

In general, however, the extended families of these Canadian respondents fell well within Litwak's typology of the modified extended family.[1] The nuclear family was the important unit in kin relations, there was no evidence of any but equalitarian relations and geographical propinquity was in no case a condition for the existence of ties with kin.[2] The modified extended family is said to provide social, psychological and economic support to its members, despite geographical mobility. The respondents in this study, whether geographically mobile or non-mobile, reported essentially the same kinds of relationships with kin. The similarities between the two groups were especially prominent in the number of relatives kept in contact with and in attitudes. The frequency of contact and the pattern of mutual aid were different for the two groups. Frequency of contact was obviously dependent on physical proximity, while mutual aid as well seemed to be dependent on this, but also may have been influenced by the fact of geographical mobility. This is not surprising, since exchange of services was not seen to be among the most important patterns in kinship relations. The relatively small proportion of respondents reporting many of the types of aid, the proportion who felt that help and advice were among the advantages of having kin and the fact that no one mentioned services exchanged when asked why relatives are "special" point to this conclusion. What was significant, however, was the emphasis, regardless of geographical mobility, on *potential help* ("when in need") and on the more intangible feelings of commitment and "sense of belonging". Not one respondent denied all psychological ties to relatives. The five respondents who were not kin-oriented all admitted either obligations or advantages, or both. The important aspect of kin relations among these respondents is best interpreted as having to do with psychological support in the sense of belonging to a group based on particularistic ties, a group able to deal with idiosyncratic situations, should such arise.

The respondents were asked whether there had been any substantial changes in their relationships with relatives and what such changes were. No changes were mentioned by 28 respondents. Four respondents considered that geographical mobility had disrupted relations with kin. Of these, two were non-mobile respondents – they had kin in the Montreal area. This has obvious implications for a definition of geographical mobility in further studies. Four others recognized the effects of physical proximity on behavior by reporting that they saw their relatives less often after moving away. Again, two were non-mobile. Three mobile respondents considered geographical mobility to further cohesiveness rather than disruption. Each stated that they felt closer to a particular relative (father, mother, or sister) after having moved away (note in this connection the remarks made above on "affection and companionship").

Two other types of "substantial changes" mentioned bring out two factors which may be much more significant in disrupting kin relations than geographi-

1 E. Litwak, "The Use of Extended Family Groups in the Achievement of Social Goals: Some Policy Implications", *Social Problems*, 7:177–187, 1960.

2 Two questions dealing with authority and with demands for geographical propinquity were asked to establish these last two points.

cal mobility. One respondent reported that after her father's death, she does not see his "side of the family" any longer. Another reported that "visits with aunts and uncles become less as one grows older." It is noteworthy that both his parents were deceased. That the death of "connecting" relatives is highly disruptive of relations was also indicated during the course of the study. Mother's siblings were found to be more important than father's siblings for contact and mutual aid. Further investigation indicated that this difference was due to the earlier demise of fathers. Respondents whose father was dead (N = 12) had less contact with father's siblings than respondents whose parents were both living (N = 24). Respondents whose parents were both dead (N = 7) had considerably less contact with their parents' siblings than the other two groups. There were no cases of widowed fathers.[1]

The other factor was specific quarrels, illustrated by two respondents. One woman had severed all connections with her relatives because of a violent and seemingly irreconcilable disagreement. Another respondent reported seeing more of his father's relatives after the father's death. It appeared that his father had had a disagreement with his kin, and only after his death did they establish relations with the respondent.[2]

These cases suggest that attitudes to kinsmen are by no means directly reflected in behavior. They support in an extreme and paradoxical form the proposition that a particularistic kinship ideology may be of great importance for the individual's emotional needs in an industrial society, though in his behavior he may be completely committed to a universalistic pattern of relationship.

---

1 Such results have a bearing on the formulation of a structural model for the "modified extended family." A series of nuclear families connected by *continuous links* (living consanguines) radiating from Ego might be postulated. The basis of kinship ties in North American society rests mainly on particularistic attachments formed in childhood, within the nuclear family. Therefore, all the attachments within an extended family are based on a series of connections with members of particular nuclear families. It is not difficult to visualize how the severing of one such connection, whether through death or other means, would greatly increase the likelihood that all attachments formed through it would disappear.

2 The possibility of such disagreements raises the question of their nature and the determinants of complete severance of connections. Also, it raises the question of reasons for refusal to be interviewed.

The Kinship Network among French Canadians[1]

RALPH PIDDINGTON

The University of Auckland, Auckland, New Zealand

PART I

1. Introduction

THIS essay is divided into two parts. Part I gives the general conclusions of my research in St. Boniface in 1962. Part II contains documentation, consisting mainly of statements by informants, as well as some supplementary notes. The documents are numbered for ease of reference.

Sociological studies of the functions of kinship have usually concentrated attention on how these functions affect the lives of local communities. Indeed this is the only type of study possible in many primitive societies characterised, until recently, by partial or complete isolation. Within such societies kinship bonds tend to form a closed system of human relations within a limited territory. There are, of course, partial exceptions to this statement, for example inter-tribal kinship relationships in aboriginal Australia. But it remains true that most studies in kinship have of necessity placed primary emphasis on kinship relations correlated with regular and often daily face-to-face contacts within a limited geographical area.

The phenomena of geographical mobility, urbanisation and industrialisation in modern society call for a wider approach. It is necessary to ask what happens when kinsmen become separated from each other by great distances, as happens frequently on the North American continent. Under such circumstances, do kinship bonds tend to atrophy? Or are they kept alive by mutual visiting, correspondence, the exchange of greetings cards and other factors to be mentioned later? And if they are severed by migration, can they readily be revived under appropriate circumstances?

---

1 I wish that I had space to thank individually all those French Canadians who helped me so patiently and conscientiously in my work, and in whose company I spent so many pleasant hours. But I feel I must thank specially M. Jean Lagassé who in 1962 (as at St. Jean-Baptiste in 1957) went to great pains to put me in touch with informants and offered extremely valuable sociological comments on my material. I also wish to thank Miss Eleanor Crosby for much valuable help in analysing the data.

The French Canadians of Western Canada and certain parts of the U.S.A., where extensive migration has been going on for many years, provide an excellent field for the study of these and related problems. I chose St. Boniface for my research in 1962 for various reasons. It is and always has been the focal point of the French Canadian parishes on and adjoining the Red and Assiniboine Rivers which were the first French Canadian settlements in Western Canada and where live to-day the vast majority of the French Canadians of Manitoba. It has acted as a "clearing house" for many migrants, particularly young men who come there from rural parishes, acquire professional or business qualifications and then migrate to some other province where they think they will find better opportunities for advancement. In Quebec particularly, their perfect bilingualism is a distinct advantage. This is why my St. Boniface material shows a number of migrations to Quebec and Ontario, whereas that collected in 1957 at St. Jean-Baptiste (Piddington 1961:13), which was based on information concerning people following for the most part rural occupations, showed comparatively few.

As previously, my work was based on the collection of genealogies, which should be the starting point of all studies of kinship. But my approach was somewhat different. I made no attempt to discover the full range of kinship awareness, the extent of which in "modern" French Canadian society has already been demonstrated by Garigue (1958:63–76) and by myself (Piddington, 1961:9). In particular, I refrained (with a few exceptions) from boring my informants by asking for the names of young children. Consequently, the named kin recorded were fewer than in 1957, the average number per genealogy being 256 for St. Jean-Baptiste and 142 for St. Boniface. Two other factors affect this discrepancy. Firstly, my St. Boniface informants were on the whole younger and a number of their siblings and cousins were not old enough to be married, which minimised the number of affinal and collateral kin who would ultimately appear in their genealogies. Secondly, they belonged for the most part to the professional and business classes. Their business and professional contacts tended to minimise to some extent their contacts with kin and therefore their opportunities to acquire, through gossip, a wider knowledge of their genealogies.

I was nevertheless impressed by the range and detail of kinship awareness of which two features deserve mention. One is the importance of *potential knowledge*. Even when informants failed to provide information on certain branches of related families, they knew where such information could be obtained. They frequently referred me to relatives who could provide it.

The second feature is the significance of *negative information*. Compare the two following pairs of statements:

(a) They never had any children.
(b) No, she was never married.
(c) I don't know whether they had any children or not.
(d) I don't know whether she ever married.

Clearly, the first pair indicates keener kinship awareness than the second, though this information is not revealed by merely enumerating named and unnamed kin. The majority of negative answers which I received were of the (a) and (b) type.

2. Migration

For almost all genealogies I recorded the names of kinsfolk who had left Manitoba and also the Canadian province, or State of the U.S.A., to which they had migrated. I then questioned informants about their contacts with these migrants and assigned to each answer a rating on a four-point scale. This was necessarily subjective, but I could think of no more exact and objective way of quantifying the data. How, for example, could one evaluate regular visits against regular correspondence? And as regards visits, it is impossible to reach any objective definition of such terms as "regular" or "frequent". Take, for example, the case of two kinsmen, one of whom comes all the way from California to visit in St. Boniface every two years, while the other comes from North Dakota, only about three hours away by train, two or three times a year. Which can be said to have the closer bond with the kinsman visited? Again, the character of visiting varies from casual visits of an hour or so to residence as a house guest for a period of days or weeks. All these considerations, and many others, must be taken into account in assessing the strength of a kinship bond, and this can only be done subjectively. The following are the broad criteria, one or more of which I took into account in assigning a rating:

Rating 1: Frequent visits. Regular correspondence. Exchange of Christmas cards, which amounts to the same thing since a letter is almost always written on the card. Economic aid. Assistance at times of crisis, e.g. birth, bereavement, sickness. Frequent long-distance telephone calls.

Rating 2: Infrequent visiting. Irregular correspondence. Regular contact through a third party, e.g. "She writes to my mother regularly, so I often get news of her; and mother sends to her news of our family". Infrequent long-distance telephone calls.

Rating 3: Casual contacts only, e.g. "I saw him two years ago at my uncle's funeral"; "I saw him when he passed through here two or three years ago". Condolence cards. Occasional contact through a third party, e.g. "I have not seen or heard from him for many years, but my uncle visited Vancouver last year and when he came back told me that he was married and had three children."

Rating 4: No direct or indirect contact for many years.

I may add that I rarely experienced difficulty in assisgning a rating on the basis of criteria such as the above, and believe that my results represent a substantially accurate assessment of the situation. A total of 299 ratings for contacts with kin living outside Manitoba[1] were recorded in 16 genealogies, with the following results:

Rating	*No.*	%
1	65	22
2	53	18
3	118	39
4	63	21
	299	100

Mean Rating: 2.59

Ratings were tabulated according to the area where the kinsfolk concerned were to be found, thus:

Region	*No. of Ratings Recorded*	*Mean Rating*
Quebec and the Maritime Provinces*	52	2.50
Ontario	47	2.64
Saskatchewan	41	2.63
Alberta	26	2.15
British Columbia	34	2.53
Central U.S.A. States	41	2.49
California	24	2.79
Other U.S.A.	21	2.62

* Practidally all Quebec.

These variations are not so marked as might be expected. They suggest that kinship as such, rather than geographical proximity and convenience of access, determine whether kinship bonds shall be maintained or atrophy. Nor is there a consistent relation between distance and intensity of contact. Thus, as we would expect, distant California rates lowest, but the second lowest area is Ontario – an adjoining province.

There is considerable variation between different informants as to the contacts they maintain with remote kinsfolk. The genealogies were classified according to the number of ratings 1 and 2 which they revealed. These ranged from 69% to 25% with a mean of 39%.

There is also considerable variation between the genealogies in regard to the percentages of kin residing outside Manitoba. These range from 32.8% to 1.3% with a mean of 12.1%. Migration thus tends to "run in families". The most important reason for this is that migrants tend to go to places to which

1 Geographically distant kin for the purpose of this study were taken to be those living outside Manitoba. This is not so arbitrary as would appear because, as stated previously, the vast majority of Manitoban French Canadians live in the region of the Red an Assiniboine Rivers centering on Winnipeg and St. Boniface (Stanley, in Wade 1960:343). With rapid communications, the French Canadians in this region form an enclave, which contrasts with the scattering of other French Canadians over wide areas of North America.

their siblings or other relatives have already migrated rather than to scatter themselves over different areas.[1] This is illustrated by the following statement: "My cousin Alphonse was the first to go to British Columbia where he became a foreman and married a British Columbian girl. He persuaded his six brothers to follow him and got jobs for some of them. When their father grew old and frail he went to British Columbia to stay with one of them."

Of 1218 marriages recorded in the genealogies, 169 (13.9%) were with persons of ethnic origin other than French Canadian, mainly with English Canadians, Americans, Ukrainians and Irish. Such inter-ethnic marriages are notoriously apt to separate the French Canadian spouse wholly or partially from his or her culture and community, especially when there is a religious as well as an ethnic difference between the spouses, though cases of this kind are uncommon. The main factor leading to ethnic alienation is language. Whereas practically all people in Western Canada understand English, only a very small proportion of other ethnic groups understand French, so that the spouses in inter-ethnic marriages tend to speak the former language and their children often grow up knowing no French – a circumstance by which they become separated from the French Canadian community.

Of the 169 inter-ethnic marriages recorded, 52 were between spouses now resident outside Manitoba. It is interesting to enquire how such inter-ethnic marriages affect contacts with French Canadian kin in St. Boniface. Though the number of cases is small, it should be noted that the mean contact rating here is 2.4, as against the overall mean of 2.59. These figures suggest the tentative conclusion that inter-ethnic marriages do not affect relations between migrant French Canadian spouses and their kinsfolk in St. Boniface.

3. Agencies of Kinship Liaison

Though no adequate comparative data ara available, it seems probable that the material presented above indicates that French Canadians maintain bonds with geographically distant kin to a greater extent than do individuals in communities of Anglo-Saxon origin[2]. In such communities, which exhibit, as

1 Thus out of 143 cases in which siblings migrated from Manitoba, only 43 (30%) broke up to settle in different areas. In the remaining cases two or more siblings migrated to the same area. As extreme examples of this tendency, there was one case each of the following: 8, 7 and 6 siblings migrating to the same area.

2 Firth (1964:81) in a recent reference to a study of kinship in London records that 51% of informants kept in touch with kin living in the British Isles but outside London. As we have seen, St. Boniface informants keep in touch with 79% of their relatives living outside Manitoba. The terms "outside London" and "outside Manitoba" are, of course, not strictly comparable and would have to be considered in relation to the distances involved, transport facilities and other forms of communication. But it may be pointed out that, in general, the distances involved on the North American continent are very much greater than in the British Isles. So far as English Canadians are concerned, the essays by Osterreich and by Koch and Bennett in this volume suggest that the difference between English and

do the French Canadians of Western Canada, a high degree of geographical mobility, it is common for a kinsman (other than a priority kinsman) to move away and after two or three years to lose touch completely with the kin whom he has left behind. What, then, are the factors which maintain French Canadian kinship bonds with distant kin, factors which I propose to call "agencies of kinship liaison"?[1] The following seem to be the most significant:

(1) Kinkeepers. Studies of kinship in modern society have revealed the significance of what Raymond Firth calls "pivotal kin" and for which David Schneider employs the term "kinkeepers". The exemplar of such persons is "Aunt Emma who knows all about the family". French Canadians have a special term for them: *défricheurs de la parenté*, which Marcel Rioux (1959) translates "kinship clearer-uppers", that is, people who can clear up knotty problems connected with kinship. I was frequently referred to them for information which my informants could not provide. Moreover, informants frequently took the initiative in consulting them about questions which I had raised. They are usually elderly women and keep up an extensive correspondence with geographically remote kin to whom they provide information about kin in Manitoba in return for news of the migrant and any kin who may be living in his vicinity. Others, particularly younger men and women with business and family responsibilities, are quite content to leave the preservation of genealogical knowledge to them,[2] but there is among some at least a definite feeling that someone should discharge this important function (D.21) to which a considerable amount of prestige attaches.

(2) Certain persons connected with rail and air transport (including the R.C.A.F.) who are able to obtain free travel which enables them to visit distant kin more frequently than would otherwise be possible.

(3) Transport workers whose duties make long journeys a regular necessity, such as members of train crews and long-distance truck drivers, may likewise visit distant kinsfolk.

(4) Employees of inter-provincial and international business and governmental organizations whose work entails much travelling and who may be transferred from one province to another and, in some cases, over the international border.

(5) Nuns, whose vocation may take them from one province to another. Lack of a family life of their own seems to give them a keen interest in their kinsfolk and, though the extent of their visiting is restricted, they frequently make contact with relatives in their new area and send home news of them. The reciprocal process also occurs.

(6) The same is true of priests, who have moreover a greater freedom of social activity.

French Canadians may be exaggerated. But present indications are that the difference exists and is sociologically significant.

1 It is not, of course, denied that similar factors operate in other societies, though probably not to the same extent.

2 Cf. what was said above about the importance of potential knowledge.

(7) Members of the armed services and the R.C.M.P. who may be transferred.

(8) Regular or casual mutual visiting with kinsfolk living in different provinces of Canada and in the U.S.A.

(9) Attendance at ceremonial occasions such as marriages, funerals and wedding anniversaries of older kinsfolk. Funerals are more significant than marriages, for several reasons: they entail no invitations or financial outlay for presents; at marriages there is always the potentiality, and sometimes the reality, of tensions of various kinds which do not occur to the same extent in connection with deaths; at weddings there is a gathering of two distinct groups of kinsfolk, many of whom may be unrelated or even unknown to each other; whereas at funerals most of those attending are related to the deceased and therefore to each other; they are united by their common grief, and kinship bonds which might otherwise atrophy are renewed and strengthened.

Wedding anniversaries, particularly golden weddings, are very important functions, usually involving the celebration of Mass in the local church. They are an occasion for the assembling of kin, some of whom travel considerable distances to attend. It is not unusual on such occasions for the celebrants to be presented with a partial genealogy showing the names of all their children, grandchildren and great grandchildren, if any, sometimes accompanied by photographs.

(10) St. Boniface possesses a large and well-equipped hospital to which seriously-ill French Canadians are brought from other parts of Manitoba and even further afield. Visits to such individuals by their kinsfolk are an occasion for renewing kinship ties with other relatives living in St. Boniface.

(11) Documentary material. Reference has been made to genealogies prepared for wedding anniversaries and I have referred (1961:18) to *La Liberté et Le Patriote*, cuttings from which referring to family events are often kept for many years. The same is true of invitations to marriages or wedding anniversaries, cards of sympathy and the like.

(12) Slides and colour films have largely, though not entirely, taken the place of the family album as a pictorial record of family doings, and have the advantage that they can be easily transported from one place to another.

(13) The prevalence of intermarriage between kin (particularly those in which siblings marry siblings) will be discussed later. But it should be mentioned here that it serves to reinforce kinship bonds between geographically remote kin.

Some comments may be offered on the above agencies of kinship liaison. In the first place, it will have been noticed that many visits to distant places where kinsfolk reside are made for purposes extraneous to the maintenance of kinship bonds. This applies both to occupational duties and to pleasure. Both Canada and the U.S.A. possess many centres of tourist attraction and a desire to visit these is often an important, or even the most important, factor leading to travel. Similarly, many Manitoban French Canadians, particularly those in poor health, go south either temporarily or permanently to escape the rigours of the Canadian winter. But travel of this kind is almost always an occasion for visiting kinsfolk; informants usually expressed regret when they had failed in this regard, producing various explanations of their defection.

Another feature of visiting is that it serves to maintain contact not only between the individuals or families directly involved, but also between other kin and those in the area visited. Much time is spent discussing kinsfolk and the returning traveller brings home news of the people he has visited, which may form the basis of future visits of others to kin with whom they might otherwise have lost touch. This kind of *indirect contact* is very important, almost as much so as direct contact by correspondence.

Another factor is the size of the sibling group, which is a marked feature of French Canadian kinship. If a person has a large sibling group and his parents and cousins are members of similar groups, the chances are high that one of the individuals will sooner or later visit more remote parts of Canada and the U.S.A. and so establish the kind of indirect contact mentioned in the previous paragraph.

4. Intermarriages of Kin

In St. Boniface, as in St. Jean-Baptiste (Piddington 1961:10–12), marriages between persons who are already related to each other are common, the most frequent example being cases where two (or even three) siblings marry two (or three) individuals from another sibling group, cases where two brothers marry two sisters[1] and sister exchange[2]. The figures for the last two types of marriage for the two studies are as follows:

	Cousin frérot marriages	*Sister exchange*
St. Jean-Baptiste:	71	14
St. Boniface:	16	9
Total:	87	23

One factor affecting the frequency of such marriages is the familial and kinship-oriented pattern of French Canadian visiting and conviviality. Thus siblings tend to visit and attend parties together and thus meet another sibling group under conditions favourable to flirtations leading to courtship (cf. Miner, 1939:72).

1 The French Canadians have a special term for the children of such unions: *cousin frérot*, which might be translated "brotherly cousins". They are said to be "rather more than cousins" because they are related through both their fathers and their mothers. I shall use the French term as a convenient abbreviation for marriages of this type, although of course it is the marriages of the parents and not of the cousins themselves which are concerned.

2 Sometimes there is a double wedding; sometimes a period of time elapses between the two marriages.

We may ask why *cousin frérot* marriages are almost four times as frequent as sister exchange. According to M. Jean Lagassé (personal communication) this arises from the essentially practical French Canadian attitude towards marriage. Romantic love is emphatically not absent, but *l'amour* tends to be thought of in terms of such qualities as a sense of responsibility, potentialities as a good mother and the observation of familial obligations generally (Garigue, 1962:87–88). Ability to get on with in-laws is also important.

A young single man, whose role it is to take the initiative in courtship, will be inclined to favour a girl whose sister's suitability has already been presumed or proved by his brother's betrothal or marriage. She "comes from a good stable" and will probably prove to possess the qualities desirable in a wife.

Three of my informants suggested other possible factors which may operate in addition to those stressed by Lagassé. They are not inconsistent with them:

(1) Among young French Canadians there is a measure of segregation between the sexes in economic and recreational life. Thus two brothers may meet a third man in a billiard saloon and subsequently be invited to his house where they meet his two sisters whom they subsequently marry. Their sisters, not acquainted with the host, would probably not be invited. The same sort of thing happens when two sisters meet another girl at work or in a sports team, with parallel results.

(2) Two brothers having met two sisters will discuss them and their families so as to assess the qualities and circumstances likely to make for successful marriage, finally reaching a favourable conclusion. Two sisters may likewise discuss matrimonial possibilities. A man would not similarly discuss his matrimonial inclinations with his sister, and *vice versa*.

(3) A brother, particularly an elder brother, adopts a protective attitude towards his sister and keeps a wary eye on her relations with the opposite sex. Such vigilant supervision may have a dampening effect on courtship activities. A man would not be similarly concerned with the romantic interests of his brother.

The bearing of marriages between pairs of siblings on kinship relations lies in the fact that in *cousin frérot* marriage a man is related to his wife's kin not only by the affinal link but by consanguineous and affinal ones through his brother. This makes for wider kinship awareness and a double interest in affinal kinship bonds.[1]

As regards migration, inter-marriages between pairs of siblings and other intermarriages between kin make for the survival of kinship relations in cases where one couple moves to another part of North America (D.48,49,50).

5. Conclusions

It may be concluded that kinship bonds are an important factor in maintaining the identity of French Canadian society outside Quebec, which is the

1 Another term for *cousin frérot* is *cousin double*. (Garigue, personal communication).

only part of North America where French Canadians are in a majority. Some contact is maintained with migrant kin in the vast majority of cases, at least in the case of the generation of the migrant. His or her descendants, however, tend to be swallowed up into the overwhelming English-speaking majority.[1] But the widely dispersed French Canadian population is constantly being renewed by fresh migrations of individuals very often related to those who have already migrated.

How this operates is well illustrated by the French Canadian community in Los Angeles. When extensive migration to California took place in the twenties, various French Canadian clubs were formed (D.52). One of these, *Le Cercle Canadien Français de Los Angeles* is still active, but its membership is no larger than when it was first formed about 1939. This fact is extremely significant. As succeeding generations of French Canadians have been swallowed up in the sprawling collection of cities known as Los Angeles, the membership of the club has been reinforced by successive new immigrants. It would be interesting to know whether this sort of thing occurs in other colonies of French Canadians in the U.S.A.[2] But the Los Angeles case illustrates a general principle – that the loss of French Canadian individuals into the wider society of North America does not necessarily mean that the survival of French Canadian society outside Quebec is doomed (cf. Piddington, 1961:21). As stated at the beginning of this section, the network of kinship relations described in this article contributes largely to the goal so dear to the hearts of French Canadians, a goal for which they have struggled for over two centuries – *la survivance.*

---

1 As we have seen, the same thing tends to happen in cases of inter-ethnic marriages.

2 It is apparently not the case in the New England community studied by Theriault (1960). But there are indications that the spirit of French Canadian identity is by no means moribund in New England. For example: "The comment that you make about the degree of organization of French Canadians in the U.S.A. and particularly in New England might be related to the recent extension of "Le Club Richelieu" to a number of centres in New England.

Le Club Richelieu is a French-speaking service club. Until three or four years ago, it had locals only in the Province of Quebec. In the last years, however, there has been an extension drive and a few locals were established outside Quebec, in the Maritimes and Ontario mainly, but also in Maine, New Hampshire and Massachusetts.

Le Club Richelieu informs me that they have locals quite active at the following centres:

Boston	Manchester
Fall River	New Bedford
Hartford	Lowell
Hollyoke	Nashua
Lewiston	Wolleston

These centres are all in the New England States of Maine, Massachusetts, Vermont and New Hampshire. A number of other locals are presently being organized. In view of the fact that the main business language of the Richelieu Club is French, their establishment in the New England States is an illustration of the vitality of the French Culture in those areas." (Jean Lagassé, personal communication).

PART II

Documentation and Supplementary Notes

Most of the following material consists of statements by informants. Unless otherwise stated, all statements were recorded in St. Boniface with the exception of one informant who lives in Winnipeg. Though the statements represent the sense of what informants told me, they are not recorded *verbatim*. For one thing, I have adopted the anthropological convention of recording relationships in descriptive terms, e.g. by using the term M.B.So. when the informant actually spoke of "my cousin" or mentioned the kinsman by name. Again, I have used certain technical terms (such as "sibling group") instead of "brothers and sisters".

1. General

There is a considerable amount of individual variation in the interest which French Canadians take in their kinsfolk and their attitude towards kinship in general. Women are more interested and better informed than men, having more time for visiting, correspondence, telephoning and otherwise keeping in touch with their kin. For example:

D.1. "We are a very closely knit family – very clannish".

D.2. "I have practically no contact with him – he is not the visiting type."

D.3. "My business contacts with kinsfolk do not affect the frequency of social contacts, which is based on personal preference."

D.4. "We have so many relatives in and near St. Boniface that we just would not have time to visit them all regularly."

D.5. "My mother's brother Maurice lives in St. Boniface but I only see him because he was a class-mate of my husband at the University."

D.6. A young professional man asked me whether I thought kinship was weaker among men in the professions than among others. I said my preliminary impression was that this was the case, because the bond set up between University class-mates to some extent minimises kinship relations in later life. "Yes, that is my experience. When I took my degree at the University of Montreal there were only three of us from Western Canada. This created a bond between us so that to-day they mean more to me than many of my kinsfolk." Another young professional man, speaking of a relative: "I have only seen him once in recent years and that was because we had been at the University at the same time. We met at a reunion of graduates."

Even when informants, at the initial interview, disclaimed interest in their kinsfolk, their statements sometimes proved to be not in accord with the facts. Thus:

D.7. "I know verry little about my kinsfolk and am not very much interested in them."

When I subsequently checked this statement against the genealogy I collected from this informant and his wife I found that I had recorded 205 named kin (compared with the mean of 142 for all the genealogies) and a contact rating (Part I, Section 2) of 2.66, only slightly below the general mean of 2.59. Moreover during the interviews I had with him and his wife he showed keen interest in the discussions and even appeared to become slightly annoyed with his wife when they disagreed on some point connected with the genealogy.

Again, the young wife of a professional man (herself a graduate) talked at length about kinship at an early interview:

D.8. "I sometimes think that French Canadians pay too much attention to kinship. If you see two people reading in *La Liberté et Le Patriote* that somebody has made a speech, they immediately start talking about the speaker's kinship relations to them or to people whom they know. They become so involved in this discussion that they never bother to read the speech. I think friends are more important than kinsfolk because you can choose them freely without feeling any obligation to associate with them. I know kinsfolk can be helpful. When I was in Montreal as a rather impoverished student, two of my kinsfolk helped me in a practical way with free accommodation and free professional services. Of course I was grateful and I always go to see them when I am in Montreal. But I don't like being under an obligation to people, and on the whole I don't think kinsfolk are very important to me."

The same informant, after a series of interviews which included a detailed enquiry into her actual relations with kinsfolk:

D.9. "You remember I told you I thought kinship was not important. Well, the talks we have had have shown me just how important kinship is." (cf. the statement in D.35 by the same informant.)

2. A Note on Surnames

A study of French Canadian surnames would prove interesting, both sociologically and linguistically. The large number of people having identical surnames is not surprising in view of the fact that the original immigrants who came to New France did not number more than 10,000 at the outside. After the conquest, immigration dropped to a trickle and the only other source of new surnames has been from Canadians of other ethnic groups who have been absorbed into the French Canadian population. Thus one of my informants told of a relative in Quebec whose name is "Campbell". He speaks no English and pronounces his name "Cambelle". But in spite of such cases it remains true that a small number of surnames are distributed widely among the population. Thus in Quebec there are gatherings of people descended from immigrants from whom they derive their surnames. Garigue (1962:26) mentions one such gathering of more than 7,000 people named Poulin and states that a number (*plusiers dizaines*) of such gatherings are advertised in Quebec newspapers every year.

Naturally this duplication of surnames is apt to lead to confusion, particularly in small nucleated settlements such as St. Denis de Kamouraska. Miner (1939:74–75) describes some of the means by which confusions may be avoided as follows:

"Some cases in point will clarify this function of names. The *curé* of the parish is called "Lallemand", the apostrophe having been dropped after the initial *L* and the article joined to the noun. The *curé* is, in fact, of German extraction; and his German surname of Fieber is still known by himself and a few of the more sophisticated parishioners, such as the local senator. Other parishioners remember having heard the name mentioned but cannot recall it. The phonemes being new and strange, the name was hard to use; and so he was called "The German" instead. To-day he signs himself with this name that society gave him. Another name of the same type is "Langlais", which has very wide distribution. In another case a German named Franck settled in the parish with his family. Fully acculturated to-day, his descendants are still called by that name, as it had a phonetic counterpart in French.

There is another type of name change even more general and pertinent to this discussion. To take three local cases: there are families called Roy and other Desjardins, whose ancestors were called Roy *dit* Desjardins; the man who opened land for the Raymond family was named Phaucas *dit* Raymond; and the family of Beaulieu is related to Hudon through generations called Hudon *dit* Beaulieu. The origins of the secondary names are largely lost. The most logical supposition is that the secondary names are added by people trying to distinguish between persons of the same name. The majority of this type of name is descriptive, like Beaulieu; and even the linking word *dit* indicates that the secondary names arise popularly. To-day in this and in surrounding parishes none of the double names is in use. However, everyone knows the history of the cases cited above.

There is another system for differentiating between persons with the same Christian and surnames; it is to state, in addition, the name of the father of each man. Two men named Paul Garon would thus be called Paul à Joseph and Paul à Baptiste, identifying them through their immediate families. This form is usually used only when the listener requests clarification."

The situation in regard to surnames in Quebec is reproduced in microcosm in Manitoba. Its French Canadian population is largely descended from a relatively small number of original immigrants who migrated westward after the downfall of the Riel administration in 1870; so one finds, as one collects genealogies, a frequent recurrence of surnames. Thus:

D.10. Statement by a lady who had recently moved from St. Jean-Baptiste to St. Boniface: "When I go to Mass at the Cathedral I see people with the same names as those I knew in St. Jean-Baptiste – the Ayottes, the Marions, the Fillions, the Desaulniers. It is just like being back in St. Jean-Baptiste."

As regards the avoidance of confusion, I did not record any of the usages described by Miner. I may have failed to discover them, or they may have existed at an earlier period. But I did record one device, which consists of changing the spelling of a name when the change does not affect the pronunciation – for example, Comeault and Comeau. Thus I received the following statement from an informant whose name is Dureault:

D.11. "The Saskatchewan branch of my family have dropped the final "-lt" in our name. This sometimes happens when the occurrence of a large group of brothers may lead to confusion among them and their offspring. Another example is the Dandenau(lt) family. A further instance of changing spelling of names (without altering pronunciation) occurred in the case of my M.B.W.F., *Omer Syrenne* who had a brother *Oscar* who worked in the same business. Endless confusion resulted over letters and cheques addressed "O. Syrenne". So *Oscar* changed the spelling of his name to Cyrenne."

3. Inter-ethnic Marriages

Reference had been made in Part I to the way in which linguistic and religious circumstances arising from inter-ethnic marriages may alienate French Canadians from their ethnic group. This is illustrated by the following:

D.12. "My uncle Omer bought a hotel in Ontario, married an Irish girl and brought up his children there. They speak no French, and three of them married Protestants. In two cases the spouses turned Catholic but in the third the husband refused and later brought up the children as Protestants. My uncle was so angry that he refused to come to the church to give the bride away. These cousins have difficulty in visiting in Manitoba where some of their older relatives speak little or no English. And their children object to such visits because they cannot understand what is being said."

But this does not always occur. Sometimes the alien spouse is absorbed into the French Canadian community. Thus the following statement by a young lady living in Winnipeg:

D.13. "My M.F. fought in the American Civil War – his F. had emigrated from Ireland. He became a captain on a boat on the Red River and later a merchant in Winnipeg. My mother married a French Canadian."

It may be added that this lady and her mother (née Flannigan) speak both English and French fluently and take an active part in French Canadian social life.

4. Dimensions of Kinship Awareness

The information which any individual possesses about the names of his kinsfolk is distributed over two dimensions – the *vertical* and the *lateral*. The former comprises the names of ancestors and their collaterals, sometimes traced back over many generations; the latter is concerned with contemporary or near-contemporary kin, the living and the recently dead. Either or both of these dimensions may be regarded as important, but in different ways. In societies of the stratified type the vertical dimension is important as validating claims to status, titles and inheritance. The lateral dimension, on the other hand, reflects the importance of interpersonal relations between living kin with all the prestations which these involve.

This distinction is important for the study of French Canadian kinship. Thus Marcel Rioux (1959) questions the suggestion of Garigue (1958:63–76) that cultural factors, rather than the phenomenon of urbanization, determine changes taking place in French Canadian kinship structures. With this issue as such we are not here concerned. What is interesting is the nature of the evidence cited by Rioux. This evidence comes from Chéticamp, a remote rural community of about 600 Acadians in one of the Maritime Provinces. Practically all of them are descended from fourteen men who settled in the vicinity towards the end of the eighteenth century, and to whom they can trace their genealogies, which record the names of from 500 to 2,000 individuals – far higher than anything found by Garigue in Montreal.

There is a keen demand for the services of *défricheurs de parenté*, largely in connection with the propriety of projected marriages,[1] that is in the lateral dimension, marriage being one of the relationships which may be allowed or prohibited between kin, subject to special dispensations by the Church. But it appears that the people of Chéticamp (or at least *défricheurs de la parenté*) take pride in their descent from the fourteen original settlers and in their knowledge of the genealogical lines through which this may be traced. In this respect they resemble English people whose ancestors came over with William the Conqueror or Americans descended from the millions of gallant souls who sailed on the Mayflower. It follows that Rioux's genealogies, sometimes spanning eight generations, include many names of people long since dead, with whom no living member of the community has had face to face relations. His quantitative data are therefore not comparable with those of Garigue, in which the lateral dimension, involving actual prestations as against sentimental interest and family pride, is all important.

What is the situation in Manitoba? Very much like what Garigue describes for Montreal, though for somewhat different reasons. The westward migration to the Red River after 1870 brought settlers from whom most Manitoban French Canadians are descended. This involved a severance of kinship relations with Quebec. Thus:

D.14. "My grandfather came here in the eighties with ten children and eight dollars. Travelling was expensive in those days, and we lost touch with people back in Quebec."

This explains why hardly any informants could name any of their great grandparents and none could name more than one or two.

---

1 The complexity of the problems involved here is well illustrated by the following case: "A man married for the third time a woman who had been married herself four times. As the two wedded had had children by every one of their respective marriages and as the woman was known to have had children during her periods of widowhood, the problem of the genealogy and kinship of all these individuals presented a puzzle that only a specialist could disentangle". (Rioux, 1959:9).

As regards the vertical dimension, there is a genealogical institute in Montreal which will trace the genealogies of French Canadians back to New France and even to metropolitan France. Only two of my informants had availed themselves of its services, though several of them could have afforded the substantial fee involved.

5. Migration and the Agencies of Kinship Liaison

The following information was obtained from a lady aged about 90 living in Los Angeles and her daughter. It illustrates the extent of migration in many French Canadian families. For the sake of convenience I have recorded kinsfolk as relatives of the mother as ego. Some of the information (referring to the family of D.H.) was sent to me by letter after I had left Los Angeles, so I was unable to enquire into the frequency of contacts for this section of the genealogy. The genealogy records 237 named kin. The following material shows a high degree of geographical mobility. All the individuals mentioned are French Canadians unless otherwise stated.

D.15. "My F. was born in Quebec and emigrated to Alberta where he married my mother who had also come from Quebec. They moved to Manitoba and then to Los Angeles. One of my daughters who was raised here speaks no French. Most of my m. siblings remained in Quebec. My M.B.So. once came from Montreal to visit us in Los Angeles. My m.b.so.w. (a widow) lives in Alberta and visits Los Angeles frequently. All my m.sis. children were born in Quebec and emigrated to Alberta. A m.sis.so.d. married a man from Montreal where she lives. She visited Los Angeles about 20 years ago.

All my F. siblings remained in Quebec except one f.sis. who moved to Ontario – I had an Easter card from her the other day.

One of my sis. remained in Alberta where her children were born. But one of her d. came to Los Angeles where she married and remained for a time. She returned to Alberta after the birth of her two children.

Another of my sis. also remained in Alberta where her three children were born. But these all moved to the region of Los Angeles where they are now living.

One of my d. (a widow) born in Alberta married in Los Angeles a man who had been born in Wisconsin. Another of my d. who had been born in Manitoba married an American and moved to Arizona. Still another d. married a man from Quebec and moved to Los Angeles.

I have some information about my D.H. family. My D.H.F.F. lived in Quebec where his children were born. My D.H.F. moved to Manitoba, where he married, and later moved to North Dakota and then to Wisconsin. Some of his children were born in Manitoba, some in North Dakota and some in Wisconsin. Of the first of these one D.H.B. married an American from Montana. Another D.H.B. married a girl with an Irish name who had been born in London, England. They moved to Montana, where he died. A D.H.B. born in North Dakota married an American girl. They are now living in Minnesota. An unmarried d.h.sis., born in North Dakota, moved to Los Angeles, where she died. Of the D.H. siblings born in Wisconsin, an unmarried d.h.sis came to Los Angeles and died here. Another d.h.sis married a man from Montana and also died here. Another also came to Los Angeles where she married an American. Another married an American from Montana and moved there. Another came to Los Angeles and married an American."

Kinship relations between people who have been separated by migration do not usually atrophy though they may become latent. For example:

D.16. "I have a cousin in Quebec who comes to Manitoba every four or five years, not to see us but to visit his brothers. However, they try to arrange some sort of social contact for us. I have two cousins in Florida. We had been neighbours in St. Jean-Baptiste. They visit Manitoba every four or five years and always visit us."

D.17. "I have no regular contacts with her, but relations are easily renewed. For example when we meet at a wedding we kiss each other and feel we have been close all our lives. We take up where we left off."

D.18. "I have not seen anything of them for many years but I feel I could always visit them and be welcome." (cf. D.33).

Family gatherings at Christmas and New Year are an important mechanism whereby kinship relationships are kept alive. They are usually held at the home or homes of the oldest surviving members of a kinship group. Married couples often alternate by spending Christmas with the parents or grandparents of one spouse and New Year with those of the other. The intervening week is spent in visiting any close kin who may live in the vicinity (D.42).

Another important activity at this time is the sending of Christmas cards. I asked a number of my informants to give (a) the total number of Christmas cards they despatched each year and (b) how many of these were sent to relatives as distinct from friends and business associates. The mean proportion sent to relatives was 38.5% of the total. There was considerable variation in the proportions among different informants. Two of them, who sent relatively few cards to relatives, made the following statements:

D.19. "We send no cards to our close relatives. We send them presents. Christmas cards are for friends and distant relatives."

D.20. "No, we don't send them cards at Christmas, but we always try to visit them or at least telephone."

The following statements give a more concrete picture of the agencies of kinship liaison described in Part I:

D.21. "We often hear about her from mother. When mother dies, we shall have to start writing."

D.22. "My sis. Cecile is the letter writer of the family, but we take it in terns writing to m. We 'phone around the sibling group first to make sure m. gets all the news."

D.23. "I get news of my relatives in Montreal from my brother. He is employed by Canadian National Railways. He has a free pass and therefore often visits them in Montreal."

D.24. "My sis. is married to a technician in the R.C.A.F., stationed in Alberta. I spent two months staying with her there last year. She came here at Christmas and Easter on an R.C.A.F. plane."

D.25. "The families of my F. and of his sis. were children together in Manitoba. The Sis. H. migrated to Trois Rivières (Quebec) where he became manager of a timber mill, while his children were still young – they all married there.

Frequent contacts have been maintained between the families. The daughter of another of my F.B. (St. Boniface) married a man who is connected with a commercial air line. He is able to obtain concessions which enable him and his w. to pay frequent visits to Trois Rivières. The wife also keeps up regular correspondence with her relatives there. My f.sis.d. visited St. Boniface last year with her family and keeps up correspondence and my sis. here. She also writes to my f.sis. who is a nun at St. Boniface.

My F.Sis.So. came from Trois Rivières with his wife to spend his summer holiday at St. Boniface last year. His sis. came here to spend Christmas last year together with my F.B.So. who had been living at Trois Rivières for two years. Another F.B.So. also spent some time at Trois Rivières, where he worked in his F.Sis.H. timber mill. He returned to Manitoba and is now living at Brandon."

D.26. "I always visit kin on business trips when I can. I always call on my relatives in Brandon and on my wife's relatives in Detroit. I used to visit my wife's sister in Montreal – she is now in California. But I only visit fairly close kin. My mother does more visiting of distant kin, but her time is free, whereas I am limited by my business. For similar reasons she stays with relatives, whereas I stay at hotels."

D.27. "A distant cousin of mine in Quebec is Manager of a paper factory. He often passes through Winnipeg and always visits us, or at least 'phones from the airport between flights."

D.28. "My f.m.sis., a nun, founded convents at Key West and in California. I used to receive little gifts from her till I was about five, when she died. When my parents honeymooned in California they visited her. She had no previously met my F. but I'm sure there had been some correspondence in the family.

My f.sis entered a convent in Montreal. She taught in academies in Winnipeg and St. Boniface. She became Superior of a convent in Ontario and later Mistress of Novices at Oakland, Oregon. She wrote to all members of the family, including me and my cousins. She is in touch with my F.B. (a retired priest) who lives on the Richlieu River, Quebec. A priest, my F.B.So., is in Montreal. He writes here regularly, particularly to his adoptive brother, who is a priest in St. Boniface. He visits his f.b.d.d. once in a while. He is in touch with his m. side of the family who live on the Saguenay River, Quebec. I have visited his m.sis. at the Saguenay and she has visited us at Winnipeg."

D.29. "Two of my cousins are nuns who live in Manitoba. They visit British Columbia every year on leave and bring back news of my cousins there. When one of these relatives had a serious accident they telephoned us at once."

D.30. "My m.sis.d. now lives in another part of Manitoba – she always has a lot of news. She raised the family after her m. died and then became a nun. I suppose the fact that nuns are cut off from the world gives them an interest in family news; also they have plenty of time to write, whereas we are caught up with practical affairs and family responsibilities."

D.31. "My F. had a m.sis. who was a nun in Montreal. My f.m. and the nun kept up correspondence. When f.m. died, F. and his two sis. kept up correspondence with the nun. In this way the nun kept my family in Manitoba abreast of news of their cousins in Montreal and *vice versa*."

D.32. "My cousin Joseph is a priest who studied for several years at a seminary in Quebec. While there he used to visit the family of my uncle (not his own father). When he used to come back on holiday he brought news of them."

D.33. "Members of families drift apart and sometimes come together again. My Sis.H. had a sister in Ireland who married an English civil engineer. They emigrated to Nairobi, and he lost touch with them. Two French Canadian Missionary priests from Kenya were visiting Winnipeg and met my Sis.H. They promised to try to locate his sis., which they did. His d. Patricia on a world tour visited Nairobi and stayed for some time with her aunt."

D.34. "My F.Sis.So. is in the R.C.M.P. and came here last year for the Musical Ride. He brought his family with him and I met them again." (Note: The Musical Ride is an impressive spectacle presented by the R.C.M.P.).

D.35. "We are the only people to have a holiday cottage at the lakes, so our kinsfolk come and visit us there every summer. One day this year we had twenty-three relatives for two meals. I had got in provisions for them and they also brought food with them. On the last day there was so much food left over that I held a sort of "auction" – no money involved of course, but I would hold up a ham and say: "Who wants this?"

D.36. "If any of our family from St. Boniface visit Detroit my sister there 'phones my cousin and they all get together."

D.37. From a lady living in Los Angeles: "My H. and I were born in Alberta where we knew one another. We came independently to Los Angeles about 40 years ago and were married here. Since then my H. has paid seven visits to Alberta, where he has 145 nephews and nieces."

When later I was collecting the names of these individuals from ego and her H. the latter remarked:

"I can't tell you the names of all of them – but I will be able to do so when I have met them all this summer."

D.38. "I am afraid that T.V. may have affected these parties." Q: How has it affected your relations with kinsfolk? "When we left St. Boniface for Saskatchewan, T.V. was just beginning. For the first year it was a novelty and did affect visiting. But now we take it for granted. I receive just as many visits as formerly, and although I watch T.V. when I am alone in the house, I would not dream of letting it interfere with visits to kinsfolk."

D.39. "My F.B.So. in North Dakota comes to St. Boniface about once a year for weddings – he has many relatives here."

D.40. "We see more kinsfolk at funerals than at weddings because the latter require invitations. Sometimes kin (not close) say they are only sent invitations to get a present from them."

D.41. "When I was a teenager at St. Malo we used to have wonderful parties. Kinsfolk would take turns at giving parties – we would often spend the night with our hosts. At Xmas all kinsfolk would assemble at my F. house where F.F. was living."

D.42. "While we were living in Saskatchewan I always came home (a 14 hour drive) to visit my parents who live near to those of my wife. One year I came ten or eleven times. We always came at Christmas and New Year, spending Christmas with my wife's people and New Year with mine, or *vice versa*. Between the two I spent time having meals with all of my sisters – they would have been annoyed if I had not. By the time New Year's Day came I felt I never wanted to see roast turkey again."

D.43. "After midnight Mass we go to the home of my wife's people for a party; there is much gaiety, but no present giving. New Year is more important. We take the noon meal with my wife's family then move to my parents' family. Only members of the families and their spouses attend, e.g. in visiting my family my wife's siblings would not attend unless they happened to be married to one of my siblings, in which case they would attend in their capacity of spouses."

Q. What if parents live in different places? "My sister Anita lives in Somerset, where her husband's parents lived. Her H.F. is now dead and it is a small family, so gatherings are not held there. One way of getting round the difficulty is to spend Xmas with one spouse's parents and New Year with the other's."

D.44. "I saw my f.b.d., who lives in Saskatchewan, about a month ago when her F. was ill in St. Boniface Hospital."

D.45. "When my uncle Edouard came from Quebec for a visit he brought slides and told us news of his family. In the same way, our relatives from British Columbia always bring slides and movies when they come to visit us."

D.46. "He went to a wedding anniversary celebration at which twenty of my side of the family were present and made a film of the proceedings. He afterwards showed it to other relatives who had not been there."

D.47. "My F.Sis.So. was overseas during the war, married an Irish girl and settled in England. Their daughter returned to Canada and lives in Montreal. I always visit her when I am there. Her parents sent us a film taken at the time of their wedding."

D.48. "I saw him last spring on a visit to Toronto. He married my wife's sister, so we correspond frequently."

D.49. "We keep up some correspondence. She visited here three years ago and I visited her in Alberta last year. Her husband is a cousin of my wife's father."

D.50. "My F.B.So. and his wife, who is my H.Sis., live in a different part of Manitoba but we exchange visits about once a month."

6. Kinship and La Survivance

It will have become clear that kinship is an important integrative factor not only in small French Canadian communities but over the whole of Canada and parts of the U.S.A. How effective will kinship and other features of French Canadian culture be in counteracting the disruptive influences which are at work outside Quebec? Both Stanley (1960) and Theriault (1960) are cautious in their predictions for Western Canada and New England respectively. But apart from the official mass media which lead the struggle for *la survivance*, many individual French Canadians are enthusiastically interested in the goal and are prepared to make sacrifices to achieve it. The following statement by a young professional man is typical:

D.51. "It is important that French Canadians should stick together and bring up their children as French Canadians. That is why I am here in St. Boniface. I have had opportunities for professional advancement in other communities, and the first question I have always asked is 'Is there a French school?' When the answer was 'no' I refused to take the opportunity."

In considering the losses of French Canadian individuals into the wider society of North America, it must be remembered that such losses are constantly being made good by the "recruitment" of new individuals. How this may happen in an environment thoroughly inimical to *la survivance* is illustrated by some material I collected in Los Angeles from an informant who had made a special study of French Canadians in that area:

D.52. "My father was an Acadian born in Maine. He went to Quebec, where he married, and subsequently moved to Alberta. I came to Los Angeles in 1929.

Early this century an attempt was made to establish on Figueroa Street a parish with a French Canadian priest. But he was transferred elsewhere and the parish ceased to be French Canadian. Now we attend a number of churches where English is used.

In 1919 Albert Lemieux, an immigrant from Massachusetts, formed *Le cercle Canadien Français de Long Beach*. About 1922 some French Canadians from Montreal formed the first *Cercle Canadian Français de Los Angeles*. A year or two later, Lemieux and some new immigrants from Massachusetts formed *Le Cercle Frontenac*. This killed the first *Cercle Canadien de Los Angeles*, many of whose members joined the new club.

In 1924 a group of women formed *Le Cercle Jeanne d'Arc*. Men used to bring their wives to meetings in cars and play poker in an anteroom during the proceedings. The women did not like this and admitted the men as associate members so that they could attend meetings instead of playing poker. About 1939 men were admitted to full membership and the name of the organisation was changed to *Le Cercle Canadien Français de Los Angeles*, which is still in existence. Attendance at meetings at first was from 100 to 150 and about 450 on special occasions – New Year's eve and 24th June (the fête of St. Jean-Baptiste). Attendance is about the same to-day. Recent immigrants from Canada since the war have shown less interest in the club. French Canadians who come here stay French for a generation and then lose touch with other French Canadians, though they stay Catholic." (Cf. Theriault, 1960).

BIBLIOGRAPHY

Firth, R., 1964, "Family and Kinship in Industrial Society", *The Sociological Review Monograph No. 8*, University of Keele.
Garigue, P., 1958, *Études sur le Canada-Français*. Montreal, Faculté des Science Sociales, economiques et politiques, Université de Montréal.
—, 1962, *La Vie Familiale des Canadiens Français*. Montreal and Paris, Presses de l'Université de Montréal and Presses Universitaires de France.
—, 1963, *L'option Politique du Canada Français*, Montreal. Les Éditions du Léverier.
Miner, H., 1939, *St. Denis: A French-Canadian Parish*. Chicago. Univ. of Chicago Press.
Piddington, R., 1961, "A Study of French Canadian Kinship". *International Journal of Comparative Sociology*, Vol. I, No. 1, pp. 3–22.
Rioux, M., 1959, *Kinship Recognition and Urbanization in French Canada*. National Museum of Canada, Bulletin No. 173.
Stanley, G. F. G., 1960, "French & English in Western Canada", in Wade 1960, pp. 311–350.
Stanner, W. E. H., 1934, "Ceremonial Economics of the Mulluk and Madngella Tribes of the Daly River", *Oceania*, Vol. IV, 156 and 458.
Theriault, G. F., 1960, "The Franco-Americans of New England", in Wade 1960, pp. 392–415.
Wade, M. (Ed.), 1960, *Canadian Dualism*, Toronto, University of Toronto Press.

Kinship and geographical mobility in Burundi (East Central Africa)

ALBERT TROUWBORST

University of Nijmegen, Nijmegen Holland

THE purpose of this essay is to describe how geographical mobility in Burundi was related to certain characteristics of the kinship structure in this country.[1] Before going into the subject itself, I will give a brief description of the local kin group, the most important kin group in Burundi, and the relations of its members to other groups and categories of kin, as well as to neighbours and friends. In another section the extent and the nature of geographical mobility of Rundi society will be discussed.

Some of the aspects of the problem in question have already been described in a former article[2]. The material presented therein will partly be reproduced here. Certain details, in particular the case histories, have been omitted however.

Throughout the article the past tense has been used, but that is not meant to imply that all the situations referred to do not exist any more. Though much has changed in Burundi since the arrival of the Germans and later on the Belgians the general pattern of the geographical mobility, its causes and its effects have to a certain extent remained the same. I did not therefore limit my discussion to either the old or the new systems. I was in that way able to use data, bearing on different times in the history of Burundi from pre-colonial times to 1958 when I visited the country. When necessary, I will indicate the nature of the changes that occured with the lapse of time.

Local Kin Groups

The most important kin groups in Burundi were the local kin groups, composed of the male married members of what might be called small lineages,

1 Field research in Burundi was carried out during the year 1958 with financial support from the Netherlands Organization for the Advancement of Pure Science (Z.W.O.). I want to express my thanks to this Organization as well as to the Institut pour la Recherche Scientifique en Afrique Centrale for its precious aid when I was in the field. In 1958 the now independant Kingdom of Burundi still formed part of Ruanda – Urundi, territory under trusteeship of the United Nations and was administered by the Belgians. Before 1919 Burundi belonged to German East Africa.

2 Trouwborst, A., (1959): La mobilité de l'individu en fonction de l'organisation politique des Barundi. Zaïre, 12, 787–800.

their wives and their unmarried male and female children, living in the same locality. There was no special term in the Rundi language to refer to these groups. Most commonly, people used the term *umuryango*, a term that referred also to the widest groups of patrilineal descendents of a common ancestor, the "clans". The term *umuryango* then was used in a rather loose way, its exact meaning in a concrete case depending on the context. These local kin groups came into being and continued to exist by the widespread custom of patrilocal marriage. Though not all Rundi did marry patrilocally it very seldom happened that not at least one of the sons of a man remained on the lands of his father. As the same was true for the sons of a son etc, many descendants of a single ancestor might live together in the same locality.

There was no formal limit to the extension of the patrilineal core of the local kin groups whose genealogical depth varied considerably from one instance to the other. Sometimes a local kin group was composed of only the members of a nuclear family, at other times a local kin group was so big that the members of its patrilineal core were not able to trace their exact genealogical relations to all other members, though they knew their relative genealogical position. The local kin group and not the clan was the real cooperative unit in Burundi. The members of a clan lived widely dispersed and most of them did not know each other. The members of a local kin group on the other hand regularly helped each other, united in the cult of the ancestors and in other religious ceremonies. They acted as a unit towards the representatives of the government and were collectively responsible in cases of murder in which a member of the group was involved. All members of the group regularly exchanged food, beer and other commodities. They sometimes gave each other cows on the basis of the patron-client relationship.

Economic cooperation outside the nuclear family was not very frequent but not without importance. Members of the local kin group helped each other occasionally with field labour, herded in turns the cattle and constructed together huts and grain bins. The Rundi themselves were very much aware of the advantages of belonging to a local kin group, especially if it was a numerous one. They even had a term for a big family whose members lived in the same locality, i.e. "*igisata*".

The advantage of being a member of such a big family[1] was, as my informants explained me, that when a man quarelled with other people, he could count on the help of many relatives. I once overheard for instance, a man in court complaining of being defenseless against his adversary who was backed by a numerous family.

Most big families Tutsi as well as Hutu exercised some kind of political influence. This was true in 1958 as it was in the past. Families who in 1958 were represented in the bodies of local judges and in administrative councils at different levels, formerly also had occupied official functions.

1 Throughout the text, the term "family" is used as an equivalent for "local kin group", except when the context requires the more precise term.

It should be remarked, however, that a man did not rely exclusively on the members of his local kin group. As to the collective activities, for instance, of which mention has been made, any non-patrilineal relative who lived in the neighbourhood might be called upon for assistance. Preference was even given to the help of a nearby matrilateral or affinal relative rather than to the help of patrilineal relatives living far away.

In all exchanges of food and beer many non-patrilineal relatives were involved. It even happened that a man had more "beerfriends" amongst his matrilateral relatives and his affines than amongst the members of his local kin group. This was true in the case for instance of a man who lived alone without any other patrikin in the neighbourhood.

All kinds of relatives were involved also in relations of patron and client by giving each other cattle and lands, and assisting each other in political affairs. It happened for instance that poor men attached themselves to a wealthy relative, their mother's brother for instance, who gave them lands to live upon and other necessities of life, in exchange of which they worked for him. Non-patrilineal relatives might participate in the informal meetings of the family councils discussing common affairs of its members.

All Rundi, except extremely poor people, had also quite a number of non-related beer friends some of whom were invariably neighbours. From the point of view of the character of the exchange relationship, the mutual rights and obligations towards these friends were the same as towards relatives though they were exercised less regularly and involved lesser amounts of goods. If a brother would contribute for instance beer and food on any occasion, a non related beer friend would contribute on certain occasions only. These exchanges between friends equally implied mutual help and advice. Friends were involved also in all kinds of more or less contractual relationships based on the gift of the lease of land or cattle.

A Rundi then did not need to depend exclusively on his family. As we shall see, it was possible for a Rundi to live without the aid of kin, but it should be added that this was not easy except when he was a wealthy man of high standing and protected by a powerful patron. Otherwise, a man without the backing of relatives would lead a miserable and insecure existence.

Geographical mobility in Burundi

First of all, attention will be paid to permanent migrations, other movements largely being the result of these.

There were quite a lot of reasons why a man might decide to move away from his community. Each of these reasons will be discussed separately though several of them often concurred in a single concrete case.

One of the most important reasons for migration was land shortage. It often happened that a man was not able to settle all his sons on his lands. One or more of them would then be obliged to apply to an official of the government for a place somewhere else. This did not necessarily mean that a son had to move away far from his father. He might remain on the same hill and would in that case be able to maintain intensive contacts with his parents. There seemed to have been however general movements of people away from certain densely populated areas. I do not have statistical material to show the extent of these migrations but I can give some indication of the direction and the nature of them.

One of the regions to which migration took place on an apparently rather big scale was Bunyambo in the south of the country where part of my research took place. It struck me there that most of the people originally came from other parts of Burundi. It might be that this migration has been accelerated in modern times but it is certain that it had started before. People showed me several places occupied some time before the German occupation of Burundi and uninhabited before. I even believe that this migration was in part a policy of the government. It is known that other regions of Burundi were occupied in the same way.[1]

Other reasons that might induce a man to leave his locality were famine or better economic prospects elsewhere. In that case people generally went to relatives faraway, who where in a better position. An important reason for a man to move away from his community presented itself when he was in conflict with his political superiors or his patron. Before leaving he would try to find another chief or patron willing to take him under their protection. As a permanent migration required the permission of the local authorities, such a migration often took the character of a flight, people leaving their place by night.

A man might decide to go away, even when he was not in conflict with his local sub-chief or chief but for instance when he had become the client and protégé of another chief who lured him with all kinds of benefits. These changes of loyalty were evidently not appreciated by a local chief and were often the cause of quarrels between the two chiefs involved.

Such a migration usually was the cause of another one. A chief who invited a man from another chiefdom seldom had available free, immediately cultivable lands and was forced to expel people from allready existing farms. The alternative would have been to give virgin land but such a gift would not have much value. Uncultivated land required long and arduous work before giving any returns. The expulsion of people sometimes was a drastic measure. A wealthy man once proudly told me that 5 people had been removed from the place where he was living now.

People rewarded in this way were not necessarily the subjects of another chief. They might be warriors or servants of the king or their own chief who after

1 In an interesting letter, shown to me by Mr. René Lemarchand of University of Florida, dated of the 20th of February 1946, written by the King of Burundi, Mwami Mwambutsa, to the Resident of Urundi, representing the Belgian administration at that time, restitution is claimed of Bugufi, formerly a province of Burundi, but ceded to Tanganyika Territory in 1923. It is claimed in this letter that Bugufi, sparsely inhabited and covered with forests, was occupied long ago by a Hutu retainer of Mwami Ntare, the King of Burundi. The descendants of this man, composing now the chiefly family of this province, as well as the descendants of numerous other Rundi are still living there. According to the text, it was clearly the intention of King Ntare that Bugufi should be populated by Rundi and conquered as an accretion to his Kingdom.

conclusion of their service received several grants from their lord, amongst others
clusion of their service received several grants from their lord, amongst others land. They might be also newly appointed officials of the territorial administration who generally received farms on their installation.

In general, appointments of all kinds involved quite an amount of moving. New chiefs took up residence in several places and were accompanied by relatives and favorites who had to be installed also. This again implied the expulsion of other people to make place for the newcomers.

Other reasons for migration were the following: Young children mostly accompanied their mother after the latter's divorce or the death of their father. Once adult they could go back to the community of their patrilineal relatives but it happened also that they stayed in the place where they had grown up. Another case was that of a man who went to live on the farm of his father-in-law when the latter did not have any sons.

Another form of permanent migration was the one involving the women who on their marriage went to live with their husbands. Matrilocal marriages being extremely rare, this form of migration involved almost all Rundi women. It should be remarked, however, that princes and other wealthy people formerly had the custom of living for the first year or so on the farm of their father-in-law before installing themselves definitively.

Most women married within a day's walking from their parents' house but not often on the same hill. There were no rules of preference for marriages between certain localities, but in practice many marriages were contracted between people on neighbouring hills.

As to the general pattern of all these permanent migrations, it should be remarked that they were mostly individual affairs. It might happen that some brothers migrated together but this was not done regularly. The picture that arises from an analysis of the geographical mobility in Burundi is that of individuals hiving off from time to time from their families to establish themselves elsewhere in a very independent way. We will return later to the implications of this situation.

However, people who left their families did not entirely cut off their contacts with them. It even happened that they returned after a number of years. A man never lost his rights on the lands from his father, and he could claim part of them on his return. A man continued to have these rights even when his father had died during his absence. These rights were never contested though many conflicts arose concerning the way the redistribution had to take place.

People who had not moved away too far continued to pay frequent visits to their parents at home. A man regularly brought a pot of beer to his father or might come around to chat a little. There were mutual visits on the occasions of birth, marriage, death and on the days of religious ceremonies. There were family assemblies also in the case of quarrels. It might happen for instance that an old and wise member of the family was invited by his relatives living elsewhere to intervene in a conflict.

It is difficult to say what distance constituted a real barrier to the continuance of these contacts. The Rundi are able to walk enormous distances in a short time. The frequency of the contacts diminished, however, the farther relatives lived away. People sometimes told men they had cut the contacts with their family owing to the far distance.

Another element in the situation was the genealogical distance. I would say that people farther than 3 generations removed from a common ancestor and not living in the same locality gradually ceased to have contacts. Contacts would be most frequent when the father of a man was still alive. Later on, with children and grandchildren born in the separated families and the nearest relatives dying, the frequency of the mutual visits diminished. It might be that this happened less soon in the past when the ceremonies of the ancestor cult were one of the most important occasions for members of a family to meet.

Still another factor was the nature of the relations between distant living relatives. Quarrels might lead to an entire cutting off of all contacts.

These three factors, geographical distance, genealogical distance and the nature of the relations between kin determined the frequency, the duration and eventually the end of the links between relatives. Gradually, new entirely independent local kin groups came into being who in due course of time even lost all memories of previous links with the original group.

Whatever may be the case, the migrations of permanent character were at least in the beginning the cause of much travelling. Many visits were paid between relatives not only on the occasion of feasts but also without a special reason. These visits were accompanied by exchanges of food and beer, symbols of good relations between people.

Other trips of short duration were undertaken by the Rundi when they had to accompany the king, the chiefs and other dignitaries. All these officials were by the nature of their office and for reasons of policy frequently obliged to make visits to different parts of their territories, to visit each other, to assist to national festivities etc. They were always followed by a whole train of followers, servants, favorites and clients. Following a chief or a patron was considered a duty, an act of subservience and an expression of loyalty. At the same time it gave prestige to a chief to be followed by many people.

The king and the chiefs received also many visitors from all parts of the country. People went to the courts of the wealthy to pay their respects, to seek justice, to pay their taxes or simply in the hope of obtaining substantial gifts. Many went also to fulfill their duties of forced labour.

The chiefs regularly sent out their messengers, judges, spies and tax collectors on all kinds of missions. The wars in which they were involved equally brought many people far from their homesteads.

It should be understood however that frequent and distant trips in connection with the political life of the country were made by only part of the population. Many simple, poor people only very occasionnally came into contact with the authorities when they paid their taxes or fulfilled their duties of forced labour. The more a man associated with people of high standing the more frequent were the occasions for trips.

A special category of trips of short duration were those made in connexion with the institution of clientship. If a man for instance had the desire to obtain a cow, he had to pay many visits to his prospective patron before he could even get a promise. The cow once obtained, many other regular visits had to be paid to bring beer and food, to work, to announce the birth of a calf etc. Given the fact that many Rundi had more than one patron frequent visits to different places were needed.

Travelling for purely economic purposes was done by small numbers of merchants who sold their own products. I met some of these people, fabricators of small arm rings that were made on the spot in the presence of the buyers.

Formerly, markets did not exist, but in 1958 they had acquired much importance. People visited them to sell the coffee they had cultivated on their plantations to Greek and Indian merchants and to buy all kinds of commodities, foreign made and indigenous. Though there were markets then all over Burundi, visiting them still required a lot of travelling.

I witnessed still another ancient form of geographical mobility in Bunyambo where, as in some other regions of Burundi people drove their cattle each summer to dry season pastures. Only part of the family of the owners accompanied the cattle, women and children staying behind. Different kinds of arrangements were made with the local people part of whom were clients of the Bunyambo cattle owners and in that position had to take charge of the cattle of their patrons.

I do not think that the overall rate of the geographical mobility had changed very much in 1958. Movements, permanent as well as temporary, required for political and administrative reasons certainly had become less frequent. On the other hand, the new administrative organs in part staffed by Belgians employed also Rundi who had to travel in their service and had to live near the administrative centres far from their homes. The missions, a few commercial and industrial enterprises and the existence of the not very numerous urban centres introduced also new types of geographical mobility. Other new factors favouring geographical mobility were the improved roads and new means of transport. All this, however, could only have strengthened the tendencies that existed allready but did not change them fundamentally.

We may conclude, that geographical mobility was a common phenomenon in ancient as well as in modern Burundi, affecting the life of many people. The ways in which these effects were felt in the local communities are analysed in the next section.

The effects of Geographical Mobility on the Local Situation in three Regions

In order to explain the ways in which geographical mobility affected the kinship system some descriptive material will be presented on the local situation in the three regions of Burundi where field research has been done.

In Kirimiro, a densely populated region in the centre of the country, Hutu cultivators constituted by far the major part of the population. On each hill, geographically rather clearly demarcated from other hills, only one or two local kin groups of Tutsi were represented. Part of the hill communities visited formerly belonged to a royal residence.[1]

The core of the population was formed by some old, numerically strong Hutu families long since established in the region. Each member of these families knew very well his relative genealogical position in relation to the other members of his own family though there was uncertainty as to the exact links between members more than 4 or 5 generations removed from a common ancestor.

These families were relatively rich, as appeared from the fact that several of their members possessed some cows, rather an exception for Hutu in this region. They did have also much influence being represented on the bodies of local judges and in former times having occupied offices as collectors of honey, beer and cows, as surveyors of forced labour and as sub-chiefs. These offices were executed mostly in the local royal residence but required occasional trips to the residences of the king at Muramvya, some 30 miles away. All these families had lost some of their members by migration which might be considered as a loss in power. Nevertheless, they had succeeded in maintaining a position of political importance and economic wealth, even in modern times.

Another politically but not numerically important group were some Tutsi families most of whom lived only rather recently in the region. These newcomers, with the exception of their servants and poor relatives who had accompanied them, occupied important functions in the region.

The founders of these Tutsi families had been followers of chiefs and other administrative officers under whose protection they had entered the region. The genealogy reproduced below shows the relations between these chiefs and will aid in the following description. The names marked with a cross (×) are those of chiefs having had part or all of their territory in Kirimiro. It should be remembered also that the kings formerly had a residence in this region.

In 1958 Mboneko was chief in Kirimiro, Mvukye was one of his sub-chiefs. Both men were considered to belong to different branches of the royal family traditionally hostile to each other. The fact that Mboneko and not Mvukye had succeeded Gahiro shows that even in recent times traditional power politics had its way.

It should be understood that Mboneko's chiefdom as it was in 1958 comprised the territory of several ancient chiefdoms joined together by the Belgian

1 It is not easy to generalise on the nature and the delimitation of the smallest local units in Burundi, now or in the past. Real villages do not and did not exist. In some parts of the country, one might speak, as is done in this study for the situation in Kirimiro, of hill communities in the sense of groups of people living on geographically rather well demarcated hill tops, sharing a certain sense of unity and sometimes constituting an administrative unit. In other regions the situation is much more confusing. In the regions personally known to me, it is best described respectively in terms of neighbourhoods, in terms of the groups of warriors formerly united under a sub-chief and in terms of the administrative units constituted by the Belgians.

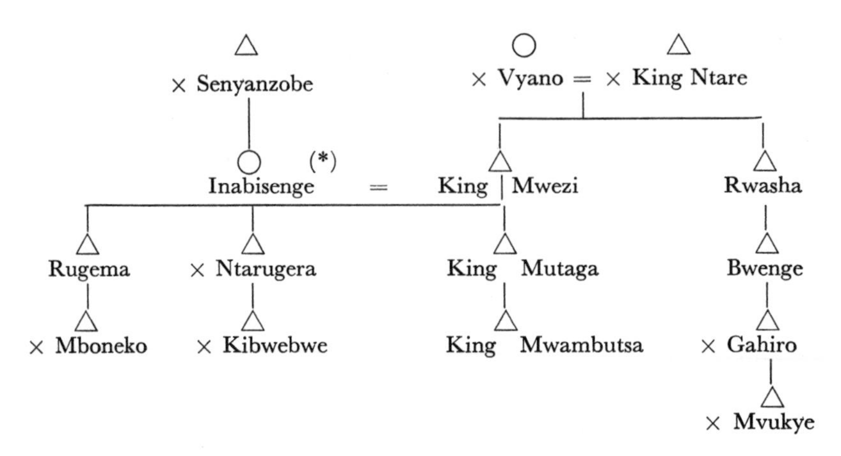

(*) Please note that I. was not the mother of Rugema, Ntarugera and King Mutaga.

administration. Not all chiefs mentioned in the genealogy were therefore successors of each other. Some of them, Gahiro and Kibwebwe for instance, reigned at the same moment in different parts of what was later one chiefdom.

The Tutsi retainers of whom mention was made before normally did not keep their favourable position after their protector had died or left the region. Many of them even left the region themselves or had to content themselves with lessened power and prestige as some of the following case studies will show.

Baransata, member of a Tutsi-Hima clan for instance had come to the region as a follower of the chief Ntarugera, who nominated him as a sub-chief. He and his sons replaced some Hutu sub-chiefs from the families just mentioned, but in their turn were replaced by nominees of the succeeding chief.

The case of Baransata is an example of the way in which a new local kin group might be founded and gain numerical importance. In 1958, the descendants of Baransata were spread over two hills and occupied numerous huts. Though they had lost their offices as sub-chiefs, they still were wealthy and had much influence in their communities.

Another Tutsi immigrant owed his influence to the fact that the sister of his father was one of the wives of the chief Gahiro. This man, wealthy in cows and lands and having several servants, was in 1958 one of the principal judges in the region and a member of the council of the chiefdom.

These immigrants did not always stay alone. A Hima man for instance who had come in the train of the chief Ntarugera, from whom he had received extensive lands, had been joined by some of his widowed sisters and their sons. Such relatives, if poor, were more or less considered as servants of the man on whose lands they lived.

I met only one Tutsi family who had since long been established in Kirimiro. This family also belonged to the Hima caste and its members had occupied in the past offices of sub-chiefs in the royal domain. Later on they had been replaced, but they still exercised influence because three of them were local judges. In 1958 they were dispersed on several hills, some having received lands elsewhere.

Even though this family did rather well in its home-country, some of its members had in the past sought their fortune elsewhere. A man called Musubare, for instance had attached himself to one of the sons of Ntarugera in another chiefdom and had become a sub-chief. He returned to his home-country after having been destituted, to settle on lands given to him by the chief Gahiro.

He was a wealthy man in 1958, having kept the cattle he had received from 5 chiefs. Being old, he took no active part to the political life of his community but his eldest son had succeeded him as a local judge.

Besides these Hutu and Tutsi families with varying degrees of wealth and political influence, many other people from poor to rather well off, inhabited the hills of Kirimiro. Most of them lived there since long, immigration being limited in this densely populated part of Burundi. There was only a small number of poor newcomers, humble servants of chiefs and wealthy Tutsi as well as others attracted for instance by the presence of a market at Mutaho, the place where I lived.

All these people, rich or poor, Tutsi and Hutu, lived dispersed amongst each other, there being no separated living quarters for the members of certain castes or classes, with the exception of the pygmoide Twa. A man's neighbours therefore were people of all kinds.

As to the different forms of collaboration I witnessed, in particular the construction of the houses and the herding of cattle, neighbours as well as relatives were involved in them. The same was true for the exchanges of beer and food, the lease of lands and the lending out of cattle.

In Bunyambo, the second region visited, the situation was different in some respects. Though the region as a whole seemed to have been inhabited long since, parts of it must have been populated very recently. By far most of the people I met were either immigrants themselves, or the sons and grandsons of immigrants. Another difference was that the proportion of Tutsi was much higher than in Kirimiro and cattle more numerous. Most important offices were occupied by Tutsi. In the particular hills I visited only one Hutu had acquired some prominence as the favorite of a chief.

Some case histories may illustrate in what ways geographical mobility affected the life of individuals in Bunyambo. First of all, I want to show how families might become dispersed in the course of a few generations.

A man called Simbare, a Hutu of the *Abarunga* clan now living at Kiririsi in Bunyambo, descended from a certain Mpoongo who had come here from the region of Mosso. His brother, though living not far from him, had left the lands of his father. Another brother had done the same and had gone to live in the territory of a different sub-chief but still in the same chiefdom. As to the two brothers of Simbare's father, these had moved to other chiefdoms, each of them to a different one. Their descendants were still living there and were visited occasionally by Simbare.

Now, Simbare's family was a humble one. Its members formerly had been cooks in the service of chiefs, but they apparently had not distinguished themselves in other ways and had remained simple farmers. Their fate had not directly been influenced by political circumstances.

The same is true of the family of Sinamenye, a Hutu of the clan of the *Abararo*. The father of Sinamenye had left his parents and had come alone in Bunyambo to serve under the chief Ruhaza from whom he had received a kraal.

Sinamenye now lived here together with his brother from a different mother. His father's divorced third wife, lived with her son, the half brother of Sinamenye at her own father's place, in another chiefdom. Owing to the conflict that had arisen between Sinamenye and this half brother all contacts had been cut. Neither did Sinamenye have any contacts with the brothers of his father and their descendants. On the other hand, Sinamenye continued to exchange beer with the brothers of his mother living at a hill nearby.

The life history of another man is an example of the way in which a politically deeply involved man and his family might move around. Bambara, a member of the Tutsi clan of the *Abasapfu*, descended from a family of milkers for the king, had been rewarded by receiving a large number of royal cattle. Several women of this family had married the sons of chiefs. Bambara himself had been a milker at the royal residence of Ibuye. He had been nominated as a sub-chief, but had left the place to accompany the king at the time many rebellions shook Burundi. Conflicts had arisen between his family and the local chief who participated in the rebellions. Later on Bambara was again nominated as a sub-chief, but came into conflict with his new chief also, this time Karabona, the cause being that this chief had seized a cow he first had given under the contract of clientship.

Bambara was nominated as a sub-chief for the third time by Mugwengezo, then chief at Bunyambo. This same chief married two sisters of Bambara. This time Bambara remained in function under the two successors of Mugwengezo but was finally destituted because of old age.

Another family I knew in Bunyambo also had become deeply involved in the political history of the region. Simbakwira, a Tutsi from the clan of the *Abayogoma*, belonged to a family of milkers for the king, whose members frequently had been sub-chiefs and had married the daughters of chiefs. His grandfather had even been betrothed to a daughter of the king, but the marriage had not taken place owing to the death of the girl.

Simbakwira had been a sub-chief himself and had married the daughter of a chief. He was nominated as a sub-chief by Bigana to replace another sub-chief, the brother of Bigana, who had reigned in the territory of his father, but later on was expulsed by Bigana. Simbakwira in his turn had been destituted when a rival branch of the royal family had got into power in Bunyambo, and had been replaced by the father's brother's son of the new chief.

These two stories, as do other life histories published elsewhere[1], show how

---

1 See note 2, page 166.

Tutsi families in particular often because involved in the rivalries between chiefs. At the death of a chief a whole re-allocation of power took place, involving not only his sons, but also his affines and other favorites.

In a region like Bunyambo, the support of a big family counted less for the individual than in regions like Kirimiro. More important were the political relations and the relations based on cattle clientship. This may be explained by the fact that cattle herding in Bunyambo was practised by almost every man, whereas in Kirimiro only the wealthy people owned some cattle. Cattle herding needing more space than agriculture, one did not find in Bunyambo such large contiguous blocks of cultivated fields as in Kirimiro. This means amongst other things that even the big families in Bunyambo lived much more frequently on dispersed holdings than in Kirimiro.

It was more difficult therefore for Hutu to attain prominence. Elsewhere, their power was partly based on their numerical strength and the wealth of their agricultural holdings. In the absence of these, Hutu did not have many means to assert themselves politically.

Another element in the situation in Bunyambo was the scarcity of good lands. I frequently heard complaints of people who had moved away from one locality in the region to another because of the poor quality of the land. The internal migrations in Bunyambo were therefore more frequent here than, for instance, in Kirimiro. This also prevented the growth of big local kin groups and may have had an influence on the position of the Hutu in this region.

On the other hand, Bunyambo being much less populated than Kirimiro, it was much easier there to obtain lands. This is the reason why it was possible for immigrants to build up quite rapidly a new and numerous kin group that, though not all of its members lived in one compact block of lands, could exercise political influence if the dispersal had a limited character.

All taken together, the tendency in Burundi of the constant foundation of new local kin groups and the splitting up of old ones showed itself clearest in this particular region.

The third region visited was situated in what formerly was the administrative centre of the country, in the neighbourhood of Muramvya, where formerly most royal residences were concentrated.

This region also was densely populated and intensively cultivated, but owing to administrative requirements more Tutsi lived here than in Kirimiro. The situation could be characterised as a mid-way position between Kirimiro and Bunyambo.

I found in this region old established Tutsi and Hutu families of considerable dimensions both attaining positions of high standing.

It should be remarked however that the standing of many Hutu families was not of the same kind as that most of the Tutsi had. Many of the prominent Hutu families formerly were charged with ritual functions at the court, but did not actively exercise real influence. An example was for instance a family of the *Abahanza* clan whose duty it was to supply a young girl to the king for the occasion of the *umuganuro*, the national festival of the sorgho. The only thing the girl had to do on this occasion was to sweep the floor and lay the parket of grass on the place the where ceremonies took place.

The members of this family derived certain benefits from what was considered to be an honour: to present to the king this gift in the person of a girl. I spoke to the father who was the last one to have done this. In gratitude, the king had allowed him to take the rank of judge without his being obliged to give the substantial gifts normally required from such a functionary. The same man was sent on some confidential missions for instance to summon peolpe who had neglected to send wood to the royal residence.

Some other Hutu families however took part in a more active way in the political life of the country. A few officials with territorial charges were of Hutu descent and were known to have participated in several wars.

As to the Tutsi in this region they often were of very high standing, belonging to families considered to be of royal descent as the *Abarango*, and the *Ababibe* or families whose wives were allowed to marry a king like the *Abenengwe* and the *Abanyakarama*.

I met only a few immigrants of low status. This probably can be explained by the fact that this was a very densely populated region, interesting only for people of high standing, who might hope to obtain political power.

On the other hand, it is certain that quite a few people had left in order to settle themselves elsewhere. I was told about men who were known to have followed the chief Busumano, brother of the king Mwezi, after his appointment in Bunyambo.

That such migrations incidentally were not always of a definitive nature is shown by the fact that some of these people who after having lived in Bunyambo for sometime had come back to Muramvya. I met one who had returned because he wanted to marry the widow of his father's brother who had died during his absence. The father of this man also had been away for a long time to serve under the chief Ntahushira, who lived in the Bututsi and equally had come back afterwards.

This comparative review of the situation in different parts of Burundi shows that geographical mobility did not have everywhere the same effects. However, it is possible to detect a number of elements common to the situation in at least the three regions visited. The next section of this study is therefore devoted to the general effects of geographical mobility in Burundi as a whole.

The Effects of Geographical Mobility on the Kinship Structure of Burundi

The immediate effect of the geographical mobility in Burundi was the dispersal of kin groups. Everywhere, members of many different clans lived together. In a hill community in Kirimiro for instance members of 10 different clans were found to be represented by their local kin groups. The members of one of these clans belonged to 6 different local kin groups of which the genealogical links, if they existed, were unknown. The same was true for two other clans each represented by two different local kin groups. It should be added that one of the local kin groups occupied 21 of the 74 huts of the community and that there were 5 local kin groups each occupying only one hut. The last ones of course could hardly be called local kin groups.

This dispersal of the members of a clan to such a degree that the genealogical links between most of them were no more known makes it understandable that the clans never acted as a unit. The significance of the clans therefore was purely symbolic. The membership of a clan only provided a rather vague indication of status.

Another feature of the kin structure of Burundi related to the foregoing was that there were no clearly demarcated kin groups between the level of the clans and that of the lineage core of the local kin groups. It seems to have happened that parts of clans changed sometimes their clan name, but this was a question of real scission and not of segmentation. The new "clan" cut off all relations with the original one, soon got the same characteristics of the other clans and constituted itself on the same level of organization. What happened also was that parts of a clan added the name of one of their ancestors to their clan name, but again these "sub-clans" behaved as all other clans. Besides, such splits occurred only occasionally and can scarcely be described as the scission of clans.

What happened in fact was that part of the descendants of a common patrilineal ancestor confirmed its own identity towards another part of these descendants. Both parts together constituting only a small fraction of a whole clan. This might for instance take place when some members of a lineage refused to assist in the arrangement of a murder case in which another member was involved, clearly demonstrating thereby that they did not want to be considered any more as part of the lineage. Normally, the scission would take place in a more gradual way, contacts between different parts of a lineage becoming less frequent in the course of time and ceasing completely at a certain moment.

When the members of such a lineage did not live together they scarcely constituted a corporate group. Even the term lineage applied to such a group looses much of its meaning. It is for that reason that I do not think that it would be useful to regard a non-localised lineage as a separate level of group organisation between the clan and the local kin group.

At this point, it is necessary to add, that even the term local kin group lacks a very precise meaning. One might restrict the term to the group of people living on single compact blocks of land obtained at one occasion by its ancestor or senior agnate, but this would exclude all other nearby living patrilineal relatives of the group who share many of its activities. I have therefore extended the term local kin group so as to include all nuclear families living so near to each other that daily cooperation is possible and in so far as they were in the past not separated by an administrative frontier.

This apparent fluidity of the kinship structure of Burundi and the absence of segmentation on different levels can at least partly be explained by the effects of geographical mobility. It is true that in certain parts of the country large families managed to stay together and to derive advantage from their numerical strength, but there were limits to their growth owing to the scarcity or to the bad quality of available lands.

It was therefore very difficult for kin groups to maintain an effective solidarity beyond a certain point in their development.

Theoretically, this solidarity might have been kept alive even between relatives geographically dispersed, but there were not many reasons why the Rundi should try to do this. Relatives living in another locality even if not too far away were not of much use in daily life. It was much more profitable for people to rely on their neighbours. Besides, the advantages of belonging to a big family, in the case of commoners at least, existed only for people living in the same administrative sub-division. The threat of leaving the territory of a sub-chief or chief for instance did have much weight only when it was uttered by the members of a localised kin group living in that territory. Moreover, members of dispersed living kin groups often were subjects of rival chiefs and might even have opposed political interest. A local kin group concentrated on its own political interests which normally were the interests of the territory in which it lived.

There was still another factor which had a counter effect on the growth of effective kin groups. Each Rundi had to a certain extent to divide his loyalties between his kin and the political authorities. This manifested itself clearly in the case of people who were on the point of leaving their home country as the follower of a chief. Such a situation might imply the choice between a political career with all its promises but also with all its risks and a relatively secure but little promising life in the midst of a family.

Once a man had opted for a political career, he could of course be of help to his kin. As we have seen, some of his relatives might be attracted by his good fortune and come to live with him. But whatever was the case, a man who left his family weakened its strength and had to be considered as a loss in many respects.

All this means that there were, besides sentimental considerations, but few reasons why a man should continue to frequent his relatives who had stayed home. As soon as the genealogical distance between him or his descendants and his home family had become too far, all relations were cut and even the sense of a family relationship at all got lost.

At the same time, a man who had left his family, immediately started to build up a new local kin group, which might become rather numerous in a few generations and in most respects wholly autonomous. This new local kin group would accrue then in members up to the time that part of these left the group again to establish themselves elsewhere.

This pattern was somewhat different in the case of members of those families, mostly princes and Tutsi, who on a high level were actively engaged in the political life of the country. Such people, less locally oriented in their political interests, did have much to gain from manipulating their family relationships, even when it concerned relatives living far away. At the same time, political revalries often also opposed near relatives to each other, as is witnessed in the frequent wars between sons of a deceased chief. Political life on this level united as well divided the members of a family.

The model to be used when describing this kind of scission in what might be called the lineage of the Rundi, clearly cannot be the same as the one used, for instance, for segmentary lineage systems. One of the characteristics of the segmentary lineage systems is that newly constituted groups do not lose their organisational links with the original group and continue to keep a sense of solidarity and belonging together with the groups at higher levels.

In Burundi on the other hand constant splits occurred originating new groups which in a rather short time became wholly autonomous. The model that could be used may be represented by a genealogy of the following form.

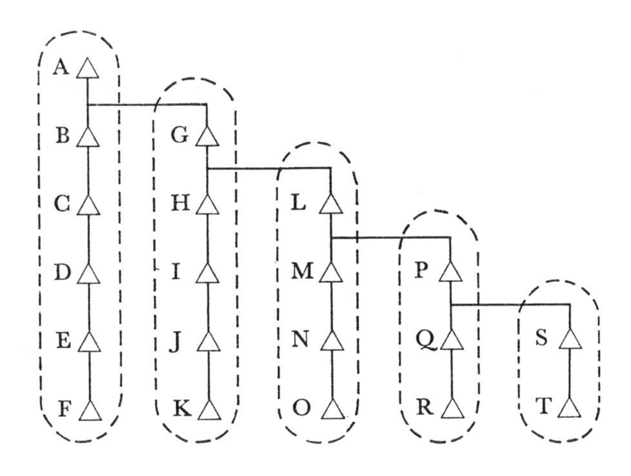

G in this genealogy would be the man who left his original local kin group to establish himself elsewhere and found a new kin group. Later on, L detached himself from this new group to establish in his turn another new one, and so on. B, C, D, E and F are the men who stayed behind and who continued the original local kin group. In such a case the genealogical links between for instance F and T could have entirely been forgotten though it might be that the memory of A would have been retained. The dotted lines encircle the men who constitute the core of the five different autonomous local kin groups that descended from A.

This model genealogy does of course represent reality in a very schematic way but it is useful to show the general tendency that constantly was at work in the social structure of Burundi.

One should keep in mind also that the model only refers to the patrilineal core of the local kin groups, and does not take into account the kinship relations between relatives other than the patrilineal ones.

In the foregoing pages mention has frequently been made of the importance in the life of an individual of maternal and affinal relatives with whom many contacts were maintained. These contacts were initiated by women entering and leaving the local kin groups. When it is realised that owing to the absence of regular marriage ties between definite localities these women came from and went to very different places and that the families of these women were affected also by geographical mobility, one can understand the dispersal of the different kinds of relatives a man had.

It was therefore difficult to foresee exactly what kind of kin relationships would be stressed in a particular case. It is clear however that distance was a very important factor in determining what was the issue.

Conclusion

The conclusion to this study of geographical molibity is that this phenomenon in Burundi was in different ways related to some particularities of the kinship structure in this country and that it was determined itself by several economic and political factors.

The high density of population in some regions and poor soils in other regions did not allow the gradual and unlimited extension of kin groups in a geographical sense and forced many people to migrate. Political factors favored geographical mobility in other ways and did contribute to the undermining of kin solidarity preventing in that way the formation of big strong kin units. It might be said from this point of view that political and economic factors did weaken kin bonds.

On the other hand, political and economic factors were operative also in binding kinsmen together. A man very often had to rely on his kinsmen for assistance in economic and political affairs. Besides, the relative security existing in Burundi in peace time, made it possible to the Rundi to visit even distant living kinsmen. Men might decide also to join themselves to the local kin groups of relatives elsewhere profiting thereby from their kin ties in distant regions.

One could not therefore say that the only effect of geographical mobility was to weaken kin bonds. It would be safer to conclude that the phenomenon was in constant interaction with a whole set of elements in a complex situation.

APPENDIX

A Note on Research relevant to the Extended Family and Geographical Mobility

S. C. CHRISTOPHER

University of Washington, Seattle, U.S.A.

It has become part of the folklore of sociology that the extended family hinders geographical mobility, that geographical mobility is a *sine qua non* for industrialization, and that therefore extended family ties are an impediment to industrialization in the developing nations of Africa and Asia. Actual research, however, does not bear out the hypothesis.

Litwak (1960) argues convincingly that the classical extended family acted as a barrier to geographical mobility when and only when they felt that such mobility was not legitimate or would lead to a break in contact. Nuclear families who had good reason to move were actually better able to do so if they had an extended family to help them than if they stood alone. The extended family, by cooperation, could raise capital to send one of its nuclear families to the urban center. This family, with its superior earning power, could then bring other nuclear families from the extended family after it. The existence of the extended family tie between the migrating nuclear family and those left behind also enhanced the mobility of related nuclear families by providing reliable information on jobs, housing, local social norms, language, and generally aiding the new migrant at the most difficult point of migration.

A number of studies show that even in the most urbanized parts of the world's most industrialized nations, the extended family is far from defunct. Young & Willmott (1957) present evidence to indicate that extended family relations provide positive advantages for working class nuclear families in industrial London. Axelrod (1956), Greer (1956), and Litwak (1958) in three independent studies of middle-class groups in large urban centers (Buffalo, Detroit, and Los Angeles) found that almost 50 per cent of the middle-class individuals saw relatives at least once a week or more. In still another study, by Bell & Boat (1957), it is reported that in San Francisco close to 90 per cent of the people said that an extended family member was also one of their closest friends. In a study in New Haven (Sussman, 1953), close to 70 per cent of the people interviewed said that they provided sufficient extended family aid so that if it were withdrawn, the recipients would suffer a loss in status. Ishwaran (1959) extensively documents the very vital role that the *familie* (extended family) plays for the *gezin* (nuclear family) in urban middle class Holland.

The case against the extended family seems to rest on two assumptions. These assumptions are: 1) the extended family is dysfunctional for an industrial society, and 2) industrialization is dysfunctional for the extended family. Both assumptions have practically been accepted as fact, when they are actually only questionable hypotheses. The evidence is not all in, but the way "returns" are going it looks like our thinking on the extended family may be in for some drastic revision.

Bell and Boat point out that approximately 80 per cent of their respondents said they could count on extended family aid in cases of illness which lasted a month or longer. The fact that such aid in industrialized economies can be given in the form of money, which is easily sent over vast distances, means that the extended family can perform a useful psychological and economic function in providing that quick and personally tailored aid which even the best-ordered bureaucracy cannot provide. It would also appear that the extended family, realizing the advantages of mobility, actually encourages and makes it possible. It need no longer fear, in this day of rapid communication, that spatial separation need necessarily mean a break in the bonds of kinship.

If industrialization were dysfunctional for the extended family, it would surely be dying out in industrialized countries. The faith that industrialization is dysfunctional for the extended family has apparently served as evidence for many who proclaim that the extended family therefore *is* dying out. The research evidence that it apparently is alive and active leads one to doubt the assumption upon which the converse of the theorem was based.

All of this has very great relevance for prediction and social planning in the developing countries. It suggests that

1) the extended family is not necessarily a hindrance to industrialization;
2) the extended family may well be a positive force in making industrialization speedier than it otherwise could be;
3) social policies inimical to the extended family should be seriously reconsidered;
4) prognostications based on the assumption that with industrialization will come the weakening and perhaps disappearance of the extended family should be supplemented by forecasts based on the contrary assumption.

In summary, accumulating research evidence indicate that both those social planners who are worried about the disorganizing effects on kinship institutions by industrialization, and those who are worried about the limiting effects on industrialization by the extended family, may well be worrying about non-existent spectres. Apparently the two are not, as was long thought, inimical to the optimal functioning of each other.

Seattle

S. C. Christopher

LIST OF CONTRIBUTORS

Ayoub, Millicent R., Ph.D., (Harvard), is Research Associate in Anthropology at the Fels Research Institute and Assistant Professor at Antioch College, Yellow Springs, Ohio. She carried out research projects on kinship among present residents of Ohio and in 1953 on kinship in Lebanon.

Beckett, Jeremy, Ph.D. (Australian National University), is Lecturer in Social Anthropology at Monash University, Melbourne. In 1957 he worked amongst Aborigines in Western New South Wales and has re-visited the area a number of times, most recently in 1964.

Bennett, John W., M.A., Ph.D. (University of Chicago), is Professor of Anthropology and Sociology, Washington University, St. Louis. Dr. Bennett has done extensive research on social organization and economy in Japan and rural North America. He has also been concerned with the application of anthropological concepts and methods to the study of industrial societies.

Gould, Harold A., M.A. (Ohio State University), Ph.D. (Washington University, St. Louis), is assistant Professor of Anthropology, University of Pittsburgh. From 1959 to 1962, Dr. Gould conducted research in North India in the areas of social mobility and culture and personality.

Gutkind, Peter C.W., M.A. (Chicago), Ph.D. (Amsterdam), is Assistant Professor of Anthropology, McGill University. He has carried out research on problems of Industrialization and Urbanization in Africa.

Hubert, Jane E. de B., B.A. (Oxon.), Postgraduate Diploma in Anthropology (Oxon.), is Research Officer, The London School of Economics and Political Science. Since 1961 she has been in charge of a team carrying out an anthropological study of extra-familial kinship in a middle-class area of London.

Ishwaran, K., M.A. (Bombay), Ph.D. (Dharwar), B.Litt. (Oxon.), M.S.S. (The Hague), D.Litt. (Leiden), is Professor of sociology at York University, Toronto, Canada. He is editor of *The International Journal of Comparative Sociology* and of the *Journal of Asian and African Studies.* He has carried out research in India, Holland and Canada.

Kohl, Seena, is Research Assistant, Department of Sociology and Anthropology, Washington University, St. Louis. Mrs. Kohl is associated with Professor Bennett's Cultural Ecology Research Program in Saskatchewan, Canada.

Nzimiro, F. Ikenna, D.Phil. (Cologne), is Lecturer in African Sociology, University of Lagos, and a post-doctoral research student in the Department of Social Anthropology, University of Cambridge. In 1960–61 he carried out research on kinship among the Ibos of Eastern Nigeria.

Osterreich, Helgi, M.A. (McGill), is Teaching Assistant in the Department of Sociology and Anthropology, McGill University. In 1963 Mrs. Osterreich carried out research on kinship among English-speaking Canadians.

Piddington, Ralph, M.A. (Sydney), Ph.D. (London), F.R.S.N.Z., is Professor of Anthropology in the University of Auckland. In 1957 and 1962 he carried out research projects on kinship among French Canadian communities in Manitoba.

Trouwborst, Albert, Ph.D. (Leiden), is Lecturer in Social Anthropology at the University of Nijmegen, Holland. He was formerly Curator of the National Museum of Ethnology, Leiden, and Assistant Professor in the University of Montreal. He carried out field work in Burundi in 1958 and in Surinam among the Matawai (Bush Creoles) during the summer of 1963.

INDEX